# PILGRIMAGE TO MECCA

For

# JAMES

As He Starts His Pilgrimmage

# Pilgrimage to Mecca

## The Indan Experience, 1500-1800

by

# MICHAEL N. PEARSON

 Markus Wiener Publishers
Princeton

FOR INFORMATION WRITE TO:
MARKUS WIENER PUBLISHERS
114 JEFFERSON ROAD, PRINCETON, NJ 08540


LIBRARY OF CONGRESS CATALOGING-IN-PUBLICATION DATA

PEARSON, M.N. (MICHAEL NAYLOR), 1941-
PILGRIMMAGE TO MECCA: THE INDIAN EXPERIENCE, 1600-1800/
MICHAEL N. PEARSON
INCLUDES BIBLIOGRAPHICAL REFERENCES AND INDEX.
ISBN 1-55876-089-X (HC: ALK. PAPER)  ISBN 1-55876-090-3(PB: ALK. PAPER)
1. MUSLIM PILGRIMS AND PILGRIMAGES—INDIA—HISTORY.
2. MUSLIM PILGRIMS AND PILGRIMAGES —SAUDI ARABIA—MECCA—HISTORY.
3. ISLAM—INDIA—HISTORY.
I. TITLE.
BP187.3.P386    1995
297'.55'08914—DC20    95-31975    CIP


THE ILLUSTRATIONS ARE REPRODUCED COURTESY OF THE
VICTORIA AND ALBERT MUSEUM AND STERLING PUBLISHERS, BOMBAY.

EDITED BY LEON KING
COVER DESIGN BY CHERYL MIRKIN
THIS BOOK HAS BEEN COMPOSED IN CENTURY OLD STYLE BY CMF GRAPHIC DESIGN

MARKUS WIENER PUBLISHERS BOOKS ARE PRINTED
IN THE UNITED STATES OF AMERICA ON ACID-FREE PAPER,
AND MEET THE GUIDELINES FOR PERMANENCE AND DURABILITY
OF THE COMMITTEE ON PRODUCTION GUIDELINES
FOR BOOK LONGEVITY OF THE COUNCIL ON LIBRARY RESOURCES

# CONTENTS

I have been working intermittently on this book for some ten years. During this time I have had helpful advice and general assistance from a range of friends and colleagues. Tim Coates at the University of Minnesota helped with bibliography. Charles Boxer as always was generous with advice and assistance. Martin Braach-Maksvytis helped with bibliography and translations. Fr. John Correia-Afonso was always hospitable in Bombay, as was my friend Fr. Teotonio de Souza during several visits to Goa. I owe a major debt to Professor A. Jan Qaisar of Aligarh Muslim University. He supervised a translation of the most important Persian text for my topic and period, the "Anis-ul-hujjaj." I fear he spent too much of his own valuable time on this task; I am very grateful to him.

Research for this project took place in a variety of libraries and archives. I remember with particular gratitude the helpfulness of the staff at the library of the School of Oriental and African Studies, University of London; the India Office Library, and its big brother, the British Library; Charles Borges at the Xavier Centre of Historical Research in Goa; P.P. Shirodkar, Director of the Historical Archives of Goa; the James Ford Bell library and the Ames Library at the University of Minnesota; the New York Public Library; and the ever-helpful staff at my home base, the University of New South Wales library. I should especially thank, at the University of Minnesota, the past and present curators of the Bell Library, that is Jack Parker and now Carol Urness, Don Johnson of the Ames Library, and Jim Tracy, Chair of the

History Department, who made possible my stay in Minneapolis in 1989.

Over the last few years several parts of this book have been tested at various conferences and seminars. To all who made helpful comments on these occasions, my thanks. I must also acknowledge that earlier versions of parts of this book were published in the following places: *Indica* (Heras Institute Diamond Jubilee Number), XXIII, 1986, pp. 143-58; *Journal of the Oriental Society of Australia,* XVII-XIX, 1986-87, pp. 164-79; *Indica*, XXVI, 1989, pp. 103-18; *Studies in Maritime History,* ed. K.S. Mathew, Pondicherry, 1990, pp. 112-26.

I note with gratitude financial assistance provided for this project over several years from the University of New South Wales' Special Research Grants committee of the Faculty of Arts and Social Sciences, and a last-minute grant from the School of History's Research and Publications Fund.

Finaly, thanks and more than thanks to Denni and James for love and support.

> *M.N. Pearson*
> *Dolans Bay, November 1994*

# Notes on the Illustrations

*Page i:* An early drawing of a pilgrimage caravan.

*Chapter 1:* A nineteenth century of the Temple at and the Kaabah.

*Chapter 2 and front cover:* Caravan to Mecca departing from Cairo.

*Chapter 3:* Plan of the city of Mecca. The city lies in a long irregular hollow among bare mountains quite effectively depicted here by a peculiar configuration which is unlike any conventional drawing of rocky landscape.

*Chapter 4:* The Sharif of Mecca with his entourage. The eminent position of the Sharif is clear not only from the umbrella over his head but also from the fact that a *pakhalder* precedes him, spraying water on the road.

*Chapter 5:* The port of Surat. The importance of Surat lay in the fact that all trade with the red sea ports was carried on from here, even before the Mughals came on the scene. Surat was also famous for its ship-building activity.

*Chapter 6:* The Syrian Caravan. The illustration shows the three-tiered composition without any attempt at perspective. The drawing of tents with two occupants seated facing each other is quite formal.

*Chapter 7:* Seascape. The sense of direction is conveyed by the different orientations of the two ships. The depiction of passengers in a row, framed individually in niches follows a cliché that was established by the 13th century in Arab painting.

*Chapter 8:* Mural from the Shiva temple at Tirupudaim-aruthur. An Arab dhow brings a cargo of horses. There is enough literary evidence to indicate the importance of Arabian horses.

*Chapter 9:* Arafat, the place of Recognition. This illustration vividly depicts what actually is the *Hajj* when on the ninth day of zu'l hijja, all the pilgrims assemble in the valley and offer *vuquf,* standing as the sun crosses the meridian. The pilgrims to Mecca are required to wear seamless white garments (*ihram*) as seen here.

# CHAPTER 1

# Introduction

# HISTORIOGRAPHY

A pilgrimage is a journeying to a sacred place as an act of religious devotion. The greatest of such journeys is the *hajj,* the pilgrimage to Mecca, which is one of the main requirements of Islam and therefore central for Muslims. For over 1300 years it has been a major event of world history, transcending in significance its importance for the Muslim Faithful. Even today it is by far the largest gathering of people on a regular basis anywhere in the world. This book presents an analysis of the *hajj* from Mughal India to Mecca in the early modern period. In a series of linked chapters we investigate seriatim the various meanings of the *hajj* and examine in detail its centrality. We look at the motivations and actual experience of those who undertook the journey and pay close attention to its political and economic dimensions. As we shall see in our final chapter, which briefly compares it with other pilgrimages, no other event has the precise characteristics of the *hajj.*

There is a second domain in which the *hajj* from India to Mecca is of unique importance. Recent years have seen a rapid expansion of interest in the history of the Indian Ocean. Most of the studies have been devoted to trade. Economic ties are usually pointed to as having produced important links all across the large maritime area by scholars who seek to present the Indian Ocean as a category and an area whose characteristics are a certain unity and coherence. Passenger traffic has been neglected as, for example, in *The Indian Ocean,* edited by Satish Chandra and in two recent studies by K.N. Chaudhuri.[1] The exception is an article by Kenneth McPherson, who provides a useful overview of all passengers before the nineteenth century, though he says little about the *hajj*.[2] What has been forgotten is that pilgrims going on *hajj* over the Red Sea is the only example we have of a regular, passenger route in the premodern period and that this traffic created religious, social, and cultural links all over the Indian Ocean world. It is true that the voyage from Lisbon to Goa and back on the Portuguese *carreira* was also a long-distance and habitual route, but its purpose was different; most of the passengers were not religiously motivated and as we see in Chapter 2, their numbers aboard the huge Portuguese ships were much smaller. In other words, in terms both of Indian Ocean history and, more importantly, of the history of the Islamic world, the *hajj* is a vital subject of study.

Sources for study of the *hajj* from Mughal India are fragmentary, scattered, and in a variety of languages, as our ensuing discussion will make clear. As with most topics for this period, we often have to proceed by inference and innuendo, and sometimes must even use fuller sources from later periods, though of course with very great care. There is also the problem that I, as a non-Muslim, am unable to undertake on-site investigations, Mecca being closed to all but the faithful. This seems to have been the case right from the beginning of the Muslim era.[3] Despite the scarcity and difficulty of the sources, what is not in question is the validity and importance of the topic. It was too important for the some fifteen percent of Indians who were Muslim, too significant in terms of activities in the Indian Ocean, and too central economically, politically and especially religiously, to be ignored. We can say little of the piety and devotion, or indeed greed, of the silent thousands who made the *hajj* in the early modern period from Mughal India; for such sources as we have are largely élite accounts. Nevertheless, even an account as scrappy and limited as the one presented here is worthwhile, because such an important phenomenon, so central in accomplishment or mere aspiration, deserves its own study.

Even at this early stage of our study, motivations, which we will be writing about implicitly throughout, require comment. W.R. Roff sketched two general social motivations in a Southeast Asian context: "These are, pilgrimage as a rite of passage, marking the transition from one state to another; and pilgrimage as a ritual of affliction, compensating or atoning for, or designed to avoid, some real or feared personal misfortune."[4] Our early modern sources for India seldom allow us to be as specific as this, but there is no doubt that both these matters were present for *hajjis* in our period also. Yet we consider it axiomatic that fundamentally the *hajj* was a religious event undertaken for religious reasons.

The present study can be justified on several grounds. Even in studies of the Muslim world in general, such as the recent overview by Ira Lapidus,[5] the *hajj* is conspicuous by its absence. The first volume of *Hajj Studies,* which appeared in 1978, contained interesting articles, all modern and mostly social-science oriented. It was meant to be part of a continuing series, but, in a way which may be symptomatic, so far as I know no further volumes have appeared.[6] Closer to home, Roff writing of the interest and importance of pilgrimage in South and Southeast Asia lamented that "Despite this, we have yet to produce a single major study of the pilgrimage from these regions."[7] Similarly, the senior maritime historian Ashin Das Gupta, wrote recently of "The Islamic pilgrimage of the *hajj [sic]* of which we still await a proper study . . . "[8] In a review of two books on the Indian Ocean, John Richards made the same sort of comment. He wrote that "The integrating force of the Islamic pilgrimage every year to the Holy Cities in the Hijaz is such a pivotal part of this Indian Ocean system that it cries out for separate treatment. Unfortunately, so little has been done that it would be difficult to identify a scholar for such a study . . . "[9] I have volunteered myself for the task in the hope that at least my

5

study will bring into focus a comparatively new area of research.

I hope that this book is a contribution to the study of the Islamic world by a sympathetic *farangi*.

The total Muslim population in the world today is well over one billion. Of these, over 300 million live in the present states of Pakistan, Bangladesh and India; many more than in the largest single Muslim country, Indonesia, and, of course, far more than the total population of the Arab world. Gaborieau and his contributors have reminded us that Islam in South Asia is an important, and neglected, area of study.[10] But it must be stressed that, unlike Hinduism, Islam in South Asia has an important international dimension. The community cannot be investigated in isolation from its links with other Muslim areas, and especially with the Holy Cities.

The final justification for this study is more theoretical and will be only implicit in what follows. Recent comparative or global studies of the early modern period of history, designed to explain the rise of the west or the creation of the third world, have been explicitly economic determinist in their approach.[11] Contrary to this, my analysis in this study is designed to show that people act for many reasons, not all of them economic. Chapters 6 to 8 of this book, which seek to challenge the notion of a *hajj* market, can be seen as an attempt to modify the regrettable trend in most recent history which connects causation with Mammon and neglects God.

It is surprising that there is so little secondary literature on the *hajj* from India in our early modern period. The only modern study I know of is a recent book on Mughal-Ottoman relations by Naimur Rahman Farooqi who covers Mughal and Ottoman political response to European threats to the *hajj*.[12] His book is particularly useful because he avails himself of the very difficult Ottoman archives as well as more familiar Mughal sources, but lack of access to the copious Portuguese documentation has limited his study. There are only occasional and casual references to the *hajj* in the standard accounts of Mughal India, or even of Islam in early modern India. S.A.A. Rizvi's voluminous books on Indian Islam in the sixteenth to nineteenth centuries are cultural and literary studies, and although several of his subjects, including Shah Abd al-Aziz and Shah Wali-Allah, made the *hajj,* Rizvi says little about this part of their careers.[13] Muhammad Mujeeb's detailed *The Indian Muslims,* and Aziz Ahmad's *Islamic Culture in the Indian Environment* both make only fleeting references to the *hajj.*[14] Peter Hardy's account of Islam in India since the sixteenth century has nothing on the social role of the *hajj,* but merely three passing references to individual people undertaking the pilgrimage, or going to Mecca.[15] Schimmel's account of Indian Islam is an excellent literary and religious compilation, but with almost no attention to any external dimensions of her subject.[16] Gaborieau's collection similarly has only two passing references to the *hajj.* This is revealing of the focus of scholarship at present, for his book is meant to reflect the state of research today on South Asian Islam.[17] The same can be said of another collective, and very uneven, survey of Islam in Asia, where again there are only very scattered and passing references to the *hajj.*[18] Two other books where one would expect to find extensive coverage of the *hajj* are in fact silent. The useful *Islam and the Trade of Asia,* edited by D.S. Richards, has nothing, yet the role of the *"hajj* market," in other words the nexus, if any, between trade and religion, has been much discussed recently. Similarly, keeping in mind our earlier comment on the role of the *hajj* in creating the only important passenger traffic in the Indian Ocean in the early modern period, it is surprising indeed that a compilation called *Mouvements de populations dans l'océan Indien* has nothing on the movement of pilgrims.[19]

The present work aims to fill this gap, indeed, in a presumptuous fashion, to give back their history to these anonymous *hajjis.* So far as I know, few other students of Indian history from any period are pursuing parallel studies. W.R.

Roff did important work on the *hajj* from Southeast Asia, which often flows over into and illuminates the phenomenon in nineteenth-century India also, as is shown in his article in Dietmar Rothermund's collection and in his later articles.[20] As Roff's articles make clear and any cursory study of standard bibliographies will reveal, there is copious documentation available for the colonial period. For example, the British government in India produced two useful official reports on the *hajj*.[21] Barbara Metcalf is focusing directly on the *hajj* in nineteenth-century colonial India, but so far her work is, for the most part, unpublished.[22] She is mainly interested in working out what the *hajj* meant to its participants and how it changed them; in other words, her prime concern is with the *mentalités* of the pilgrims. Her research is based on an impressive mass of actual accounts by people who made the *hajj* and felt compelled, whether for reasons of didacticism or self-glorification, to write about and publish their experiences.

For the early modern period we have a few comparable accounts by participants. Nevertheless, there is a potential problem with such sources. As is well known, pilgrims in Mecca engage in a set of rituals and ceremonies whose format was laid down to a very large extent by the Prophet himself in his "pilgrimage of farewell" in 632.[23] Over the subsequent thirteen centuries, descriptions of *hajjs* show a remarkable similarity. During the central days of the *hajj* pilgrims are told specifically what to *do;* indeed the manuals produced by and for pilgrims, and the guides who chaperon particular groups, are designed precisely to achieve uniformity of conduct. Each group of pilgrims, depending on place of origin, has with it a semi-official, or official guide called a *mutawwif,* who advises and leads the visitors through their time in Mecca.[24] Even today in Mecca, pilgrims from different countries group together in particular localities where their language is spoken and their own food is available.[25] It is significant that in a seventeenth-century illustrated manuscript a

*mutawwif* appears in each of the depictions of pilgrim caravans in Mecca.[26]

The problem appears when we consider the nature of the
accounts of returning *hajjis*. My own acquaintance with some
of them leads me to suspect that the pilgrims are also pro-
grammed as to what to *feel*. They feel awe and fear in Mecca,
love in Medina and so on, simply because this is what they
know is expected of them. In the early modern period few
comment on the prevalence of flies and endemic disease in
Mecca or the way Meccans fleeced pilgrims. Such secular
inconveniences were nullified by the intensity of the religious
experience. In short, these personal accounts could be considered to be as normative as the official and semi-official
guides for pilgrims which have been used for centuries.

Several fruitful studies of the *hajj* from Southeast Asia
have appeared. A.H. Johns has suggestive things to say about
the role of the heartland of Islam, that is the Hijaz, in his
studies of Islam and especially *sufis* in Indonesia.[27] Matheson
and Milner published and commented on several nineteenth-
century Malay accounts of *hajjs*.[28] There is also a recent
detailed study of the *hajj* from Malaysia from 1860 to 1981,
only part of which has so far been published.[29] The early part
of Harry Benda's seminal book focused on the role of Islam,
and the wider Muslim world, in nineteenth-century
Indonesia.[30] Vredenbregt and Meulen[31] provided good
accounts of the *hajj* from Indonesia, based on Dutch sources,
while W.R. Roff was, until recently, working on the *hajj* from
the Malay world. Some years ago he proposed a series of very
useful general ideas to be investigated. Among other topics,
he noted the importance of regional variations in the Islamic
world, and suggested that while the *hajj* was especially
important as a vehicle for Islamic identification in Southeast
Asia, in some Muslim areas other things, such as fasts, could
be more important. He also commented on the way the *hajj*
in the Malay world can be seen as fitting in to pre-Islamic
custom (as indeed it does in Mecca itself, for this city was of

9

course a pilgrimage centre before Islam).[32] He notes the Malay custom of "merantau," or going away, and suggests that the *hajj* then is an "Islamic re-articulation of pre-Islamic practices."[33] Other Southeast Asian specialists have even evaluated the *hajj* as a form of tourism.[34] Indeed, the *hajj* can be many different things;[35] it was an important transmitter of disease, in Iran today it has major political implications, and we are told that the number of pilgrims from Nigeria has risen recently but that this is mostly for corrupt reasons, such as drug trafficking, smuggling, and foreign exchange dealings.[36] The *hajj* has even been subjected to a multiple-regression model in order to predict the future numbers of pilgrims, and another thoughtful study on the future of the *hajj* is concerned that its spirituality is being lost, or that modern technology has made it too easy.[37]

There is quite a large body of literature on the *hajj* from the Middle East and the Maghreb. Pride of place must go to a very recent and distinguished study by Suraiya Faroqhi published in German, *Ruler over Mecca: The History of the Pilgrimage.*[38] This important work is based on the Ottoman archives and marks a major step forward for academic studies of the *hajj.* Faroqhi concentrates on the Ottoman period, though there is also sketchy coverage of more modern times. However, her concerns are, a little different from mine. She concentrates on the political and organizational aspects of the pilgrimage rather than its religious role and has little to say about India. Two recent collections focus on Muslim travel, including pilgrimage; both have several articles of comparative interest.[39] A quite different work is the vast and sumptuous series of publications by Kammerer devoted to the Red Sea area in general. In five volumes making up seven books he provided an enormous accumulation of data on the Red Sea and the surrounding area up to the seventeenth century. Numerous illustrations, often in color, enhanced his lavish work.[40]

We may next note three useful accounts in encyclopedias.

The obvious first place to look is in the *Encyclopedia of Islam*.[41] A useful collaborative account of pilgrimage in general, and in most of the world religions, is to be found in the *Encyclopedia of Religion*.[42] Another short account of pilgrimage in Asia in general by Paul M. Toomey appears in the recent excellent *Encyclopedia of Asian History*. A recent book by Barber provides a short but intelligent overview of pilgrimages in general.[43] Strongest on the religious aspects of pilgrimage are two older French works. First is the collaborative collection *Pèlerinages,* which covers ten sorts of pilgrimages. The contributors worked to a common set of questions, and Muhammad Hamidullah's account of the *hajj,* is excellent on the actual rites and their meanings. The same applies to Gaudefroy's detailed account.[44] Among the academic and analytical literature, we note a useful analysis of the *hajj* in Mamluk times,[45] and an excellent detailed study of the Egyptian caravan to Mecca.[46] Long's useful work a Westerner's detailed and sympathetic account of the modern *hajj,* covers its social, medical, and religious aspects, while Birks's comparable account deals mostly with West Africa, the author being an English social scientist.[47] King's article would be an excellent place for a novice to start an investigation of the *hajj*. He provides useful maps, a bibliography, and a reliable account of the geography and history of the Hijaz and the *hajj*. But there are gaps: he ignores pilgrims from South and Southeast Asia; there is no discussion of the economics of the *hajj* in history, nor of the role of the Holy Cities as diffusion centres crucial for the vitalization and reinforcement of correct Islamic conduct.[48] Equally useful as an introduction to the whole topic is a chapter in von Grunebaum's *Muhammadan Festivals*. It includes some illustrations, and is good on all religious aspects of the *hajj,* such as the rituals, the cosmology of the site, and the origins of the rites. It does not cover social, economic and political aspects.[49]

Non-academic accounts by actual *hajjis,* whether Muslim or not, are numerous. There is a whole series of nineteenth-century classics, mostly by Westerners who successfully disguised themselves as Muslims. The account of the great traveler, and skilful self-publicist, Richard Burton is probably the best known. There are, however, other valuable accounts by Doughty, Hurgronje (this one having a very important political implication), Keane and Burkhardt, and translations of Muslim accounts, notably that of Ali Bey, and of a pilgrim from Mauritania.[50]

The revival of Western interest in the Muslim world has happily produced a considerable number of modern accounts of the *hajj,* some of them very lavish productions indeed. Two stand out, one by Guellouz and one by the great Kenyan photographer Mohamed Amin; both have brilliant photographs.[51] Even better for a visual impression, especially if one is a non-Muslim and cannot gain access to the Holy Cities personally, are several of the documentary films on the *hajj*. The best I have seen is "Mecca, the Forbidden City," the film made by an Iranian crew in the 1970s, which brilliantly conveys all the fervor, rapture, and devotion of the *hajj*. Among other recent accounts is the book by Kamal,[52] which is a modern version of the age-old guides and handbooks for intending *hajjis,* with the text in both English and Arabic. Also available are two Pakistani versions of these guides, and an eighteenth-century version in French.[53] Eldon Rutter has given us a detailed personal account by a Westerner, while Khalifa's little book is a charming personal account by an Englishwoman married to an Egyptian.[54] Equally personal, and captivating, is Stegar's often moving, and very individual, account. The author went on the *hajj* in 1927, but published her book in Australia some 42 years later, when she was 87 years old.[55] There have been several accounts in English of recent pilgrimages from South Asia, and also one very detailed and valuable account by the Nawab of Bhopal from early in this century.[56] A very eminent Hyderabadi, Nawab Sir Nizamat Jung, even published a series of poems inspired by his *hajj*. One stanza will serve to give the flavor of them all:

Kingdoms and Empires may decline,
Of pomp and power and splendour reft.
Here is no change—the spark divine
Still in these hills and sands is left![57]

So much for a quite sketchy description of the historiography in general available for the *hajj*. Many other works can be traced from standard Islamic bibliographies, and especially from J.D. Pearson's invaluable *Index Islamicus*.[58] Few of the accounts so far discussed can be of much use for writing a history of the *hajj* from Mughal India, yet one proviso must be made here. The actual ritual of the *hajj* has changed very little indeed over the last thirteen centuries; the whole point is for the modern pilgrim to follow precisely the actions of the Prophet on his "pilgrimage of farewell" in 632. Thus while the social context of the *hajj* has obviously changed (varying greatly over time and depending on who is undertaking it[59]) what the *hajji* does has not. Therefore when we are talking about this we can use data from any period.

What, however, of the sources for our period and area, that is for the *hajj* from early modern, or Mughal, India? As we noted, there are vast gaps. I think I can claim to have used all the available indigenous Indian sources, pitifully few though they are. I would be surprised if I have missed any Persian or Arabic source describing the *hajj* from Mughal India. There is no doubt occasional mention of Indian pilgrims in the copious Middle East sources in Arabic and Turkish. I have used these accounts either in translation, or at second hand. Thus in the case of Ottoman Turkish sources, we can now rely on two excellent recent books, by Farooqi and Faroqhi,[60] which have used these difficult archives exhaustively. Some examples of accounts by pilgrims not from India may be noted first. The great traveler Ibn Battuta spent some time in Mecca, and his account is useful for the ceremonies he did; yet we get little sense of what he *felt,* there is no sense of devotion or piety in his account.[61] Ibn

Jubayr's twelfth-century narration of his long journey from the Maghreb and of his *hajj* is an excellent and devout description of his experiences.[62] Puey Monçon, a Spanish Muslim pilgrim of about 1600, has left us a poem describing his adventures. It gives an excellent impression of the piety of this *hajji,* the difficulties and dangers of his long voyage, and the sense of awe and wonder he felt in Mecca. [63] Bernard Lewis published two short, agreeable accounts, one by a fourteenth-century African ruler, and one by a fifteenth-century Spanish Arab diplomat.[64]

Several early European accounts by people who made the *hajj* disguised as Muslims, or at least traveled in the Red Sea area, are also useful. William Foster published a number from the late seventeenth century in his book. One of his travelers, Pitts, who definitely did do the *hajj,* probably in 1685, and who is at pains to correct previous incorrect accounts by those who had not, points out that "I speak from knowledge, they only by hearsay," and "I speak of what I know and have seen."[65] These accounts supplement and add to Varthema's sketchy narrative from the early sixteenth century, and a less known but very valuable anonymous account from about 1580.[66] Various other Europeans claimed, or are reputed, to have made the *hajj* in disguise. In 1183 a band of crusaders under Renaud de Chatellou penetrated the Red Sea area, and was annihilated one day's march from Medina. Of the survivors, some were taken to Cairo and executed, and possibly some others ended up in Medina, or even Mecca.[67] In the late fifteenth century the Portuguese king sent two emissaries by land to investigate the Indian Ocean area, this effort being in tandem with the better known sea expeditions. One of these travelers, Covilham, may have got to Mecca, though his modern editor shows some hesitancy in asserting this, and Kammerer is quite dubious about the claim.[68] Purportedly three other Europeans also got to Mecca in the period from the mid fourteenth century to the 1560s.[69] There is little evidence to back up by these claims. In any case, the

Europeans left no useful information about their travels and discoveries.

There is also a large literature by people who, while not claiming to have been to the Holy City, did present themselves as well informed about it. Padre Roger in the mid-seventeenth century said he had received a first hand account of Mecca and Medina from a Christian apostate, who spent five months in Mecca before reconverting to Christianity. Roger's account does not inspire respect, for he claims Muhammad reigned as king of Mecca for nine years, and died in 683![70] Around the same time, in the 1640s, Olearius was secretary to a mission despatched by the Duke of Holstein to Moscow. He spent several years in Persia, and his account of the *hajj,* while of course second hand, is relatively well informed.[71] An example of what was available in the way of information for Europeans early in the eighteenth century can be found in Reeland's compilation, while the Dane Niebuhr traveled with pilgrims over the Red Sea in 1763, and left a detailed account of what he saw and was told. He was hardly a sympathetic observer, but he was factually well informed.[72] These and many other accounts by European travelers will be used, and quoted extensively in this work. With all their faults, they are still prime sources for us, especially in the absence of many indigenous records.

What we really need, of course, are accounts by Indian Muslims who made the *hajj* in our period. This is precisely what we do not have. There are several brief mentions in the standard Mughal chronicles of people going on *hajj,* but these say nothing of what they did there, and in any case usually refer to members of the élite only. Even Indian accounts tend to be very brief, presumably because the writers thought it would be impious to say much or because they assumed that everyone knew already what happened on *hajj.* Thus Gulbadan Begum gives no useful information at all in her *Memoirs.*[73] A second account by a contemporary participant, Hajji-ud-dabir, is again very brief, and the translation from the Arabic original is so mangled as to make the meaning almost obscure. He did the *hajj* in 1574, and merely tells us that he entered Mecca, did the perambulation of the Ka'ba, the genuflections at Maqam and Safa, and the running.[74] The narrative of a *hajj* from Damascus by a Kashmiri, translated by Gladwin, is again succinct to the point of being useless. The Kashmiri made the journey in the 1740s and merely said "we reached Medina, where we paid our devotions at the shrine of the holy prophet, and other sacred tombs in that neighbourhood. When we had performed all the usual ceremonies at Medina, the caravan proceeded; and on the 6th of Zulhejeh we arrived at Mecca. When I had completed my pilgrimage, I visited the most remarkable places in and about Mecca." He then made a series of casual remarks, such as that the present Sharif of Mecca was well liked, and that "The women of Mecca wear green apples about their necks, and think them very ornamental." He stayed three months in Mecca, then went on to Jiddah, and really told us nothing of what it was like.[75]

Marshall's standard Mughal bibliography lists no other likely sources, except for one which I will describe presently, and two which appear to be of marginal importance: a short account by Faizi, the famous poet of Akbar's court, of the pilgrimage undertaken by Abu Turab Wali in 1578-9, and a sixteenth-century poem describing Mecca and Medina.[76] The important account is the "Anis-ul-hujjaj," by Safi bin Wali Qazvini (Mulla Safi-ud din). In translation this covers 71 pages. Qazvini made his *hajj* in 1087-88 AH (1676-7 CE).[77] It is by far the best account we have by a contemporary Indian Muslim. This is not to say that it gives a detailed account of the actual *hajj*, for it does not, but it is invaluable for its account of the Holy Cities, its detailed narrative of the voyage to the Red Sea, and its advice to passengers making the voyage. This maritime part of the account has been well used by Professor A. Jan Qaisar in his fascinating study of life at sea in the seventeenth century, a subject to which a recently published seventeenth-century travel account also contributes.[78] Qazvini's importance was reinforced for me recently by Barbara Metcalf, who wrote in 1990 that the written accounts left by the earliest travelers from India to the Hijaz date from the late eighteenth century. The general assumption is that the very first was by a disciple of Shah Wali-Allah in 1787.[79] This of course merely reinforces the unique value of Qazvini's much earlier (over one hundred years), and obviously much neglected, account. A scholarly edition and translation is much to be desired.

It appears that all these pilgrims assumed there was nothing new to say about the *hajj*. Qazvini wrote that he would not say much about the *hajj* itself, or Mecca and the Ka'ba, "on account of the brevity of this treatise and availability of the relevant details in many books and compilations . . ."[80] Annette Beveridge, the translator of Gulbadan's sixteenth century *Memoirs*, observed in a footnote that Gulbadan left no account of her time on *hajj*, and commented, "Some day perhaps a pious and enlightened Musalman will set down the inner meaning he [*sic*] attaches to the rites of the pilgrimage. How interesting it would have been if our princess had told us what it was in her heart that carried her through the laborious duties of piety she accomplished during her long stay in her holy land! She might have given us an essential principle by which to interpret the religious meaning which devout women attach to the rites commanded on the pilgrimage."[81] The modern historian can only echo this lament.

Our other main contemporary source is the records of the early Europeans in India. These can be difficult to find and use. Most of them are untranslated from the original Portuguese, Dutch, and Spanish, and many are unpublished. Nevertheless, they have been invaluable in this study, as will become clear as we proceed. I used especially the Portuguese records, for the seventeenth-century English and Dutch documentation has little for our purposes. The Portuguese records are conventionally divided into two categories, missionary records and records generated by the Portuguese government in Goa. As to the first, most of them are published, and they contain valuable insights and descriptions. The missionaries were of course trying to make converts, and so they were particularly interested in the religious activities of their potential clients. They aimed to know and understand the opposition the better to subvert it. And they were particularly interested in Muslims, the main religious and political opposition they faced. Muslim proselytizers were at this very time doing very well, especially in Southeast Asia, and their activities there were a source of morbid fascination for the various Christian orders. Thus, the missionary accounts are relatively full, relatively perceptive, and, of course, thoroughly hostile.[82] Their characterizations of Islam and the Prophet are redolent with prejudice and hatred. I will quote them frequently, but I trust their vigorous animosity will not be offensive to modern readers, especially Muslims. It would be incorrect to suppress or soften their denunciations, for this antipathy was real and cannot be ignored.

The accounts of the Portuguese governors and captains, and official chroniclers, are less useful. Frankly, this is a problem for me. As is well known, the Portuguese aimed to control and tax all sea trade, especially in the Arabian Sea, and also to prohibit trade in certain items, notably spices. They also forbade passage to Turks and Arabs, seeing these two groups as inveterate enemies. Their accounts are full of stories of stopping and looting or sinking huge Muslim ships bound for the prohibited area of the Red Sea. We get frequent descriptions of what cargo was on board, and how many soldiers and crew were there, but I have found almost no references to the existence of pilgrims on these ships plundered by the Portuguese. Yet they certainly were often on board, as the evidence I will present in the body of this study will make clear. A tentative answer may be that the Portuguese merely considered the pilgrims to be beneath notice; also when they sank a ship, as they often did, they of course got no clear idea about who was on board. We can also remember that *hajjis* did not necessarily look very different from other passengers, and indeed they certainly would fight as hard, or harder, as anyone else on board. Yet the fact remains that it is extraordinary that the secular Portuguese accounts have been of such little use. This is, however, an inconvenience rather than a crippling problem. As we will see, there is plenty of other evidence from which it is possible to reconstruct the role of the *hajj* from Mughal India.

## PROBLEMS OF PERCEPTION

To start this section, it is instructive to look at the work of the great modern historian Fernand Braudel. For a start, he writes of "the ships of Mecca," ignoring the obvious fact that Mecca is not a port.[83] His coverage of the whole matter is an example of the sorts of problems we find in contemporary work. Braudel claims "And indeed the pilgrimage to Mecca was the biggest fair in Islam,"[84] and later notes a very valuable caravan going "from Aleppo to Suez, Mecca and beyond . . . "[85] Leaving aside his irritating use of "Islam" (What does this mean? Does it include say Indonesia?), a glance at any map will show how improbable this route would be. Why should a land caravan from Aleppo go across to Suez? In fact they went more or less due south, through modern Jordan and so to Arabia. And where is beyond? The virtually impassable, and thoroughly hostile, deserts of Southern Arabia? And it is interesting to see that the only source Braudel gives for this sentence does not mention Mecca at all. Note the confusion in another account from Braudel.[86] In writing about the Red Sea spice trade in the sixteenth century he says Jiddah was a great port. "And this brought to the port near Mecca enormous concourses of caravans, of up to 20,000 people and 300,000 animals, at a time. Meat was never scarce in the holy city if wheat was often hard to come by. From Jiddah ships and boats sailed to Tor, the starting-point for the caravans that took nine or ten days to reach Cairo." Here he has mixed up Jiddah and Mecca, or indeed seems to think they are the same. And he has conflated pilgrims and trade; the 20,000 people were certainly not primarily traders but rather pilgrims.

These problems are found to a much greater extent in contemporary European records. A good example is the following description by Daniel, from 1700-01. We will first quote his account, and then analyze it. "They solemnize a festival here [at Mecca] once a year, being on the three and twentieth of May, where meet four caravans—one from Egypt on [sc. and] the coast of Barbary, another from Constantinople, one from Persia, and the fourth from the country of Yemen; which meeting there together are computed to be near 400,000 souls, who come there as pilgrims and under pretence of religion, but merchandising is their chiefest business, each caravan bringing the commodities and product of their respective countries, which they barter one with another, this fair during [sc. lasting] twenty days; at which time the dervisees are wholly employ'd in distributing and selling that holy water to the ignorant people."[87]

Several problems are at once apparent with this account which, it is to be stressed, is by someone who did not get to Mecca, but merely traveled down the Red Sea. First, the *hajj* is not done on a day which equates each year with a day from the Christian calendar. Second, there was no large caravan from Constantinople; he presumably means the Damascus one. Third, 400,000 seems a wild overestimate. Fourth, his claim that religion was merely a cloak for trade is at least open to question, as we will see. Fifth, "dervisees" (darvishes) would be unlikely to engage in trade, or selling holy water. What he is referring to here is the provision of the water of the well of Zamzam to pilgrims. This was not done by darvishes, and this "trade" needs to be clearly distinguished from more usual trade in secular products.

There is confusion in European sources over both the significance of Mecca, and names. Many Europeans thought
that the tomb of the Prophet was located at Mecca, and that
to visit it was the object of the pilgrimage. A European traveler in Damascus in 1432 made the usual claim that the
prophet's body was buried at Mecca, and added, gratuitously,
that some pilgrims after seeing it blinded themselves for they
felt there could no longer be anything in the world worth seeing. A German in the 1490s, who probably did not, despite his
claims, really get near to Mecca, thought that Muhammad's
body was buried in the Ka'ba, and a French priest in the
1640s wrote a long and, of course, totally spurious account of
the "Great Temple" of Mecca and Muhammad's tomb there.
The Dutch merchant van den Broecke, usually well informed
and regarded as an important source today, even so noted
that the "false prophet" Muhammad was buried in Mecca.[88]
Some even thought the tomb was miraculously, or by sleight
of hand, suspended in the air at Mecca. A Jesuit traveler in
the 1660s refuted this vigorously: "Here I wish to draw attention to the mistaken belief the world over, that the body of the
odious Muhammad floats in the air by virtue of the walls of
his temple, it is said, consisting of load stones. When I spoke
about it to the Arabs who had visited Medina, they laughed
at those who believed in such things . . . "[89] An English
account confused both names and significance when it noted
the return of a person "from Mocha, sanctified by the addition
of Hadgee, attayned by holy pilgrimage to Mahometts shrine
. . . ",[90] for of course the pilgrimage is to Mecca, not Mocha,
and consists of various rites and actions in Mecca, while
Muhammad's tomb is in Medina. This confusion over this
most basic fact of Islam is even to be found in the modern
work of a great Jesuit historian, who wrote of "Jidda, the harbor for pilgrims going to Mecca, who had come from all over
the Islamic world to visit the tomb of the Prophet."[91]

Further confusion comes from European claims that the
great Muslim festival, that is the ceremonies of the *hajj*, took

place on a certain day each year. The normally careful Pires wrote of "the time of the Jubilee, which is held every year on the first day of February . . . " while nearly two hundred years later Daniel, as we saw, thought it was on a fixed date.[92] So also for the usually well-informed Jesuit traveler Manuel Godinho, who noted "Mecca, where Muhammad was born, and world famous on this account, and also for the universal fair held there each year during August and September, at which gather by land and sea goods from all over the world."[93] A slightly earlier account in 1652 by the Frenchman Sanson, "géographe ordinaire du Roy", of France, made a very similar mistake as to the date: "The City [Mecca], filled with six thousand well-built houses, for its magnificent Temple, is beautiful . . . At the end of May, time of the great Mohammedan Festival, over fifty thousand foreign men and almost fifty thousand Camels are to be found at the fair held there."[94] In 1780 Capper similarly seemed to think the pilgrimage took place according to a solar, that is Western, calendar.[95]

The problem is that the Islamic year, being based on the moon, "loses" eleven days each year compared with the Western solar calendar; in other words the time of the jubilee or festival, that is the *hajj*, "moves" through the Western calendar and so cannot be on the same Western day each year. We can then see these claims as early examples of a Western failure to appreciate different cultures and different customs. On the specific matter of assuming that the *hajj* was performed on a particular day in the Christian calendar, these observers presumably were simply assuming that Muslims were like Christians, and held their festivals at set times each year, failing to recognize that the Muslim year is calculated on a different basis. Some of the others appear to have thought the *hajj* was some ritual that could be done at any time, just as they could go to church whenever it suited them.

This problem, however, is not just a matter of dates. We have to treat European accounts, even by those who had, or who claimed they had, actually been in Mecca with great caution. As one example of the sorts of things Europeans wrote, which remind us very powerfully of Said's warnings in *Orientalism*, and which earlier Norman Daniel described in his important work,[96] consider the following. One of the major features of the area around the Ka'ba itself is the well known as Zamzam. Qazvini, a seventeenth-century Indian pilgrim, described its importance. As part of the whole ritual of the *hajj*, the pilgrim "should then proceed to the well of Zamzam and take out one bucket of water and drink as much as he can. The rest is to be used for bath or it may be poured on the head and face." Later Qazvini tells us that "Drinking the water of Zamzam and looking inside the well is an act of piety. There is also no harm in taking bath or performing ablutions from the water of Zamzam. Nothing except pure things should be washed by it. It is reprehensible to use it for washing after defecating or urinating. It is virtuous to take it to other parts of the world."[97] Around 1600 a Spanish Muslim pilgrim wrote of "this true water, which is a purifier for sins and neglect."[98] An *hadith* notes that "l'eau produit les effets que l'on espère en la buvant," and indeed in 1611 a grill was placed over the mouth of the well to stop people from committing pious suicide by throwing themselves in as an offering to Allah.[99]

Compare these accounts by believers of the significance of the well with what a sixteenth-century European, who apparently did make the pilgrimage, has to say: "The women of the place [Mecca] are courteous, jocund, and lovely, faire, with alluring eyes, being hote and libidinous, and the most of them naughtie packes. The men of this place are given to that abhomenable, cursed, and opprobrious vice, whereof both men and women make but small account by reason of the pond Zun Zun, wherein having washed themselves, their opinion is, that although like the dog they returne to their vomite, yet they are clensed from all sinne whatsoever . . . " Later he tells us that after the Ka'ba has been circumambulated seven times, and the black stone kissed, "After they go unto the pond Zun Zun, and in their apparell as they be, they wash themselves from head to foote, saying, Tobah Allah, Tobah Allah, that is to say, Pardon lord, Pardon lord, drinking also of that water, which is both muddie, filthie and of an ill savour, and in this wise washed and watered, everyone returneth to his place of abode . . ."[100]

In the eighteenth century, generally speaking, European accounts become more detailed, and more accurate. At the same time they reflect the beginnings of European dominance in the Indian Ocean and Middle East. Accounts before the mid-eighteenth century are usually ill-informed, but at least written from a stance of rough equality. The reverse is true from around 1750, when we begin to get precisely the phenomenon that Said identified: the creation of a history of the Middle East and Asia by materially dominant European powers.[101]

A good example of the former is the following long quotation from Olearius, who had spent several years in Persia. It is worth quoting quite fully, for it shows mistakes to be sure, but very little sense of superiority, and it is an excellent example of the degree of knowledge available to educated Europeans around the mid-seventeenth century. He wrote from Persia in April 1637:

It is about this time, that the *Persians* go to do their Devotions at Mecca, as well as the *Turks*. . . . The men put on a particular Coiffure for this Voyage, which is a kind of Turbant of White Wool; in regard their Law forbids them to wear it of any Colour, or of silk at that time. They call this kind of Turbant *Elharam*, and they cover their Heads therewith, only as they go; so as that one part of it falling down on one side of the Head, passes under the Chin, and is fasten'd on the other side.

They commonly take their way through the City of

*Jerusalem*, where they do their first Devotions. Thence they passe through *Medina*, where they continue them at the Sepulchre of *Mahomet*, which they kisse with a profound Veneration, and then they conclude them at *Meca*, or Mount *Arafat*. From *Medina* to *Meca*, they are cover'd only with a shirt, nay some go naked down to the waste. In this posture they march continually, and after a very particular fashion. For they are oblig'd to go, after the rate of a trotting Horse, or rather that of a Camel galloping, and that with such earnestness, that they hardly take the leisure to eat and drink, or yet to sleep: and all, out of an imagination, that the Sweat caus'd by that Violent Motion, and forc'd out of their Bodies, carries away with it all their Sins, and cleanseth them of all their filthinesse. The Women, who might not be able to bear the inconveniences of such a march, have the privilege to swarth up their Breasts with a Skarf, which hath a particular name, and they call it *Scamachtze*.

The tenth day of the month of *Silhatza* is that of their great Devotion. That day, all the Pilgrims go to Mount *Arafat*, which, they say, is the place where the Patriarch *Abraham* should have Sacrifiz'd his Son, and there they spend the whole night in Prayers. Towards the dawning of the day, they come down, and go to the City of *Meca* . . . . After all these Ceremonies, they go in Procession about the *Mosquey*, they kisse a Stone, which was left after the finishing of the Structure, and they take of the Water, which passes through a Golden Chanel over the *Mosquey*, and carry it away as a Relick, with a little piece of a certain Blackish Wood, of which Toothpicks are made. When the Pilgrims are return'd from their Pilgrimage, they are called *Hatzi*, and they are as it were *Nazarites*, dedicated to God, in as much as it is unlawfull for them to drink Wine ever after.[102]

25

Another account, from the 1750s, shows an advance in knowledge but not in prejudice, for Grose got the real meanings of the rites quite well. He wrote of Muhammad:

a mere man, subject to all the failings and passions of one, and so far from addressing him as a saint, is that in their moschs and orisons, they do not pray to him, but for him, recommending him to the divine mercy: nor is there any such thing, as what has been vulgarly believed, of pilgrimages to his tomb: these being in a religious sense, solely directed to what is called the Cahabah, or holy-house, at Mecca, which, having long been an idol-temple, was by Mahomet dedicated to the unity of God, and wherein he retained, in compliance to the idolators, the famous black-stone, which had been worshipped by them as representing Akbar their *greatest* god. The prophet's tomb is at Medina, visited by Mahometans purely out of curiosity and reverence to his memory; but the Indian Moors frequently return without ever seeing it at all, though it is so near Mecca.[103]

This improved knowledge was to an extent a result of better education and travel opportunities for Europeans through the eighteenth century. The negative side of this was contempt and suspicion, based on European technological superiority. Middle Eastern boats are now described as hopeless compared with European ones. A passenger on the Jiddah to Suez voyage in 1782 wrote with heavy sarcasm that "The construction and management of the vessels are equally singular and I fear any description of them will fall infinitely short of the originals; they were I believe, designed by those who built them to bear some resemblance to ships, but having very few of the properties of those machines proceed on a principle totally different from any I before beheld . . ."[104]

Nor was trade to the Red Sea now of any importance. Here is an example of the sort of ethnocentric and scornful writing that had become the norm late in the eighteenth century. A brash young Englishman, reflecting all too faithfully the growing dominance of his country, wrote:

> The trade of India wholly exists in the spirit and industry of the English. While their vessels are exploring the islands that border on the Pacific Ocean, and return with a freight that renders our settlements the mart of oriental productions, a ship or two is sent yearly to Judda by the nabob of Arcot. These vessels, indeed, carry a cargo, and import in exchange, the products of Arabia. But this is the captain's care. The only benefit which the nabob looks for, is the prayers of two or three hundred pilgrims, who are transported at his expence, to perform their vows at the mosque of Mecca! his ships were so crouded this season with these idle mendicants, that through the nabob's interest with the owners, we had the company of above twenty of them in our vessel. This was an honour we were by no means ambitious of; and from which we readily disengaged ourselves at Mocha, where they were landed to prosecute their journey in the best manner they could."[105]

Such examples could be multiplied endlessly.

W.R. Roff has written compellingly of the problem of subjecting events which have important religious significance for others to social science analysis. Any analysis by a non-believer must try to come to terms with the central religious significance that these events have for the participants. A social scientist will of course be interested in analyzing the economic, political, social, and ideological implications of the pilgrimage, its role in ideological dissemination or status enhancement, but these quite appropriate concerns must not be allowed to obscure the central religiosity of the event for those who participate in it. Roff quotes an Islamic scholar, Abu Yazid of Bistan, as saying of his pilgrimages "On my first pilgrimage I saw only the temple [*sc.* the Ka'ba]; the second time, I saw both the temple and the Lord of the temple; and the third time I saw the Lord alone."[106] The first applies to the Western social scientist who ignores the religious centrality of the event, the last to the devout, suffused in the religiosity of the event. My aim is to emulate Abu Yazid on his second pilgrimage, to see both the mundane and the spiritual aspects of the *hajj*.

## NAMES

The matter of names and their spelling is, of course, a general problem for anyone writing on non-Western history, for transliterations have varied greatly over the centuries, and our European sources frequently provide very garbled versions indeed. I have chosen to use the most familiar spellings of places, even if in some cases they are no longer strictly correct. In the Red Sea area, the strictly correct spellings (though even these are not universally accepted) would be Makkah, Al Madinah, Jiddah and for the important southern Red Sea port Al Mukha or Mukhkhah. But I will use respectively Mecca, Medina, Jiddah and Mocha. For that matter, strictly speaking the *hajj* is the *haj* or *hadjdj*, but again I will use the more familiar form.

This term, *hajj*, is completely central to our discussion, so it is worthwhile to clarify precisely its meaning. The word literally means "setting out," or "tending towards." From the time of the *Qur'an* it has meant "pilgrimage to Mecca," referring then to one of the "Five Pillars" of the Muslim faith. It is universally used in this sense in Islamic works, and defined in this way in Persian and Arabic dictionaries and glossaries. The usual word for pilgrimage in general is *"ziarat,"* and *hajj* is restricted to the most important one, that to Mecca. It is, then, an obvious solecism to write of the "pilgrimage of the *hajj*," for this means the "pilgrimage of the pilgrimage to Mecca."

Equally important for our discussion is the particular matter of two names, Mocha and Mecca. The possibility of confusion is great, for the modern transliterations are very similar, namely Makkah and Mukhkhah. Indeed, according to Tibbetts, Muslims as well as Europeans often confused the two.[107] We noted above a seventeenth-century confusion of the two, in the English account of a person sanctified after being in Mocha, a port just inside the Red Sea which has no religious significance at all. Modern editors have also had this problem. Irvine's edition of Manucci notes that people "reached Mecca [?Mokah]".[108] Irvine is obviously wrong; Mokah in the original must be in fact Mocha. This matter is of considerable importance. We read very frequently in the sources of the ships from Mecca. Now this is an obvious absurdity, even if it is to be found in some modern works, because Mecca is not a port. What we need to know is whether this means ships from Mocha, or whether the authors mean ships carrying goods from Mecca which were actually loaded on board ship at the port nearest to Mecca, that is Jiddah. The Portuguese sources write frequently of the ports of Mecca, the trade of Mecca, Mecca merchants, but often it appears they use Mecca in error for Mocha, or that Mecca is a generic term for the Red Sea; how else to explain the "ports of Mecca"?[109] A Jesuit traveler in the 1660s clarified this matter, but then added to the confusion by locating Mocha incorrectly: "Christians are not allowed to enter it [Mecca], and when they say that the Portuguese and other European nationals are proceeding to Mecca, it actually means the port of Mokah that is nearest to Mecca, which is situated inland."[110] Dutch sources also write of the ship or ships from Mecca.[111] But what of the way some modern authors write of people "sailing from Mecca in a boat of Arab merchants . . . " or of shipping having Mecca as their destination?[112] In these cases modern authors have carelessly followed their sources without reflecting on the fact that Mecca is not a port, and that often when a source writes

Mecca or some variant of this word it actually means Mocha.

## PERIODIZATION

This study is essentially concerned with the *hajj* from Mughal India. The period under review is the sixteenth to the eighteenth centuries. However, I will on occasion use sources from before and after this period, especially when I am writing of the ritual and ceremonies of the event. As noted, these changed very little over the centuries; Ibn Jubayr's twelfth-century account is very similar to that of Pitts from the seventeenth, or indeed Burton or Hurgronje from the nineteenth century. However, leaving aside the actual practice of the pilgrims, our period has a marked unity in other areas, and can be easily justified as a unit of study. In the early sixteenth century several events influenced the *hajj*. This was the time when the Hijaz was incorporated into the powerful and expansionist Ottoman empire. Since the fourteenth century the Hijaz had been dominated by Mamluk Egypt, at least to the extent that the Sharif of Mecca, the traditional and hereditary guardian of the Holy Cities and the Hijaz area in general, owed nominal political allegiance to Cairo. The Mamluks were defeated by the Ottoman Turks in 1516-17, and in July of the latter year the Sharif of Mecca, Sharif Barakat II, accepted the inevitable and recognized the overlordship of Istanbul.

As a result, the main towns and ports of the Hijaz became subject to relatively detailed Ottoman supervision, and this had its effect on the *hajj*.[113] As Raymond puts it, the *hajj* "took on a heretofore unprecedented importance during the Ottoman era. The very dimensions of the empire, its political unification, and the efforts engaged in by the Ottoman government and its local representatives to facilitate the fulfilment of the *hagg* [sic] made possible the travel of caravans of pilgrims difficult to number but estimated at 30,000 or 40,000 for those converging on Cairo and at 20,000 to 30,000 for those assembling in Damascus. To the exchange of goods directly induced by the moving of these human masses alone during a trip which lasted one year was added the commercial activity carried out through the medium of the caravans, on the way to the Hedjaz and back, which concerned the most distant regions of the empire."[114]

Meanwhile, in two other major Islamic areas comparable events occurred. In both India and Persia important Islamic dynasties took power in the early sixteenth century and established law and order and strong Islamic states. In Persia the Safavids took over very early in the century, and not only established political control but also imposed *shia* Islam over the area they ruled. In India the Mughals gained control of northern India in the 1520s, and after a brief period of uncertainty became in the second half of the century, under the great ruler Akbar, the dominant power in north and parts of central India. As Das Gupta has argued, there was then an "Islamic peace" established in all this vast area. Stability and relatively advanced administration promoted prosperity, and this in turn made it possible for more people to go on *hajj*.[115] The establishment of this stability early in the sixteenth century makes an obvious starting point for our investigations.

The choice of a concluding date is also relatively straightforward, for the situation was very radically altered late in the eighteenth century. Two facets are important here, one general and one particular. The general factor is of course the decline of all three of these Islamic empires in the eighteenth century. While it is true that recent studies have been concerned to show some progressive and innovative factors in the eighteenth century in the Islamic world, so that we are learning not to look at this period as one of unrelieved decline, anarchy and degradation, the fact still is that these empires did decline, and this did mean more precarious law and order, more difficult traveling conditions, and less state patronage for the pilgrim caravans and sea travelers. In turn these declines can be seen as a result of, or perhaps a pre-condition for, the rise of Western dominance in the Islamic world. While none of these areas were colonized in the eighteenth century, except for parts of India, the global balance did change radically, so that while we are justified in seeing these three empires as the most powerful in the world at around 1600, this was certainly no longer the case two hundred years later. By 1800 the Islamic world, and indeed Asia in general, was being incorporated into a world system centered on and dominated by capitalist western Europe. Asian subordination to the West, and especially to England, had diffuse but very important consequences for all aspects of the pilgrimage. In the broader sphere, the politics and economies of the Muslim world were transformed, often destroyed, by this new subordination, and this was writ small in the area of the *hajj*.

The more particular reason which impels us to conclude this study late in the eighteenth century is the rise of the reformist Wahhabi movement in Arabia itself. This movement, which has been dominant in Saudi Arabia since the 1920s when their political allies, the Saud dynasty, took power in the area, began in the eighteenth century as a reaction to what its founder, Muhammad ibn Abd-al-Wahhab, saw as innovations in Islam. He died in the early 1790s, but his opposition to the worship of saints, and other practices which, according to him, were not sanctioned at the time of the Prophet, was carried on by his followers. The movement became political and militant, and in 1802 the Wahhabis seized, sacked, and purified the great *shia* center of Karbala. A year later Mecca, and in 1805 Medina, received the same treatment. The influence of these wild, intimidating Puritans on the *hajj* [116] is made clear in accounts from the early nineteenth century. By 1819 their political power was lost at the hands of Muhammad Ali of Egypt, acting for the Ottoman sultan, but their influence on religion remained strong, and indeed extended to most parts of the Islamic world. In this they constitute an example of the way Islam as practiced in Mecca has always had a certain prestige in the rest of the Muslim world; but for our present purposes the point is merely that their rise, together with the general decline of the Muslim world in political and economic terms, makes a suitable terminal point for our study.

# CHAPTER 2

# The Early Modern *Hajj*

The most important Muslim pilgrimage is that to Mecca at the prescribed time, that is the pilgrimage correctly referred to as the *hajj*, but Muslims make many other pilgrimages to other places of religious significance. Muslims frequently visit shrines, many of which are tombs associated with some notable Islamic figure. These visitations are called *ziyarah* or *ziarat*, and can involve large numbers of people. Xavier de Planhol noted 250,000 at a shrine in Senegal in 1937, several hundred thousand at a site in the Nile Delta, and nearly 100,000 at one in Algeria. As a comparison, the numbers doing the *hajj* were 300,000 in 1912, and in 1927 225,000.[1] The most famous tomb is that of the Prophet at Medina, and a visit there is usually combined with the actual *hajj*, but equally important locally are the tombs of *sufi* saints considered to have some special property, such as the ability to forgive sins, to bring worldly success, to ensure the birth of a male child, or some other specific attribute. An account from the early thirteenth century lists a vast array of holy sites, from Spain all the way to Iran, which were the foci of pilgrimages.[2] These journeys were undertaken by women more than by men, and included visits to *sufi khanqahs*, shrines, mosques, tombs and mausoleums of Muslim saints, *pirs*, martyrs and notable *sufis*.[3] Muslims on a journey would take time to call in at any notable shrine or other place of religious significance *en route*. Sidi Ali Reis, in his travels to and from India in the 1550s, seems to have hardly missed a tomb or shrine on his travels.[4] Puey Monçon, around 1600, spent some time sight seeing and visiting shrines in Cairo on the way to Mecca.[5] In Mecca and Medina there was, of course, a vast array of places, apart from Muhammad's actual tomb, associated with the Prophet and his immediate family and followers and companions. Qazvini lists among other places in Mecca the houses of Khadijah, 'Aisha, and Abu Bakr, the birthplaces of Muhammad and Ali, and various mosques and tombs.[6]

Such visits and longer pilgrimages were voluntary, and this distinguishes them from the *hajj*, which is not. When a pilgrim got to Mecca he or she could do three different pilgrimages. Most of course came to do the *hajj* itself, but if they were lucky they could do the *hajj akbar*, or *hajj al-Akbar*. This was an especially auspicious *hajj*, because in certain years the time of the standing at Arafat was considered to be likely to fall on a Friday. When this was the case about double the number of pilgrims could be expected. But it was difficult to predict when such an event would occur, as the whole calendar was governed by the moon, and so could not be predicted with any great certainty. A French traveler in the early seventeenth century described this well for the Maldives. "This solemn fast [of Ramadan] begins at the new moon, and ends at the new moon of the following month. It does not, however, commence exactly at the time of the new moon, but when they first observe it; so that in some attollons and islands it begins a day sooner or later, according as they descry the crescent. The months are reckoned in the same way; it is not counted a new month till the moon is seen, which is very uncertain when the sky is thick and cloudy. Sometimes the months are different in different places."[7] Thus one could not be certain of going on a *hajj al-Akbar* until the new moon for the month of Dhu al-Hijja was sighted. Our Indian pilgrim Qazvini was one of the lucky ones; he noted that "It is one of the fortunate moments of this year that Arafah was on Friday and sacrifices were performed on Saturday. According to most of the people, especially those of Mecca, this year's hajj was hajj-i Akbar as it had been in the past in the year of the conquest of Mecca."[8]

The normal *hajj* has been much described; references concerning the actual rituals and ceremonies can be found in the various accounts mentioned in Chapter 1. The *hajj* was and is performed in the first ten days of the Muslim month of Dhu al-Hijja, the twelfth month of the Muslim lunar year. It will be remembered, however, that compared with the Western solar calendar the Muslim calendar "loses" ten or eleven days a year, so that in the space of 32 or 33 years it goes through the whole cycle of the seasons. Sometimes it will be performed in cool weather, but slowly the time of the *hajj* will move until the unfortunate pilgrim undertakes it in the hottest season in Arabia. About fifteen years after this the *hajj* will be back to cooler weather, and so on in this cyclical fashion. The crucially important rituals take place from the eighth to the tenth days of Dhu al-Hijja. Most people, however, take longer than just these three days.[9] Indeed, some authorities consider the central *hajj* to last for five, or even six, days. Thus one modern account claims that it starts on the eighth, includes the ninth at Arafat, the stoning of the devils at Mina on the tenth, returning to Mecca and again circumambulating the Ka'ba, with the actual *hajj* concluding only on the thirteenth of Dhu al-Hijja.[10]

The third type of pilgrimage is the lesser pilgrimage, or *umrah*. This can be done at any time in the year, except during the time of the *hajj*. There are, however, certain times of the year when it is better to undertake an *umrah*; thus the month of Rajab has associated with it an important *umrah*.[11] It involves merely circuits of the Ka'ba, and the running between the hills of al-Safa and al-Marwa. Usually people would do both. Richard Burton did an *umrah* just after he had completed his *hajj*.[12] Over six hundred years earlier, Ibn Battuta spent four years in Mecca, from 1327 to 1330. Apart from the times of the *hajj*, he tells us that "I led a most agreeable existence, giving myself up to circuits, pious exercises and frequent performances of the Lesser Pilgrimage."[13] In the sixteenth century Gulbadan, a Mughal princess, similarly stayed some years, and did a series of *hajjs* and *umrahs*.[14] Indeed, even today many *hajjis* linger in Saudi Arabia, combining a holiday and sightseeing with their religious obligations.

Two other variations can be briefly noted. First, Qazvini says there were three sorts of *hajjis*: those who did the *hajj*; those who did only the *umrah*; and those who did both.[15] In the more leisurely time in which he wrote, some people would undertake both types as a matter of course, and would nearly always also undertake the journey to Medina in order to visit the graves of the Prophet and the various other Islamic notables buried there. But those on the great state-supported caravans from Cairo and Damascus, that is the majority of pilgrims, were not, as we will see, allowed this sort of lingering, for they were on a very tight schedule indeed. Second, while pilgrimages are obviously central and important, any visit to Mecca at any time is meritorious. The town, redolent with associations with the life of the Prophet and of later Islamic history, is itself in a sense holy, sacred. Even if the minimal rites of the *umrah* are not undertaken, it is still, for example, meritorious to pray in the Great Mosque, and perhaps kiss the Black Stone in the Ka'ba. As Puey Monçon wrote in his poem describing his *hajj* of around 1600, "Thus we arrived at Mecca, this hallowed city, whose entrances are blessed, and walls godly; its roofs are splendid, and the whole town is blessed, for whosoever goes there receives pardon."[16]

The *hajj* itself has been recognized as being central in the town of Mecca. As Hurgronje noted, "We see how in Mecca the whole social life finds its central point in the Hajj. Nowhere has the Moslem calendar with its lunar year greater practical significance than here." The whole life of the town in fact revolved around the pilgrimage month.[17] But its significance far transcended its role in the town in which it occurred. It is of course one of the so-called Five Pillars of the faith, an obligation on all Muslims who are at all capable of undertak-

40

ing the journey. Its importance is laid down in the *Qur'an* itself, where the faithful are enjoined to "Perform the pilgrimage and the visit [to Mecca] for Allah . . . " or alternatively "Perform the hajj and the umra for Allah." Similarly, believers are told that "pilgrimage to the House [of Abraham] is a duty unto Allah for mankind . . . " Finally, the holy book says "And proclaim unto mankind the Pilgrimage. They will come unto thee on foot and on every lean camel; they will come from every deep ravine." [18]

The *hajj* was all sorts of things: a social event, a mechanism for solidifying and purifying Islam, perhaps an economic event, it had various political implications, it was an arduous and exciting journey, it was a great transmitter of disease. A fourteenth-century Egyptian said that the caravan from Cairo took with it food and water supplies and, ominously, medicines and drugs, physicians and oculists, and washers of the dead, this in the context of a death on *hajj* guaranteeing admission to paradise. [19] Dr. John Fryer noted in 1677 the return to Surat of the Jiddah fleet, "freighted with Religion and Pestilence." [20] The performance of the *hajj* resulted in a rise in status, and perhaps some people undertook it for this reason. But first and foremost it was a religious event. [21]

The *hajj* could mean different things to different people. For the majority of simple *sunni* Muslims it was an overwhelming religious experience, the event of a lifetime. For a *sufi*, the set ritual of the *hajj* was less important than the heightened mystical state which could be achieved by pilgrimage to and meditation at places associated with the greatest guide of all, the Prophet. [22] These *sufis* would follow the prescribed rituals and ceremonies to be sure, but they would claim that the quality and nature of their experience was far more intense, personal, spiritual, than was that of the ordinary Muslim. The *hajj*, then, and the whole Meccan experience were in a way similar to other mystical practices, such as meditation, song, dance, and breath control; ultimately all of them were designed to bring the adept closer to unity with God. The Prophet, and his son-in-law Ali, were recognized by nearly all the *sufi* orders as themselves great *pirs*; thus ritual laid down by the Prophet, and places associated with his life, were excellent for the needs of *sufis*.

For *shia* Muslims it was again a little different. Apart from the well-known doctrinal differences (for example a *shia* would not visit the tombs of the three first *khalifs*) the whole matter seems to have had a more mystical and devotional atmosphere for *shias*. A seventeenth-century English traveler said of Persian pilgrims that "those of them that think the best Tribe not clarified till they have enobled it by some Religious Act, are not at rest till they have wiped off these Stains; which set them on foot so often to Mahomet's Tomb; returning whence all former Taint is abolished, and they become pure Musselmen indeed, which is the strongest Confirmation after Circumcism: For That is a time of Jollity, This of Labour and Travel, whereby they approve themselves what their Parents only Sponded for them; and this is a Task imposed mostly on their new Proselytes."[23]

Modern scholars agree on the significance of the event, though their emphases vary considerably. Marshall Hodgson put it in a nutshell when he wrote, in *The Venture of Islam,* "In the hajj itself, every wealthy Muslim planned to participate as a major life's excursion, not only for piety but for adventure and perhaps learning or personal retreat; and even occasionally as a political expedient." He ignores possible economic implications.[24] William R. Roff has noted, drawing on the work of Victor Turner, some of the sociological elements of the *hajj*. He writes of "The ambiguity of a journey from the hearth to the centre, which is at once penitential and an escape from the ordinary constraints of life; the shedding of individuality in a shared 'communitas' of enjoined ritual; the acquisition and reinforcement of Islamic ideas; the symbolism of entering the Holy Land clothed in the *ihram* and the return home clothed in Arab dress; all bear witness to a transmutation which . . . carries with it profound meaning for Islamic beliefs and attitudes, and for the performance of certain roles within the *umma.* "[25]

These various strands were quite well combined in a relatively informed and sympathetic English account from the late eighteenth century. Rooke wrote

> The zeal shown by Mussulmen, and the toils and sufferings undergone by them for the sake of paying this compliment to their prophet, are wonderful; they flock to Mecca from all parts of the Mahometan countries, and perform the most laborious journies: the poorer part of these pilgrims, depend on charity for their support, which rarely yields them anything better than a scanty allowance of bread and water. Vanity, religion, superstition and commerce, are the four principal causes of these annual pilgrimages. A Mussulman that has been at Mecca, gains thereby a degree of honor amongst his countrymen, with the term of Hadge added to his name whenever he is spoke to; his attendance there at least once in his life is required by his creed: many visit it in compliance with vows made at some time of impending danger, or conditionally on the attainment of a desirable object; others who have lead dissolute lives go there for absolution; and with an intention to reform; and others for the purposes of traffique: all fancy themselves the better for having been there; and from that conviction, perhaps many really become so.[26]

How did pilgrims get to Mecca in the early modern period? The short answer is, with difficulty. No matter which route was taken, the journey was long, arduous, and dangerous.[27] As an extreme example, before this century intending pilgrims from West Africa took at least two years, and sometimes eight, to complete the return journey.[28] Indeed, it is interesting, as we will see, that a much longer time was spent on the journey than was spent in Mecca itself, for sometimes a journey of six months or more would produce only a month in Mecca and Medina. And the journey was expensive, even for those, the majority, who traveled as simply as possible. Qazvini had sponsorship from Aurangzeb's daughter Zeb-un-nisa, the great patron of scholarship and the arts during his reign, but his pilgrimage still cost him about Rs. 1000.[29] The commitment of those who undertook it is thus not to be underestimated. Nor, however, should the element of adventure and novelty be ignored. The journey was an adventure, a long break from everyday cares, and one of course sanctioned and approved because of its religious importance.

The rise of Islam had caused profound changes in trade routes in the Middle East. Mecca had been a trade center of some importance before and during the time of the Prophet,[30] but the expansion of Islam, and especially the requirement of pilgrimage, caused some changes in existing routes. Old routes were expanded, as the increasing numbers of Muslims caused a rise in the pilgrim traffic. This applies to those linking Mecca with Egypt, Syria, Yemen and the Persian/Arabian Gulf. But new routes appeared, those joining Mecca to Iraq, Persia, and Oman. The rise of Islam also resulted in a unique focus on one town, Mecca, and at a particular time of the year; that is the caravans would all be timed to reach the city early in the month of Dhu al-Hijja.

This requirement had to be rigidly met, for otherwise the correct time for the *hajj* would be missed, and the whole point of the exercise nullified. Pyrard got this right, though he also made the common mistake of thinking the point of the pilgrimage was to visit Muhammad's tomb in Mecca. He wrote of "the holy day upon which the Mahometan pilgrims assemble at Mecca to visit the sepulchre of Mahomet. More ceremonies are then performed than during all the rest of the year: on that day they come from all parts of the world, and sometimes when they have arrived too late, and it is over, they have to await the return of the festival for ten or eleven months."[31] We have a detailed account of the 1565 caravan from Cairo.[32] The caravan left Cairo on May 9, 1565, and reached Aqaba on June 5. It reached Yanbo, the port of Medina, on June 22 and arrived in Mecca on July 3, 1565. On July 23, with the *hajj* completed, the caravan left Mecca and spent the first four days of August in Medina, before returning to Egypt. This was precisely timed, for in this year July 3 to 23, the time of their stay in Mecca, coincided in the Islamic calendar with Dhu al-Hijja 4 to 24 in the year 972 AH. The main rituals of the *hajj*, it will be remembered, are performed from the 8th to the 10th of this month. In the 1740s a Damascus *hajj* caravan was attacked by bandits and three of its members killed. The chief of the caravan "wanted to assault the place, and revenge the death of our unfortunate companions; but was dissuaded from the enterprise, by the interposition of the principal people of the caravan, who represented to him, that in case of delay, the season for the performance of the pilgrimage would elapse before we could reach Mecca." [33]

Mecca, rather than being a through station, became a terminus, a place where people arrived, did their *hajj*, and then turned around and went back again. But there were variations over time, dictated especially by the security situation on the routes. If the political situation was fluid, marauding beduin had more scope. Plunder was a problem, and consequently the number of persons who ventured on the journey was reduced. This situation was acute until the early sixteenth century, before the establishment of a certain *Pax Ottomanica*, and again in the late eighteenth century as Wahhabi opposition to many aspects of the traditional *hajj*, and Islamic practice in Mecca in general, became influential. After the sack of Mecca in 1803, there were no regular caravans for several years.[34]

We have accounts of each of the major routes used to reach Mecca in our period. For the sea route from India, we have a detailed description in Qazvini's narrative. The part of

his account which deals with the sea voyage from Surat to
Jiddah has been analyzed by A. Jan Qaisar and the reader is
referred to this for an impression of the inconveniences, dangers and hardships of this route in the later seventeenth century.[35] In all his *hajj* took twelve months. He reached Surat
on the 3rd Ramazan, 1087 AH. (9 Nov., 1676). Forty-two days
later, on the 15th Shawwal he boarded the "Salamat Ras,"
which finally set sail with five other ships. They reached
Mecca on time, that is they entered the city 46 days after
leaving Surat, on the 3rd Dhu al-Hijja; on the 8th, again right
on time, they were at Arafat. The great Egyptian caravan left
for Medina on the 25th of Dhu al-Hijja, and the Syrian one a
few days later, on 2nd Muharram 1088. Qazvini, however,
was long delayed in Mecca, and finally left for Medina, after
49 days in Mecca, only on the 23rd Muharram (28 March,
1677).[36]

Qazvini noted the showy and prestigious caravans from
Damascus and Cairo, and indeed these two were always the
largest and richest.[37] This was in part because of Ottoman
patronage, but also because they drew on the two great population centers of Islam. We have an excellent contemporary
general description of them from the late eighteenth century:

> Those annual caravans which go from Aleppo and
> Cairo to Mecca, are often composed of thirty or forty
> thousand people, and are under military government,
> an officer being appointed by the Grand Signor, called
> the Emir Hadge, who conducts and commands them;
> the order of march is regular, and by ranks; the disci-
> pline is very exact, and a guard of Janissaries with
> field-pieces form the escort: they have regular times of
> marching and halting, which is done by signal. When
> they take up their ground for the night, tents are
> pitched, kitchens, cook-shops and coffee-houses are
> immediately erected, and a large camp is formed;
> everything is as quickly packed, and the camels are
> loaded in the morning to be ready for gun-firing,

46

which puts the whole body in motion. The caravan from Cairo performs its journey to Mecca in forty days, where having staid about a month to celebrate the Hadge, a festival in which both the interests of trade and religion are equally consulted; it returns in the same order, stopping at Medina in [*sic*] the way back, to pay a visit to and make offerings at the shrine of Mahommed, that having been the place of his internment, as Mecca was of his nativity."[38]

We have several detailed accounts of the great journey from Cairo. Ibn Jubayr's account dates from the twelfth century, Puey Monçon's from about 1600, Ali Bey's from the early nineteenth, and Burton's from the middle of the same century.[39] Ali Bey went by land from Cairo in 1806-7 in a caravan of 5000 camels and 2-300 horses, but at Suez transferred to a ship for a traumatic voyage down to Jiddah, which took 21 days and left him shaken.[40] Cairo was the great collection center for all pilgrims from Egypt and north Africa, and even for those from west Africa.[41] The journey to Mecca was usually made overland, though neither Burton nor Ali Bey did this. The vast camel caravan crossed the Sinai peninsular and went along the coastal plain of western Arabia, that is the east bank of the Red Sea, thus bypassing Medina, which was usually visited on the way home. This journey from Cairo to Mecca took about 40 days, or more, even up to 50.[42] A modern account says there were 36 resting stops between Cairo and Mecca, 20 days were allowed in Mecca, it took 10 days to get to Medina, where 2 days were allowed, and then 36 days back to Cairo. At a minimum the round trip took 110 days.[43] African Muslims from the area of the Sudan and further south and west would usually not go all the way north to Cairo, but rather make their way to the Red Sea and cross it to either Jiddah, the port of Mecca, or Yanbo, the port of Medina. A sixteenth-century Portuguese chronicler noted Alcocer (probably Quseir, or Kosseir, or more correctly al-Qusayr, on the west coast of the Red Sea), a port sixty leagues south of Suez, where "most of the Muslims from the west, when they go on their pilgrimage to Mecca, collect together in this port in order to avoid traveling to Cairo."[44]

The second great caravan, that from Damascus, consisted of pilgrims from all over Syria, Turkey and parts of Persia. Raymond notes the importance of Ottoman patronage. "The Takiyya [convent] and the Madrasa [school] of Sulayman showed, in a most spectacular way, the sultan's interest in the pilgrimage, of which Damascus, along with Cairo, was a rallying point."[45] The journey to Medina was 1300 km, and took some 40 days, and then ten more days to Mecca.[46] Varthema claimed the journey to Mecca from Damascus took forty days and forty nights.[47] A mid-eighteenth century account by a participant said the journey was 718 farsangs, each farsang representing an hour's travel.[48] A modern account stresses the rigorous timetable enforced on this caravan each year. The journey from Damascus to Mecca was to be covered in 39 days, with ten rest days added, and ten days were allowed in Mecca after the pilgrimage was completed. The whole round trip took 152 days.[49] There may be a lack of concordance between these estimates of time, for if indeed they are compatible the caravans would be traveling more than fourteen hours a day. However, Gladwin's account does expatiate on the very long stages traveled on this caravan, while Varthema noted that the journey took forty days and forty nights, implying that the caravans traveled day and night.

The arrival and departure of *hajj* caravans were major holidays and occasions for festivities. We have an eyewitness account by a Christian of the return of the Damascus caravan in 1432. It consisted of 3000 camels, and was welcomed outside the town by the governor and other dignitaries. It carried a copy of the *Qur'an*, which

> was enveloped in a silken covering, painted over with
> Moorish inscriptions; and the camel that bore it was,
> in like manner, decorated all over with silk. Four

musicians, and a great number of drums and trum-
pets, preceded the camel, and made a loud noise. In
front, and around, were about thirty men - some bearing cross-bows, other drawn swords, other small har-
quebuses, which they fired off every now and then.
Behind this camel followed eight old men, mounted on
the swiftest camels, and near them were led their
horses, magnificently caparisoned and ornamented
with rich saddles, according to the custom of the country. After them came a Turkish lady, a relation of the
grand seignior, in a litter borne by two camels with
rich housings. There were many of these animals covered with cloth of gold. The caravan was composed of
Moors, Turks, Barbaresques, Tartars, Persians, and
other sectaries of the false prophet Mohammed.[50]

Hazards must also be stressed. The *Qur'an* itself had negative things to say about the beduin: "The wandering Arabs
are more hard in disbelief and hypocrisy, and more likely to
be ignorant of the limits which Allah hath revealed under His
messenger."[51] The Portuguese governor Albuquerque told his
king how, around 1500, both the Mecca caravan and the town
itself had been plundered by tribes called "benybraem."[52]
At almost the same time, in 1508, a Christian pilgrim in
Palestine noted that beduin, with a fine religious impartiali-
ty, had attacked both his band and the *hajj* caravan. He
described them as "a naked, miserable, bestial, wandering
people, who alone can dwell in the desert which is uninhabit-
able to all others, attack, harry, and conquer all men alike,
even to the king himself, the most puissant Sultan of
Egypt."[53] Things had not improved a century later, for in
January 1610 an English traveler went from Aleppo to Tripoli
with a one-thousand strong caravan of pilgrims "who were
bound for Mecha, where there great Mahomet was then resident [*sic*]: whereas else we should have trauelled in great
danger and hazard of our liues, by reason the Countrey is so
full of theeues."[54] (This caravan would have to hurry, for it

49

had at most only about 40 days left to get to Mecca in time for the *hajj*.) Later in the seventeenth century similar problems were reported, though we should assume that in general this period, the highpoint of Ottoman control, was less dangerous.[55] A pilgrim noted the castle of Ala, and another of Khyber (probably 'Al 'al, and Kharja, in modern Jordan), both on the the Damascus caravan route to Medina. In both of these areas Christian and Jewish bandits attacked his caravan; later marauding Arabs were a problem.[56]

The following extended account from 1741 is an excellent description of the dangers, the fervor, the organization, and the discomfort to be found on these vast caravans.

"In the month of Shawal the pilgrims assemble in the city of Damascus, and the Pasha of Damascus is always appointed by the edict of the Emperor of Turkey, Meer Haaj, or conductor of the caravan of Mecca. Without a considerable escort it would be impossible to pass the desert; and even when the caravan is strongly guarded and the pilgrims are very numerous, the wild Arabs hang in such a manner upon their march, that if any straggle from the caravan, they are sure to be plundered. Another advantage from the appointment of the Meer Haaj is that by obliging everyone to pay implicit obedience to the regulations for marching and halting, the confusion is prevented, which would otherwise be unavoidable amongst so large a body without a head. The following are some of the regulations for the caravan. Every one has his station assigned him in the line of march, which he must preserve during the whole journey. The people of Iran, and their camels, always form the rear. When the caravan halts, a particular spot is assigned for every string of camels, and where the master of them is allowed to pitch his tent. No one is allowed to infringe any of these regulations. When the stages are very long the caravan travels day and night; stopping an hour at each of the times of prayer, when the camels are allowed to lie down with their burthens upon their backs; and at midnight they halt in like manner another hour. In order that those at the rear may know at night when the caravan is going to halt, the Meer Haaj lets off a rocket . . . . The troops of the Meer Haaj guard the caravan on all sides . . . . When the caravan arrives at Musseeret, the third stage from Damascus, they purchase necessaries for passing the desert, which the wild Arabs bring to that place for sale: after having bought what they want, they pursue their march. The stages of this journey are longer than what are traveled in any other country, inso-much that the camels of Syria, which are larger and more powerful than those of any other place, are fatigued almost to death. At the same time, the zeal of the pilgrims who go all the way on foot, keeps up their spirits, and they perform the journey with surprizing ease and alacrity."[57]

Apart from these large Damascus and Cairo caravans, there were numerous other smaller ones; from Yemen, and from other parts of Arabia, and also from southern Persia. A Portuguese chronicler noted that the town of Lasah (al-Hasa), which included the port of Bahrain and was forty leagues from Bahrain Island, was the collection point for Persians, and the Arabs of the area, when they went on *hajj*. They, like the others, traveled in caravans because their route, in this case through the deserts of Yemen, was fre-quently subject to attack from the "Alarves," or beduin, who lived there; hence the need for strongly defended caravans.[58] What sorts of numbers are we talking about in this early modern time? Today of course the *hajj* is a vast assemblage of people, with over two million people present on each *hajj*, even though the Saudi government limits numbers by allow-ing only 1,000 pilgrims per million Muslims in any one coun-try. In 1985 it was estimated that about 3 million made the *hajj*, in a total Muslim population world wide of about 750 million.[59] In July 1988 there were about 1.5 million present, and this after the Saudi authorities had tried to restrict numbers, while two million took part in June 1991. The numbers have risen greatly since World War II. The number of non-Saudis involved has gone from 29,000 in 1930 to 50,000 in 1935, 101,000 in 1950, 286,000 in 1960 and 875,000 in 1975.[60] Total numbers rose from 108,000 in 1950 to 919,000 in 1974.[61] In 1977 392,000 Saudis, 496,000 non-Saudis resident in Saudi Arabia, and 740,000 non-resident foreigners made the *hajj*, a total then of 1,628,000.[62] All this has an effect on the host country of Saudi Arabia. In 1976 the *hajj* contributed $US156 million to the Saudi economy. Expanding the infrastructure of course more than took up this sum. Six motorways have been built between Mecca and Arafat, a distance of 22 kilometres; they are used for only three to five days a year.[63]

Our data for earlier periods is obviously not very precise. Faroqhi in fact refuses to even speculate on this matter.[64] Nevertheless, we need to at least try some sort of estimate. King provides a useful overview. He notes that in 1279 it was claimed that 40,000 came from Egypt, and a similar number from Iraq and Syria. In 1324, 15,000 Negroes from south of the Sahara were estimated to be present. Numbers rose under the *Pax* Ottomanica in the sixteenth to eighteenth centuries, only to decline as Wahhabi influence grew. In the eighteenth century the Damascus caravan may have included 40,000, but in the nineteenth century only less than 10,000, and later in this century less than 1,000. Totals in the eighteenth century may have reached 200,000, in the mid-nineteenth century about 50,000.[65]

Exact data for our period is hard to find. Too often we merely have such statements as Varthema's, who wrote early in the sixteenth century that "Truly I never saw so many people collected in one spot as during the twenty days I remained there [in Mecca]."[66] An estimate from around 1580 found over 200,000 people there,[67] but a century later we are told there were a very great number, but not as many as 70,000.[68] Two other estimates from around the middle of the seventeenth century found totals of respectively 300,000 and 200,000 at Mecca; the former is from a Christian priest who, while claiming to be well informed, never got beyond Palestine, while the latter is from the Turkish traveler Cheleby Evliya and so may be preferable.[69] A French work from the 1650s, a compilation but one with a degree of reliability, found "plus de cinquante mille hommes estrangers,"[70] and to this of course one would need to add a much larger number of locals. A century later again, in the 1770s, a French traveler claimed "not less than five hundred thousand pilgrims each year at Mecca . . . ",[71] which sounds extravagant in the extreme.

We have a few more precise figures to show numbers from the three main areas, that is Cairo, Damascus and India (remembering, however, that in the first two cases these cities acted as collection points for very wide areas). A modern estimate by Raymond cautiously finds 30,000 to 40,000 from Cairo, and 20,000 to 30,000 from Damascus;[72] perhaps as many again came from Arabia itself and other Muslim areas. A report from about 1580 found 50,000 people coming from Cairo on 140,000 mules and camels,[73] but Qazvini ninety years later claimed only 20,000 from Egypt, and another 10,000 beduin, and this was a year of *hajj akbar*.[74] In 1782 Rooke, a well-informed traveler, estimated thirty or forty thousand from Cairo.[75] These figures appear to be irreconcilable. As for Damascus, Varthema in 1503 noted 35,000 camels and 40,000 people.[76] Padre Roger claimed at least 25,000 from Damascus and the Holy Land in the mid seventeenth century, and in the 1780s Rooke estimated thirty or forty thousand from "Aleppo," by which presumably he meant Damascus, Palestine, and the Levant generally.[77] A modern estimate cautiously says that in the eighteenth century between 20,000 and 60,000 made the *hajj* from Damascus each year.[78]  Perhaps this sort of imprecision is the best we can hope for.

The data from India is a little fuller, and much more important for our purposes. However, several qualifications must be made immediately. First, we have some numbers of pilgrims traveling from western India, and especially from the central port of Surat, but we know that others left from other west coast ports, patronized by the rulers of Bijapur and Ahmadnagar, and that ships also went to the Red Sea from the east coast ports of Golconda and from Bengal too. Second, we also have data that shows that pilgrims from the Malay world often traveled via Surat, or other Indian ports. As Schrieke noted, "From the sixteenth century on, Surat was one of the fixed stations for people from the East on pilgrimage to Mecca."[79] They would be included in the numbers we are about to quote for pilgrims from India, but there is no way to separate them from those who came from India. Third, we have no data at all on the numbers who made the journey overland via the northwest of India. *Sunni* theologians discouraged this route, as it involved travel through *shia* territory, but we cannot estimate what effect this had. Fourth, I have been unable to find any data at all on either numbers of ships or passengers going to the Red Sea from Malabar.

Roff says, quoting official British sources, that around the middle of the nineteenth century some 5-7,000 Indian Muslims made the *hajj* each year; by the 1880s this number had risen to at least 10,000.[80] We noted above that numbers in general in the nineteenth century were low, indeed from Damascus had fallen from perhaps 40,000 to 1,000. Thus on this basis alone we could expect rather more from India in our period than was the case in the middle of the nineteenth century.

We can begin our survey by noting that several Indian rulers at the time sent one or more ships each year to the Red Sea specifically to carry pilgrims, though rich cargoes were also on board. In the early seventeenth century Terry saw one of these ships, which went from Surat to Mocha and had 1700 people on board, "the most of which number goe not for profit but out of devotion to visite the sepulchre of Mahomet at Medina neere Mecha [*sic*] . . . "[81] In 1612 Middleton saw the "Rhemy" ["Rahimi"] of Surat, which belonged to the Mughal Queen Mother and was laden with Indian commodities for Jiddah, and some 1500 passengers;[82] we can assume the vast majority of these also were *hajjis*. Another account of this English expedition operating off the mouth of the Red Sea says that in April and May of 1612 they took, among others, two Surat ships. One was of 600 tons, and had 800 passengers, the other of 200 tons.[83] Four years later a Dutch merchant at Mocha saw a big ship from Dabhol with 1000 pilgrims on board.[84] Faroqhi notes a ship belonging to the Queen Mother of Bijapur carrying 1500 pilgrim passengers.[85] In 1618 one of the King's ships, that is of the Mughal emperor Jahangir, reached Surat with 6-700 *hajjis* on board and a valuable cargo.[86] In 1638 Mandelslo in Surat wrote of the ships that went to Aden and Mecca: "They sometimes carry above a thousand persons together, who for the most part go upon Pilgrimage to *Meca*, that at their return they may be put into the number of their *Hoggoi*, or Saints."[87] Later in this century Aurangzeb sent two of these huge pilgrim ships, of 1000 tons or more, to the Red Sea each year.[88] In the 1580s at least Muhammad Quli of Golconda sent a ship of 600 tons each year to the Red Sea, laden with pilgrims, goods and merchants. These ships from the east coast were rather smaller than the comparable Mughal ones.[89]

All of these are examples of the huge royal ships paid for by the king or a top noble. A great noble under Akbar, Abdur Rahim, Khan-i khanan, provided at his own expense no less than three ships to take people on *hajj*. Two of them, the "Rahimi" and the "Salari", each weighed in at a very large 1500 tons, according to a detailed survey by the English merchant Saris.[90] He paid for the crew, and also provided provisions for the voyagers from his own funds.[91] We also have some evidence of other ships proceeding to the Red Sea carrying pilgrims which were not patronized by anyone; there could be large numbers on these too. Early in the seventeenth century a Portuguese fleet inspected an "Arab" ship which was going from Diu to "Mecca," and which had 700 passengers, most of them people going on *hajj*.[92] In 1613 the English captured off Surat a Gujarati ship of 300 tons coming from Mocha. It had a rich cargo, 12 large artillery pieces on each side, and over 300 sailors and passengers.[93] Qazvini gives us some very suggestive estimates. On his own ship, the "Salamat Ras," there were 472 people, and more than forty others who were not recorded. His ship was one of six which left together from Surat for the Red Sea, all of them with pilgrims, merchants and goods on board. Later he noted a ship leaving Jiddah for Surat with over 800 pilgrims and traders on board. Other numbers of people on board range from 500 to 1000 on each of the ten ships which altogether made the voyage from Surat to the Red Sea each year.[94] We are justified in assuming that most of these people were not merchants or sailors, but were going on pilgrimage, for Indian ships never carried crews of anything like this size. For example, Das Gupta has data for the crew on three medium size ships. One had 48 men on board to sail from Malacca to Batavia, and the other two had respectively 46 and 66.[95]

To sum up, we are justified in finding 1000 pilgrims on each of the huge state-sponsored ships going to the Red Sea, and we can estimate six of these each year. Then we must add all those, apparently a considerable number, who traveled on other ships. Qazvini's account produces, at ten ships with 500 on each, 5000 more pilgrims. To this must be added those from places where we have no, or only very incomplete, data, notably Malabar, Coromandel and Bengal. Then we have to add those who went overland, and subtract those we have counted who, in fact, were from southeast Asia. We have at least 10,000 "certainties," and to take account of the two totally unguessable categories, that is those from eastern India, and those who went overland, we should add at least another 5000. In other words, the above data leads me to make a conservative estimate of 15,000 Indian Muslims making the *hajj* each year in our period. Nor is this extravagant when we consider Roff's more precise nineteenth-century data, for our estimate then would point to a smaller fall from India than from Damascus.

**CHAPTER 3**

# The Centrality of the *Hajj*

everal methods within Islam create a sense of community, and solidarity, within the very diverse and scattered Muslim world. At a more local level two of the five pillars of the faith are important: the fast during the month of Ramadan, and the five daily prayers. During the fasting month no believer in Muslim areas takes food during daylight hours. All the faithful are united and bonded in the observance of this pious obligation. Similarly with the prayers: at five set times each day observant Muslims pray, individually to be sure in most cases, but all at the same time, and all facing in the direction of the Holy City and the Ka'ba. This process is even more manifest in the case of the midday prayers on Friday, which are said communally, at least by men.

The *hajj* does these things too, but even more dramatically. It has been generally recognized as absolutely central for the faith. Cragg describes how "by this annual 'congregation' Islam is bound together in a visible sacrament of unity, geographically realized from the ends of the earth. In history the pilgrimage has profoundly served the solidarity of Islam and helped to a strong cosmopolitanism in architecture, tradition, and society, through the contacts it afforded. Each recurring year it mediates through the body of the faithful a vicarious experience of the symbol of Mecca, in that pilgrims share with their neighbours the thrill and emotion of their venture both in retrospect and prospect. In the actuality of the ceremonies themselves in and about Mecca there resides a powerful realization of the incorporate community of Islam, in time and place."[1]

The *Encyclopedia of Islam* notes under the entry "hadjdj" notes that "the pilgrimage helped to produce a mingling among the élite of the Muslim world; scholars on the way to Mecca would stay temporarily at places on the way, forming friendships with colleagues or themselves teaching in the local mosques." More generally, "The wandering scholar is a familiar feature of medieval societies: the pilgrimage ensured that the wanderers met, at a determined time and place. It provided the Islamic world as a whole with a center and forum, which contributed greatly to the formation and main-tenance of an Islamic consensus - almost, one might say, an Islamic public opinion." The *hajj*, in fact, creates "a height-ened awareness of belonging to a larger whole. This aware-ness is reinforced by participation in the common ritual and ceremonies of the pilgrimage in Mecca and Medina, and the communion with fellow-Muslims of other lands and peoples. The physical mobility of important groups of people entails a measure of social and cultural mobility, and a corresponding evolution of institutions."

In short, Islamic cultural unity and solidarity, a tangible sense of being an *umma*, were very largely created by the *hajj*. K.N. Chaudhuri, in his recent wide-ranging study of the Indian Ocean area, very appropriately describes Mecca as "a primate city with virtually unlimited spatial domain."[2] An account from a recent *hajj*, that of 1991, described how "Every year during Haj, the holy city of Mecca becomes the most cosmopolitan of all Islamic cities, with an international choice of cuisine, a variety of shopping and a nightlife where Muslims from all over the world meet each other, often for the first time. At an Indonesian take-away, an Indonesian pil-grim introduces his new Senegalese friend to 'hot soup with meatballs.' The Senegalese has never eaten anything but his local food before. Both men are farmers and they discuss, in Arabic, the cost of living at home, their farming techniques, and their experiences over Haj."[3]

Anthropologists have put the matter in slightly more theoretical terms. Geertz notes the great growth of the pilgrimage from Indonesia in the nineteenth century—from 2,000 in 1860 to 10,000 in 1880 and 50,000 in 1926—and comments that this "created a new class of spiritual adepts: men who had been to the Holy Land and (so they thought) seen Islam through an undarkened glass."[4] Other accounts from our period paint a similar picture. Belon, a hostile observer, wrote of the Dervishes, whom he disliked, and stressed how their status among the Turks rose after they had made the pilgrimage.[5] Similarly, Ducket noted of Persia in 1574 that "They have among them certaine holy men whom they call Setes, counted holy for that they or any of their ancestors have bene on pilgrimage at Mecha in Arabia, for whosoever goeth thither on pilgrimage, to visite the sepulchre of Mahumet [*sic*], both he and all his posteritie are ever after called Setes, and counted for holy men, and have no lesse opinion of themselves."[6] A modern scholar writes of the significance of the *hajj* in pre-Mughal India: "The community of Orthodox Indian Islam in this early period, like that of other distant Muslim regions, depended for doctrinal guidance, reinvigorated piety, and communal solidarity upon regular connections with the great shrines of the Muslim world—especially through the annual pilgrimage to Mecca. Every year thousands upon thousands of pilgrims from India traveled on the Haj to fulfil their once-in-a-lifetime obligation by circumambulating the Ka'aba [*sic*]."[7]

In all this there are three elements which need to be distinguished. First is the centrality of Mecca, an obvious and generally accepted matter. Mecca was seen as the fountainhead, the source of correct Islamic doctrine and conduct.[8] People from this area arrogated to themselves great religious prestige and authority, claims widely accepted elsewhere. Persons from the heartland apparently often felt that, even if they moved, there was no need to acculturate or adapt in any way to local customs. Eaton notes *sufis* coming to Bijapur from Arabia and Iraq who firmly retained their own customs and habits, who continued to write in Arabic, made many pilgrimages and sent gifts back to Mecca. One Arab *pir* even brought his own Arab *murids* with him: "The biographical notice clearly portrays him and his *murids* as exemplary models of Islamic behaviour in Bijapur."[9] Eaton has also given us the biography of a similar foreign religious specialist, who died in 1631-2 and whose career illustrates both the centrality of Arab, and especially Meccan, norms and the international character of such prestigious religious authorities. Shaikh 'Abd Allah 'Aidarus was born in the Yemen, went to Mecca and Medina, and was inducted into several *sufi* orders. In 1616-7 he went to Gujarat, where he was welcomed by his uncle, whose father had moved to India. This uncle was also a famous *sufi* and author. Our sheikh then moved on to Bijapur, but he remained Arab, and devoted to Arabic culture, and never acculturated to India.[10]

The very experienced Captain Hamilton, writing of the inhabitants of the area now called Somalia, contrasted Meccans and black African converts. He said that "The *Arabians* from *Mocha* [*sc.* for Mecca], and other parts of *Arabia* the *Happy*, who reckon themselves *Mahomet's* best Disciples, and who have travelled much to teach and confirm them in the Religion and Philology, declare them to be the greatest Schismaticks and obdurate *Hereticks* that profess the *Mahometan* Religion."[11] Portuguese accounts similarly point to the prestige and authority of any person, or directive, or even item, from Mecca. In 1551 a Jesuit noted with glee that they had converted, in Hurmuz, a daughter of a king of Arabia, a relative of Muhammad, a sayyid ["parente de Mafamede, da casta de Zaid"] who had recently come from Mecca, and whom the locals considered to be of great sanctity. [12] A year later another letter from Hurmuz described how "a letter from Mecca for the king of Hurmuz arrived, written by a principal sayyid ["ceyde"] of the house of Mecca, one closely related to Muhammad, ordering that he [the king] enforce a fast on certain days for all his people, big and small, because God was very displeased with them . . . "[13]

Similarly, the ruler of the powerful Muslim state of Aceh in Sumatra sent presents to Mecca and received legitimation in return.[14] As for inanimate objects, any book or relic from Mecca was treated with veneration. The lengths to which this could be taken were revealed in 1582, when the Portuguese captured a very strong ship from the Red Sea off Surat. It was very rich indeed, and when the *cacizes* (Muslim divines) on board saw the situation was hopeless, they threw overboard 30,000 Venetians worth of alms, which had come from Mecca, in order to avoid their falling into infidel hands.[15] Even Meccan dirt was redolent with holiness. In the mid-eighteenth century the ruler of Bengal, the pious Siraj ud-daula (soon to be overthrown by Clive) "erected a large *imam-bara* [a building where shia Muslims celebrate Muharram] in Murshidabad, excluding Hindus from the participation in the construction to preserve the purity of the building; its centre, the *Madina*, was filled six feet deep with earth from the sacred soil of Mecca."[16]

The second aspect of the centrality of Mecca that needs to be distinguished is the impact of the *hajj* on all who undertook it. The Dutch savant Snouck Hurgronje noted that even for those Indonesians and Malays who merely did the *hajj*, the result was an increase in their feeling of Muslim solidarity, and also "The politico-religious might of Islam, hitherto known to them only from popular legends . . . has proclaimed itself as a living reality."[17] Great prestige attached to *hajjis*. Fernão Mendes Pinto met in Mocha "a *qasis* of theirs, a *maulana*, whom they regarded as a holy man because he had recently returned from a pilgrimage to Mecca. Sitting in a carriage, protected from the sun's glare by a silk awning, he was bestowing blessings and salaams on all sides . . . "[18] In the Maldive Islands in the early seventeenth century those who had been on *hajj* were allowed to wear their beards in a distinctive style. "Those who have been to Arabia, and have visited the sepulchre of Mahomet at Mecca [*sic*], are held in high respect by all the world, whatever be their rank, and whether they be poor or rich; and, indeed, a great number of the poor have been there. These have peculiar privileges: they are called *Agy* [*sc.* for *hajji*, one who has done the *hajj*]; and in order to be recognised and remarked among the others, they all wear very white cotton frocks, and on their heads little round bonnets, also white, and carry beads in their hands without crosses; and when they have not the means to maintain themselves in this attire, the king or the nobles supply them, and fail not to do so."[19]

The effects of a visit to Mecca could be various indeed. Regrettably, it sometimes led to an increase in intolerance. In the 1630s Lobo traveled by sea from Suakin, on the west coast of the Red Sea, to Diu.

> The ship carried many people, most of them pilgrims to their accursed, detestable house, by which I mean that of Meca, where Mafoma [Muhammad] is buried [*sic*]. Once these people have visited it, they receive from the Xarifes there an indisputable pass to Heaven; and when they leave Meca in this sanctified state, nothing is more loathsome to them than to meet with Christians, for they believe themselves contaminated if they see or have any dealings with us, so pure in body and soul do they consider themselves when they leave that place. For this reason they very much begrudged our being on that ship, imagining that their purity would be spoiled by our presence there, for they avoided all communication or conversation with us, so that when they arose in the morning and their eyes were unavoidably struck by the sight of us . . . they would immediately spit in the other direction as if they had seen the vilest thing in the world . . . "[20]

Two English accounts point to a more agreeable result of making the *hajj*, an increase in sophistication, and an at least temporary attack of scruples. In 1612 an English merchant wrote resignedly of the situation at an island off Mozambique. "The people for aught I can see are sociable and not treacherous, and very willing to sell their provision to us, and much better would it be were it not for the King who hath been at Mecca on pilgrimage and by that means is come to the knowledge of the worth of silver, otherwise heretofore we might have had anything for knives, tin spoons, glass beads, little looking glasses, leaden brushes and such like . . . "[21] The second instance concerns an important Mughal noble entitled Masih-al-Zaman, who after falling out with powerful people at court took refuge by going off on *hajj*. On his way back in 1623 he was inadvertently involved in hostilities between the English East India Company and local Mughal officials, and had some money seized from him. Unfortunately for the English, twelve years later he became governor of Surat, and was still annoyed that he had never had restitution. In fact, however, he had been offered compensation some years before, but his claim had been admitted in a rather dubious fashion, and so he had refused to accept what he considered to be tainted compensation, "from scruple of conscience when hee was newly returned from Mocha [*sc*. for Mecca], sanctified by the addition of Hadgee, attayned by holy pilgrimage to Mahometts shrine [*sic*]; which having now laid aside in the execution of accustomed injuryes and oppressions proper to all Governors, hee challenged this money."[22] So much then for the centrality of Mecca, and the dignity and status acquired by those who visited it for the *hajj*. A third matter was much more powerful, that is the effect on those who stayed for some time in the Holy Cities, who did several *hajjs* and numerous *umrahs*, and who studied in the great centers of Islamic orthodoxy in Mecca and Medina, and elsewhere in the Middle East. Hurgronje again stressed "The great difference between those who have only made the Hajj and its customary accessories, and those whom a stay of years in Mekka has made participants in the

Arabic-Muhammedan civilisation . . . " Later he wrote "There live in Mekka the choice few who have thrown themselves into the very source of the stream of the international life of Islam to be purified and strengthened in its waves." He commented on how "many individuals live in Mekka from purely religious motives; they have desired to study the holy lore in the holy place, to live in the neighbourhoods of renowned pious learned men or mystics, to atone for old sins, to purify dirtily acquired property by partly pious spending, or to pass their last days on holy ground."[23]

This was by no means only a nineteenth-century phenomenon; Mecca had always acted as the center, and had always been in part populated by those from all over the Islamic world who wanted to drink at the source. Ibn Battuta (1304-1354) spent four years in the area, as did many Indian Muslims whose role we will describe presently. In the twelfth century Ibn Jubayr noted a great number of settled pilgrims [*mujawir*] and those whose stay had been long.[24]

Any religious specialist, whether primarily an *alim* or basically a *sufi* (nearly everyone was a mixture of both) added greatly to his status, prestige, and acceptability if he had sojourned and studied in the Holy Cities, or if he came from the Hijaz and was perhaps a sayyid. In a way this is a circular statement, for anyone who was, or hoped to be, a religious authority would of necessity go to the Hijaz; conversely, if this journey had not been made one had little chance of popular acceptance, or of fulfilling one's own religious aspirations. People from the Hijaz, or more often persons who had spent much time there studying and doing *hajjs*, were seen in outer Islamic areas as cynosures of the faith, people uniquely qualified to be listened to and emulated. Hurgronje again gives us a succinct, albeit rather cynical, statement on this matter. He described how in Mecca there are Malays "who, after having become more or less Mekkans [after a long residence], when their money is spent make a trip home to sell rosaries, Arabic books, scent etc. or attempt to profit financially from their wisdom (learnt in Mekka), their mysticism, or merely from the aroma of their Mekkan sanctity."[25]

An example from Southeast Asia will serve to introduce the matter. 'Abd al-Ra'uf of Singkel's career, investigated by A.H. Johns, gives a clear picture of the many ties, networks and connections established in seventeenth-century Islam, and of the centrality of the Holy Places in their formation. He was born in North Sumatra around 1615, and in about 1640 moved to the Hijaz and Yemen to study. In Medina his main teacher was the Kurdish-born Ibrahim al-Kurani. He spent a total of nineteen years in Mecca, and gained very considerable prestige. In particular, he taught hundreds, even thousands, of Indonesians there, and initiated many of them into the Order of which he was a distinguished member, the Shattariyya. He returned to Sumatra, to Aceh, in 1661, where he was a revered teacher for nearly thirty years. He kept in touch with Ibrahim in Medina, and taught what he had learnt from him to the many Indonesian, especially Javanese, pilgrims who stopped for a time in Aceh on the way to the Red Sea.[26]

Another Asian example stresses the role of Medina, and again shows Islam's extreme cosmopolitanism, in this case in the eighteenth century. Muhammad Hayya, a teacher of the great reformer al-Wahhab, had himself been taught in Medina by scholars from India, Persia, Algiers, Morocco and other places. Apart from al-Wahhab, his students came from Turkey, India, Yemen, Jerusalem, Baghdad, Damascus and other Muslim cities. As Voll notes, "The Medinese scholarly community in general was able to contact people from throughout the world of Islam because of the Pilgrimage."[27]

There are numerous comparable Indian cases from our period.[28] Hajji Ibrahim Muhaddis Qadiri, born near Allahabad, did the *hajj*, and then studied in Cairo, Mecca and Syria. He was away 24 years, but when he returned to India he settled in Agra, and was a prestigious teacher until his death in 1593. Another *sufi* of the time did seven *hajjs*, while another, born near Lucknow, studied in Gujarat and then went to Mecca. He stayed five years in Medina, each year doing the *hajj*, and then returned to Ahmadabad.[29] The international character of Islam at this time, and the pattern of a career for a Muslim religious specialist, is well illustrated in the history of a founder of the Suhrawardiyya *sufi* order in India. Shaikh Baha'ud-Din Zakariyya was born late in the twelfth century near Multan. He memorized the *Qur'an*, and undertook further study in Khorasan for seven years. Then he traveled to Bukhara, did a *hajj*, and subsequently studied *hadith* for five years in Medina. Later he traveled and studied and taught in Jerusalem, and Baghdad, where he joined his order.[30] Another case shows how international Islamic learning was, with much of it, however, focused on Mecca. The great master of *hadith* in Delhi in the early seventeenth century was Abdulhaqq Dihlawi, who died in 1642. He had studied in Mecca for some years, where his teacher was Abdulwahhab Burhanpuri who, in turn, was a disciple and famulus of one of the great Indian immigrants to Mecca, namely Ali al-Muttaqi (or Shaikh Ali Muttaqi) of Burhanpur, who arrived in Mecca in 1534 and died there in 1568.[31] Thus Dihlawi brought back to India, at second hand, the ideas of an Indian authority.

A stay in Mecca usually increased the orthodoxy, and dogmatism, of those exposed to its scholars. In sixteenth-century India Shaikh Abdu-n-Nabi was at first strongly influenced by *sufi* practices and ideas, being a member of the Chishtiyah *silsilah*. Then he went to Mecca and Medina several times, and as the orthodox chronicler Badaoni tells us with some satisfaction, "he there studied the traditional sayings of Muhammad" and as a result gave up *sufi* practice: "objecting to the ecstatics and vocal music he followed the rule of the traditionalists and buried himself in outward piety, cleanliness, purification and devotion." Subsequently he returned to India and became, as sadr-us-sudur, a powerful and conservative force at Akbar's court. His rigidity finally led to disgrace in 1580; ironically, he was exiled by being sent off on *hajj*.[32]

Other examples of people being made more orthodox in Mecca are legion. Maulana Muhammad Tahir, a Gujarati Bohra, spent some time in Mecca, "and after his return, imbued with purist zeal, undertook the reform of his fellow Bohras," engaging in a vigorous rectification campaign.[33] Another *sufi*, Shah Sibghat Allah, was a member of the Shattari order. Born in Broach, he had his training and his *pir* in Ahmadabad. Late in the sixteenth century he did a *hajj*, which, as usual, seems to have caused him to change his opinions, for subsequently he led a puritanical and reformist campaign in Bijapur.[34] Two later examples of Indian scholars who led reformist campaigns at home after going to Mecca to study and do the *hajj*, are the well-known reformers Shah Waliullah in the eighteenth century, and Saiyid Ahmad of Rae-Bareli in the nineteenth.

Some South Asian examples show, however, that Mecca did not always have the effect of increasing orthodoxy. Late in the fifteenth century Sayyid Muhammad of Jaunpur was a great scholar. Finally his studies convinced him that he was the Mahdi who would appear to cleanse the world before the year 1000 of the Muslim era, that is, 1591-2 CE. The local ruler of the time, Sultan Mahmud Begada of Gujarat, at first liked his ideas, but then, perhaps swayed by the opposition of most of the *ulama*, he asked the Sayyid to go to Mecca. This was done, and the *hajj* was performed in 1495-6, but the effect was the reverse of what was hoped. Apparently this experience merely confirmed his opinion of his role, and he proclaimed himself to be the Mahdi.[35] Once back in India, he led a large movement whose members all accepted his claims.

In the sixteenth century, as his movement grew, the authority of Mecca was brought into play to counter its appeal. The counter attack was led by Shaikh Ali Muttaqi (whom we have just met as Ali al-Muttaqi), who was born in Burhanpur in 1480. In 1534 or 1536 he traveled to Mecca, where he stayed for a long time. On one occasion, in an action that showed the prestige associated with scholarship from Mecca, he bought a famous manuscript, called the "Mawahib Laduniya," made several copies, and sent one of them back home to Gujarat. "Further copies were made from this in India, and in the sixteenth and seventeenth centuries the work became famous in the sub-continent." More to our point, once the shaikh returned home he tried hard to counter the appeal of the Mahdawis. Despite "fatwas issued by the ulama of Mecca and Medina which the Shaikh carried with him to strengthen his case," his attempt to enforce Meccan norms failed; the Mahdawis were not impressed, and the shaikh went back to Mecca.[36] His rectification efforts were, however, picked up by Abdu-l-Wahab Aqziu-l-qazat Qazi, a Gujarati who went on *hajj*, studied in Mecca with this same Shaikh Ali Muttaqi, and became an expert, as the contemporary account puts it, in piety, asceticism, and the science of tradition. "When he returned to his native country, he did away with the heresies in belief and practice which had become prevalent in his tribe, and he laboured to put down the Mahdavi sect of the followers of Saiyid Muhammad of Jaunpur." He was killed in 1578.[37]

There were other cases also where a Meccan experience apparently led to greater tolerance or, at least, no increase in orthodoxy. In the later seventeenth century a scholar called Sayyid Sa'd Allah, who had studied for 35 years in India and was also a *sufi*, proceeded to Mecca and spent twelve years there studying and teaching the standard Muslim works. As one would expect, he also did the *hajj* eleven times. A very pious and abstemious man, he was for a time close to the Sharif of Mecca, but he left Mecca for Surat when the Sharif ignored some of his advice. Aurangzeb heard of him and patronized him lavishly for a time as a prestigious returning local scholar, but eventually he proved to be too tolerant. Hindus as well as Muslims revered him, and this strained his relationship with the emperor.[38] Even more famous was Akbar's guide, Sheikh Salim Chisti. He made two extended journeys to the Middle East, on each occasion basing himself in Mecca but also traveling widely in the Muslim world. Every year, however, he would return to Mecca to do the *hajj*.[39] These experiences no doubt contributed to his high reputation when he finally settled down in India; on the other hand, his *sufi* ideas were apparently not affected by all this.

Indian Muslims did not always accept the authority of Mecca. In the 1680s we find an illustration of this. Qazi Mir, an important and scholarly noble at Aurangzeb's court, "composed a new work drawn from the Old Testament and the Evangelists . . . . When it was finished, my friend Qazi Mir prayed for leave from Aurangzeb to travel to Mecca, since no one can be refused this, as it is a pilgrimage. On his arrival there he showed the book to the principal learned man of the Mahomedan faith, who is called the Xerif [Sharif]. He collected all the most famous men of learning for the examination of Qazi Mir's opinions, and to decide whether it was right to lay them before the public. After some months spent in examination, all of them with one accord said openly that what Qazi Mir had written was correct. The verdict was attested to by the principal men—the Sharif and the other learned men of Mecca—with their seals and signatures."[40] But on this occasion the strong-willed Aurangzeb was not impressed. He still considered the book unsound, and Qazi Mir was imprisoned on his return home.

Only in a very small minority of all those who stayed in Mecca became great scholars. There was often a large settled population there of ordinary Muslims, many of whom had probably simply run out of money and so were stranded. On other occasions people who accompanied élite pilgrims had perforce to stay in Mecca until their patrons decided to go home. This was the case with the large numbers of Muslims attached to the party of Gulbadan Begum in the late 1570s. Indeed, the Ottomans became concerned at the overcrowding and pressure on food supplies that these people caused in Mecca and took steps to force them to leave.[41]

Our final illustration of the centrality of Mecca has to do with conversions. Islam in our period was expanding vigorously, especially in Southeast Asia, but also in India, where it was locked, in some areas, in a fierce battle with a newly-arrived group of proselytizers, namely Roman Catholic missionaries.[42] Again the Hijaz, Mecca, and the *hajj* are important here, for often the most prestigious Muslim *cacizes* came from the Hijaz, or had studied and trained there. The Portuguese accounts, more often complaints, show clearly the techniques used by Muslim missionaries to convert Hindus and others in India and elsewhere. What emerges is a close nexus between trade and religion, and a strong impression of the role of the Hijaz area and the Red Sea, that is the heartland of Islam, in this conversion process. As a Jesuit lamented from Goa in 1560, what was most disturbing and lamentable "is to see how the *cacizes* ["cequaces," Muslim divines] of the accursed and abominable sect of Muhammad confound us, because they come from Mecca and from Persia and from many other places to infect and corrupt the poor Hindus ["gentios"] who are almost tabula rasa," and their message has had a very great appeal indeed. Often they won by default; what was needed was more Christian missionaries to counter these overly successful Muslims.[43] The same Jesuit added that "the partisans ["sectatores"] of Muhammad don't sleep, rather their *cacizes* make themselves into seamen, and thus can go around preaching their accursed sect; and they have done so well that it seems incredible the number of gentiles that in a few years have here submitted to this evil sect, and I believe that here they have a great advantage over us."[44] Another Jesuit of the same time expanded on this Muslim conversion technique, describing again how they travel as "lascars, which is the same as sailors," on Portuguese boats even, and sowed their evil seed wherever the boat called, even as far as China, Siam and Java. Their success was disturbingly great; indeed Fr. Dinis could see only one ray of hope. These Muslims had, of course, to tell their converts that pork was now forbidden, and this was turning out to be a major stumbling block to conversions in China and neighboring areas, for pork was much consumed there.[45]

In these cases it seems clear that the missionaries came from the Red Sea by and large. However, it is well known that southeast Asia was mostly converted by new Muslims from India, especially from Gujarat and other coastal areas. Again the Portuguese records describe this process in detail. The conversions were undertaken by people who were themselves relatively new converts. The mechanism was trade and the use of the sea as a highway for the spread of Islam. In the port of Rander were Naiteas [navayats], "great robbers and pirates, who are the lowest caste of Muslims; they are all skilled sailors, pilots and masters: they follow the Arabs in their religion, and it was from them that Islam entered the kingdom of Cambay [*sc.* Gujarat] and from there spread all over India and then all over the East, both on the mainland and in the islands of Sumatra, Java, Borneo, Banda, the Moluccas and all the others where their ships called; like men zealous about their false sect, they did their trade and preached their religion and converted an infinite number of idolators and gentiles."[46]

Not, however, that it was only *cacizes* who traveled in disguise on the boats of their enemies. From the time of Albuquerque, early in the sixteenth century, we have a case, so far as I know unique, of a Portuguese impersonating a *caciz*. Fernão Dias, who had been captured by Muslims in the "strait of Gibraltar, and knew well the customs of the Muslims, and especially of the *cacizes*, and their legends and prayers." Escaped from captivity and, subsequently, volunteered to go overland to Portugal from India to take news to the king. Traveling in disguise as a *caciz*, he was helped by his excellent Arabic. Sometimes his prayers were so convincing that he was given alms. "In this way he travelled, preaching the *Qur'an* and doing everything just like a holy *caciz*,

75

and finally he got to Portugal . . . " Later he came back to India, "and went many times as a spy to the Red Sea in Muslim ships dressed as a *caciz*, and he did many services in the times of other governors, yet he died very poor; I knew him."[47]

The way to stop the real *cacizes*, urged the religious, was to prohibit trade with the Red Sea and so cut off this conversion drive at its source. But to the extent this was done, and we will discuss the matter in detail in the next chapter; it was opposed by the secular arm of the Portuguese enterprise in Asia. In 1559, an official noted that while the religious no doubt acted with the best of motives, the fact was that Goa's customs revenues had fallen catastrophically as a result of the failure of merchants "from Mecca [*sc*. the Red Sea], Persia and many other diverse parts" to come to Goa.[48]

Other Portuguese records provide good information on other aspects of the conversion drive in India. In general, the missionaries on both sides did best with people who belonged to no major formal religion; those whom the Portuguese described as "gentiles", which could mean low caste Hindus, or unsophisticated followers of folk practice. But sometimes the Muslims even, in a very threatening success, were able to get Christians to come over. In 1579, a Jesuit said that local Christians converted to Islam in Bengal because of the evil behavior of the European Christians.[49] But a long and informed account from Malabar describes both the mix of trade and religion which proved so successful, and the way the Islamic stress on the equality of all believers fostered conversions, producing the indigenous Muslim Moplah community. Correa, in an account of how Islam spread in Malabar, noted the dominance of the Nairs there, and the degraded position of the lower castes. Muslims, presumably from the Red Sea area, the major trading area for Malabar, pointed out to the rulers that the low caste porters were unable to move about freely in the area, because if they ran into Nairs they would be killed. But if these low caste Malabaris converted to Islam "they would be able to go freely where they wished, because once they became Muslims they were immediately outside of the law of the Malabaris, and their customs, and they would be able to travel on the roads and mingle with all sorts of people." This argument, plus a few bribes, convinced the rulers, who gave their consent. The actual conversion of these much-oppressed people was easy, for they thus could live where they pleased and eat what they wanted. They also received clothing from the Muslims. The result was a great success for this Muslim conversion drive, which in turn spilt over into trading success, especially in the spice trade to the Red Sea.[50]

A traditional Muslim account of conversion in the same area of Malabar provides an interesting contrast. It claims that a group of Muslims, including a sheikh, arrived in Malabar, presumably from the Red Sea area:

> an intelligence of their arrival having reached the King, sending for them into his presence, he manifested towards them much kindness, conversing with them without reserve: and enquiring of them their circumstances and condition, the Sheikh, encouraged by the King's condescension, related to him the history of our prophet Mahomed (upon whom may the divine favour and blessing ever rest!), explaining also to the monarch the tenets of Islamism; whilst, for a confirmation of their truth, he narrated to him the miracle of the division of the moon [which purportedly Muhammad did]. Now, conviction of the Prophet's divine mission, under the blessing of Almighty God, having followed this relation, the heart of the King became warmed with a holy affection towards Mahomet (on whom be peace!), and, in consequence of this his conversion . . .

many others also became Muslims.[51]

In areas ruled by the Portuguese the situation veered

between conflict and cooperation between Muslims and Christians. In Hurmuz there was a puppet king, and the missionaries could work fairly freely. In 1551, a Jesuit complained that in terms of food and drink, and in conversation by night and day, there was no difference between Muslims and Christians. In this same year a Jesuit father was gravely ill and no cure seemed possible. A Muslim Arab promised to cure him in three days and in despair the priest put himself in his hands. The Arab offered a candle each day to Muhammad, and another to Ali. In a surprising denouement, the Jesuit recovered but then turned around and converted his healer to Christianity.[52]

Two final examples will illustrate further the complex Muslim-Christian relations at this time. From Hurmuz again we have an example of what seems to be almost playful competition. True, the Muslims here stoned the processions that a priest and his converts took out at night, but in a more friendly way, when the Christian processions cried out "Jesus Christ, have mercy on us," the Muslims competed by crying out "There is no God but God ["Hum soo hé Deus, Deus hé hum soo"] . . . Whatever we did, they undid."[53] An example of what was more usual, Portuguese intolerance in an area where they had undisputed political control, relates to Murmugao, in the territory of their capital city of Goa. A Jesuit noted with glee that the political authorities had destroyed a mosque in a village near Murmugao, and this was very much to be applauded, "because in it Muhammad was worshiped by the Hindus of Salcette with offerings and other ceremonies, and by the Muslims of these areas with their accursed rites. They go to it at certain times of the year to preach [?fazer seu falar], and they have in it a school in which they teach the children their *Qur'an*."[54]

# CHAPTER 4

# The Politics of the *Hajj*

A t the commencement of our period, in 1500, the Hijaz was governed by a sharif who controlled Mecca, Medina, and their ports of Jiddah and Yanbo, though he was nominally subject to the Mamluks in Cairo. As Guardian of the Holy Places, the position of the sharif was a prestigious one. The 'Alid line which ruled the Hijaz from the 960s to the nineteenth century claimed descent from Ali via his son Hasan.[1] On the other hand the Mamluk rulers claimed the title of *Khalif* as successors to the Abbasid dynasty of Baghdad. The sharif's position vis à vis the Mamluks was not totally autonomous. At times the Mamluks took their position as *khalif* seriously, and showed interest in fostering the pilgrimage. They were also concerned about security in the Red Sea and events in the Hijaz because the very lucrative spice trade from the Arabian Sea to the Middle East and on to the Mediterranean passed through this closed waterway, and so overland from Suez to Cairo and Alexandria. The Mamluks then were concerned both in the broader sense of continuing the spice trade and protecting the Holy Places, and the narrower one of protecting, for both religious and political reasons, the pilgrimage.

The arrival of the Portuguese soon both of these aspects put at risk. They were keen not only both to oppose Islam but also to monopolize the spice trade. As Couto noted, right from the start they tried to patrol the Red Sea entrance and block the "pilgrimage to the accursed house of Mecca." Typically, service to their God also meant profits for themselves; they did this "as much to annoy and vituperate the Muslims as to make profits for the Portuguese state,"[2] for the ships they captured yielded rich booty. In this they conflicted very directly with the Mamluks. As early as 1502 da Gama captured a great ship called the "Meri," which was owned by the Mamluk ruler. It had left Calicut loaded with spices, and "because it was so large and secure, many honoured Muslims went in it on pilgrimage to their abomination of Mecca, and it returned with these pilgrims and also a very rich cargo." Da Gama's forces captured the ship, and destroyed it despite the offer of a huge bribe. One of the pilots on board was allowed to survive for the sake of his expertise, and some twenty children were saved so that they could be converted.[3] Another particular damage inflicted by the Portuguese was that their patrols in the Arabian Sea, and even cruises in the Red Sea from time to time, cut off the passage of a great ship, apparently belonging to the governor, under the Mamluks, of Damascus, which each year carried charitable contributions fron India to Mecca.[4]

Accounts of a battle between the Portuguese and a Calicut fleet in 1504-5 mention a ship (in another version two ships) loaded with alms of gold and silver, this being the one sent every seven years by Indian Muslims to the sharifs of Mecca.[5] Thanks to the Portuguese, such contributions now had to reach Mecca by other routes. Portuguese aspirations were very grandiose. There was talk of diverting the waters of the Nile, so that Egypt would become totally desert, and of capturing Mecca and holding the body of the Prophet for ransom. (This latter project derived from the doubly erroneous belief that Muhammad's body was suspended in the air at Mecca.)

Barros described the general Muslim reaction to the arrival of the Portuguese and their depredations: "Thus these kings and princes, as the merchants through whose hands ran the commerce of spices and oriental riches, seeing that with our arrival in India, in the brief space of five years, we had taken control of the navigation of those seas, and they had lost the commerce which they had dominated for so many years, and especially we were an insult to their House of Mecca, since already we had reached the gates of the Red Sea, seizing their pilgrims, all of these things were so serious for them and so sorrowful, that not only those directly offended, but all of them in general so hated us that they each in their own way sought our destruction."[6] A brother of Zain-ud-din, author of the famous *Tohfut-ul-Mujahideen*, wrote a long poem from Malabar early in the sixteenth century which noted how the Portuguese "forbade ships to set sail for Mecca, and this was the worst of the calamity," and they "restricted vessels from sailing on the sea, especially the vessels of the greater and lesser pilgrimage."[7]

The method used to oppose the Portuguese was the well known attack in 1508-9 by Amir Hussein, an Egyptian admiral, who combined with Indian forces led by Malik Ayaz in Diu in an attempt to expel the Portuguese from India. He acted on behalf of the Mamluks, and they in turn were motivated by both economic and religious hostility to the Portuguese. His defeat at Diu in 1509 was decisive for the survival of the Portuguese in India.[8] This same mixture of profit and piety seems to have determined Mamluk relations generally, and extended even to the sharifs of Mecca and the Hijaz area. An account by the Portuguese chronicler Barros of a little known punitive expedition of 1508 shows the mixture nicely. In 1508 Amir Hussein traveling down the Red Sea to enter the Arabian Sea and engage the Portuguese, stopped off at Yanbo, sixteen leagues (about 100 miles or 170 kms) from Medina, attacked the town and killed the sheikh who was lord of the whole area through which Muslims going on pilgrimage traveled. He levied a head tax on "all the cafilas of these pilgrims" but in reality he merely fleeced the caravans. Finally, the pilgrims complained to Cairo. The Mamluk sultan agreed with the sheikh that he would be given a fixed sum each year for the sheik in return for leaving the caravans alone, adding that he was doing this out of charity in order to help the sheikh. "But the truth was that it was money, because all the pilgrims who left from Cairo, or the lands of the Sultan, in the caravan, were registered by his officials, and paid two soltanis [a soltani equalled a Portuguese cruzado], one which they had always paid for portage, and the other which he said was to be handed over to the sheikh . . . But he found it hard to give the 12,000 soltanis to the sheikh, and so for four years he had not paid this, which caused the sheikh to turn again to robbery. The sultan, moved by a concern for the common weal, and by the fact that he was *Khalif* and so should right wrongs done to pilgrims to the house of Muhammad, ordered Amir Hussein to remonstrate with the sheikh and if this did not work, to take the port of Yanbo, which was the wealthiest thing that the sheikh had, and the best rent, because of the coming and going of the caravans of pilgrims there, and its sea trade."[9]

These sorts of concerns for the continuance of the pilgrimage, both mundane and spiritual, continued after the Ottoman Turks conquered Egypt in 1516-7 and also became overlords of the Hijaz.[10] The ruling sharif, Barakat II (1495-1524), sent his thirteen year old son Sharif Abu Nomay to Salim, and his family was confirmed as rulers, under the Ottomans, of Mecca, Medina, Jiddah and indeed all the Hijaz.[11]

Ottoman sponsorship fostered the *hajj*, whose numbers grew impressively thanks to state patronage and protection. The theme of Faroqhi's important book is that the Ottomans legitimized their rule and integrated their empire by spending money on Mecca and on the pilgrimage.[12] In both Ottoman Egypt and Syria important nobles, in the latter case the governor of Damascus after 1708, were designated *amir-ul-hajj* and took personal command of the pilgrimage caravans each year. A traveler in 1763 noted that the sultans sent pensions to the sharif of Mecca and his family and "With these pensions, and the freight of four or five large vessels, which he sends every year to Jiddah, laden with provisions,

84

he supports almost all the inhabitants of Mecca and Medina. During the whole time, while the pilgrims remain in the city of Mecca, as much water as two thousand camels can bear is daily distributed gratis; not to speak of the vast number of presents with which he adorns the *Kaba*, and gratifies the descendants of Mahomet."[13] A modern account said that the Ottomans had twelve boats in Suez, which each year took grain to Jiddah.[14] Among the titles of the Ottoman sultans were not only *khalif*, a dignity which they claimed by right of their conquest of Mamluk Egypt, but also *khadim-al-haramayn al-sharifayn*, that is servant of the holy sanctuaries.

This position meant that the Ottomans also were concerned by the depredations of the Portuguese. While religious matters were often put forward in public as the reason why the Ottomans hated the Portuguese, economic factors were as important for them as they had been for the Mamluks. A letter to the sultan in 1525 from the Ottoman commander in the Red Sea was virulently anti-Portuguese, but the complaint against them had nothing to do with the *hajj*; rather it stressed political and economic matters, and especially their interference with the spice trade.[15] In 1538 this concern led to sending a fleet to help local opponents drive the Portuguese out of India, starting with expulsion from Diu, their key fortress. The Gujarati noble who initiated and coordinated this offensive, Khwaja Safar, had seen his own interests seriously disrupted by Portuguese activities. He appealed to his nominal overlord, the sultan of Gujarat, for help against the Portuguese, citing various reasons, "and above all because they have affronted our religion and impeded the pilgrimage to the house of our Prophet."[16] His appeal to the Ottoman sultan was fuller and more revealing. If the Portuguese were expelled, commerce would be free as it had been before the Portuguese came, and the pilgrimage to Mecca would again not be impeded as it was now owing to the way the Portuguese had closed the Red Sea.[17] It is possible that at this time the Turks also wrote to the powerful Muslim

85

ruler of Aceh, in Sumatra to enlist his help in blocking Portuguese trade. Pinto claimed there was a pact between the two, and that the Turks had promised military aid if Aceh attacked the Portuguese.[18]

An Ottoman fleet under Sulaiman Basha al-Khadim, the governor of Egypt, duly arrived in 1538. The sultan's instructions to the commander were to "set off for India and hold those Indian ports; cutting off the road and blocking [the] way to the sacred cities of Mecca and Medina, you will avert the evil deeds of the Portuguese infidels and remove their banners from the sea."[19] But alas, the Portuguese fort of Diu held out, in an epic siege, and the Basha sailed home again. Typically, he took advantage of the fact that he reached Jiddah on the 20th of Shawwal to make a pilgrimage after which, while his fleet proceeded up the Red Sea, he accompanied the pilgrim caravan back to Egypt.[20] He cast aspersions on the quality of Islam in Gujarat claiming that he had received very little assistance from the Gujaratis, during the siege and that the ruler of Gujarat failed to the least acknowledgment of his help. Finally, he decided to leave the ingrates to their own devices.[21] This was something of a self-serving gloss on what really happened. He *had* been helped by Gujarati forces, there was nothing much wrong with Gujarati Islam, and he had left because the Portuguese had defeated him. Even so, this expedition does show that the Ottomans took seriously the threat from the Portuguese, and, more generally, their obligation to defend the Holy Places.

This position was apparently quite widely recognized by other Muslim rulers. Sher Shah, who replaced the Mughals in North India from 1540 to 1545, once said that after he had completed his conquest of Hindustan he wanted to attack the *shia* Safavid Persians who had blocked the *hajj* to *sunnis* from India. He hoped to get the Ottomans to coordinate an attack with him so that the Persians would be caught from both sides.[22] Similarly, in 1566 the Muslim ruler of Aceh, in Sumatra, appealed to the Ottoman sultan Selim II for help against the Portuguese. He addressed the sultan as the *khalifa* of Islam. In response Selim II did prepare a fleet to send to Aceh, but it was later diverted to crush a revolt in Yemen.[23]

This is not to say that the Indian Ocean and the Portuguese were ever the Ottoman's most important concern. Their priorities were overwhelmingly inland, while to the extent that they were concerned with maritime matters they looked first to the Mediterranean. As Guilmartin notes, after they beat off the Portuguese at Jiddah in 1517, they "never threw their whole weight into this conflict. Tax revenues based on land ownership were more important to them than commercial profits and Suleiman I consequently elected to move against Hungary rather than the Portuguese in the Indian Ocean," and further "The Ottoman Empire was primarily a continental power, mainly concerned with the expansion of its control over land areas. The Ottomans had no particular aversion to trade, but since maritime commerce was mostly carried out in the Ottoman Empire by non-Ottomans acting in their own interests, maritime commerce was regarded as a political and economic tool which could be manipulated at will."[24]

Nevertheless, they did continue to complain about Portuguese activities, and not without reason for the Portuguese did mount one more major expedition into the Red Sea, in 1541. The Portuguese aim was quite specifically to block the pilgrimage, and indeed the Ottomans had already had to put up with a flood of complaints about how the faithful were unable to "go to the house of Mecca, to take their alms and fulfil their pilgrimage, because the Christians take them at sea, and also within the Red Sea, and they kill and rob them and the least that they do is to capture them . . ."[25] It is nevertheless unclear whether their concern was primarily religious or economic. An exchange in the 1540s seems to show that trade and revenue were most important for the Ottomans. In 1546 they conquered Basra, and so moved much closer to the Portuguese fort at Hurmuz. But the next year an envoy from Basra's new ruler made it clear to the Portuguese that his master wanted to "make Basra very prosperous through commerce, so that it might yield a large revenue to the Great Turk" and that "the Turks wanted very much to establish a flourishing trade in Basra."[26] Similarly, Ozbaran's detailed account of Portuguese-Ottoman relations in the Persian/Arabian Gulf area in the sixteenth century, based on both Portuguese and Ottoman records, says nothing of religion at all, but rather deals very usefully with military, strategic and commercial competition.[27]

More support for the primacy of trade over religion comes from an important incident in the early 1560s, little known to historians.[28] In 1562 the Turkish governor of Basra sent an envoy to Hurmuz to make peace, for the Ottoman concern was now totally with trade. This led, in 1563-4, to a Portuguese embassy under António Teixeira de Macedo and negotiated with the sultan, Suleiman the Lawgiver (for Europeans "the Magnificent"), for a peace treaty. The Ottoman proposal was that the Turks have free navigation all over the Indian Ocean, and be allowed to have factories in certain places, paying duties on their trade there to the Portuguese. In return, the Portuguese could have factories in Ottoman areas, notably Basra, Cairo and Alexandria, and be allowed into the Red Sea area. The Portuguese turned down these proposals, as they feared they would not do well in free competition with the Ottomans; anyway they were afraid that all this was just an Ottoman attempt to get a foothold in the Indian Ocean area. Once this was achieved they could easily drive out the Portuguese, so hated by the local people.[29] What emerges most clearly from this very frank Portuguese assessment is that there is no sign that the Ottomans raised the matter of the pilgrimage, or religion, at all. The proposals as reported had to do entirely with trade.

The same applies if we consider evidence from the Ottoman side concerning these negotiations. In September 1564 the sultan wrote, after Teixeira had left, a letter to the king of Portugal which again says nothing about religion, but a lot about secular matters. In particular, he told the king that "you shall establish, on land and on sea, safety and security for the people and the merchants of our well protected dominions, who are in the land of India, in the region of Jezayir [?] and in other lands. Your present ambassador has—without delay—been accorded our noble permission, and, with our imperial letter, he has been sent back to that land. Now it is needful that, when [this letter] reaches you, you shall, without delay, despatch to us your ambassador, who shall be sent for this laudable purpose, that is, for the bettering of the conditions of the people and for the good ordering of the affairs of state."[30]

By now Ottoman concerns were no longer backed up by expeditions of the size of that commanded by Sulaiman Basha, but the Ottomans remained concerned, even if powerless to do more than fulminate. In October 1565 Suleiman, apparently now despairing of any hope of a treaty with the Portuguese, wrote again to the king of Portugal in these terms: "Recently reports of your aggression against Muslim pilgrims and merchants coming from India to our territories have reached us . . . It is imperative that after receiving my exalted letter you should, in accordance with your desire for peace, immediately stop all atrocities on the Indian pilgrims and traders. If you continue to disturb peace in that region [of India] then appropriate steps will be taken against you."[31] But the Portuguese took no notice, so in 1568 Sultan Suleiman wrote to his governor of Egypt complaining of them and their seizures of Indian ports and harassment of pilgrims. To counter them he had prepared a fleet in the Mediterranean, and now wanted to consider carving a channel between the Mediterranean and the Red Sea so that this fleet could get to the Arabian Sea and attack the Portuguese.[32] Nothing came of this project but, apart from being a curious anticipation of the notion of a Suez Canal, it demonstrates also the logistic problems the Ottomans faced, centerd as they were in the Mediterranean. Exactly why religion was now given at least public primacy is unclear; what these negotiations in the mid 1560s do show is that the Ottomans seldom complained of any Portuguese threat to the *hajj* traffic; indeed, their concern seems to be much more with trade. From this time on relations between the two were peaceful enough, based on a mutual desire for trade.[33] Yet the Portuguese continued to keep a watchful eye on the Turks. In 1605 the king wrote to the viceroy that he had heard from a person who had been released after being a captive of the Turks for sixteen years that there were revolts against the Turks in the Red Sea area, and also that the Turks were possibly contemplating an attack on Melinde. The viceroy was told to collect information, even if some expense were involved.[34]

The Ottomans then were able to do little, and apparently cared little, to help Indian pilgrims directly, in part, no doubt, because, as we will see, Portuguese activities were not nearly as detrimental to the pilgrimage as some accounts have claimed. If sometimes, at least, the Ottomans tried to help Indian pilgrims, Safavid Persia was an obstacle. This was partly due to geopolitical hostility between Persia and Mughal India. There was more or less constant tension between the two in the northwest of India and Afghanistan, then part of India, focused on the strategic fortress of Qandahar. But doctrinal differences were also important, for the Safavids were strict, and proselytizing, *shia* Muslims while the Mughals were, to varying degrees, committed *sunnis*. An indication of this sort of conflict was the way, in 1544, Shah Tahmasp of Persia forced the exiled Mughal ruler Humayun to convert to *shia* Islam before he would try to help him regain his throne. Subsequently, the Safavids frequently impeded the passage of Indian pilgrims.[35] Indeed, *sunni* visitors in general appear to have been subjected to slights and insults in Persia. For example, the *sunni* Turkish traveler Sidi Ali Reis was challenged three times on sectarian

90

grounds.[36] The *sunni* response in India to all this was to counterattack. Some of the more orthodox *ulama* at Akbar's court took the extreme step of claiming that the *hajj* was no longer obligatory, because if it were done by sea it was done under the patronage or tolerance of Christian Portuguese, and if by land through *shia*, virtually infidel, territory.[37]

It seems that the overland route was usually not the first choice anyway, except perhaps for those intending *hajjis* who lived in the far northwest of India. The sea route was comparatively easier, and this was the way most Indian pilgrims traveled. However, in the sixteenth century this route was to an extent controlled by the newly-arrived Portuguese. We will investigate the degree and effectiveness of Portuguese hostility, but first we will sketch the general Portuguese, and especially missionary, attitude to Islam. The position of the clergy was, predictably, one of more or less unrelieved hostility, based partly on doctrinal grounds, and partly on the fact, as we saw in Chapter 3, that Islam was doing very well indeed in converting people, especially in Southeast Asia.

Anti-Muslim feeling was of course rife among the Portuguese. They had reconquered their own land from Muslims, completing the task only late in the thirteenth century. In neighboring Spain independent Muslim power had lasted till the end of the fifteenth century, and the last Muslim revolt against Spanish Christian rule was to come only in 1568. In the fifteenth and sixteenth centuries, as Portugal expanded down the west African coast and then around into the Indian Ocean, some Portuguese were engaged in a long and bloody struggle, punctuated by appalling atrocities, with Muslims in North Africa. Indeed, there was frequent interchange of personnel between the two areas; many of the Portuguese commanders and troops in India had served earlier in Morocco.

Anti-Muslim feeling then was visceral, innate almost, among the Portuguese. A very powerful way to malign an opponent was to say he was soft on Muslims, or acted like a

Muslim. As one example, which powerfully brings to mind the sorts of prejudices cited in Daniel's important book,[38] the great Portuguese governor Afonso Albuquerque was accused of being as bad as Muhammad. An opponent wrote that, among other crimes and misconduct, "When he came from Malacca he got himself together in Cochin [in 1512] with sixty whores that he had brought from Goa, and he put them in a tower, and as soon as he finished dinner he went to them, and this he did all this winter [i.e., the rainy season from June to September] so that no one could talk to him or do any business; Muhammad did not have more delectation with virgin girls than he did."[39]

The antipathy went both ways. We have noted many times the way the Portuguese talked of the Prophet and of Islam, routinely using adjectives like abominable, accursed, and so on. Most of the Muslim population of Goa was killed in 1510 when the city was retaken, and subsequently Muslims were persecuted in Portuguese areas. Such visceral hatred was often paid back with interest by Muslims. A poet writing from Calicut, center of the resistance to the Portuguese, wrote:

> It is this, the worst of all creatures, the follower of the
>     most unclean ways
> The bitterest foe of Allah and His apostle, His religion,
>     and His apostle's community
> The Frank who worships the cross and prostrates before
>     pictures and idols
> Of ugly appearance and form, blue eyed like that of
>     Gorillas [Ghouls]
> He passes water like a dog, and whosoever purifies him-
>     self, is rebuked and excommunicated
> He is cunning, disobedient, deceitful and filthiest of all
>     creatures of God.

Or the following from the same poem:

They destroyed Islamic buildings and basic principles of
  Islamic traditions
They dominated the local rulers like the domination of a
  master over his slave . . .
How many Muslims are chained in their prison and how
  many are tortured with severe trials
How many they orphaned by their homicide and how
  many girls and women they made widows
How many ships they set on fire and how many vessels
  they sunk in the sea
How many Muslims they have converted to Christianity
  [by force] and even Sayids have been made prisoners
They have blocked all routes of land and sea to the
  Muslims who are still frightened
So the people have begun to live above the hills and even
  there they walk in trepidation
They have burnt the Qur'an and Mosques and in their
  places they have built their own places of worship
They beat the Muslims with their shoes and desecrate
  and defile the mosques with their urine
They dug up the graves of Muslims and in their places
  they have built their own places of worship
They have raped women in the presence of their impris-
  oned husbands and relatives
They drove the fettered, frightened and tortured prisoners in the market
They ordered them by force to carry filthy and impure
  objects and imprison them in unclean places.[40]

In the town of Ponnani, near Cochin, there lived in the
1580s a *caciz* (a Muslim divine) who was bitterly opposed to
Christians. His hatred was such that he ordered that when
he died he was to be buried on his stomach, with his face
down, so that he would not be able to see any Christians.
Every Friday he would make Christian captives in the town
draw lots, and the loser would be taken to the mosque and

there ordered to convert to Islam. Those who refused had their heads cut off, so that the mosque ran with blood. It was claimed that he had martyred some 200 Christians in this way.[41]

The Church of course was most open and most vehement in its opposition to Islam, and especially to the pilgrimage. The Provincial Councils held at Goa later in the sixteenth century passed a series of anti-Muslim decrees, their effectiveness being dependent on the extent to which the secular arm enforced them. At the first, in 1567, decree 30 recommended that non-Christians employed by the state not be allowed to take off one day a week "for the observance of their false religions." This applied especially to Muslims and Fridays.[42] Decree 35 of the same Council said "Many Muslims and other infidels come to our ports with books of their sects, and their false relics that they bring from the House of Mecca, and other places they hold to be holy, and they pass through our territories with these things to their own areas; the officials of the customs houses are ordered that when these books and relics are seen, they should not be cleared but rather the prelates or vicars should be informed and they should examine them and if they find them to be such, should burn them."[43]

The Third Provincial Council, of 1585, was concerned directly with the *hajj*. Under the subheading "That one not give cartazes or licences to go on pilgrimage to the house of Mecca or to the pagodas of the gentiles," the decree ran: "This Synod, in conformity with the Vienna Council, declares that cartazes and licences, either verbal or written, must not be given to Muslims so that they can go on pilgrimage to the house of Mecca to their false Muhammad . . . " Nor were infidels (Hindus) to be given licences to go on pilgrimage to their pagodas or false gods. The captains of Hurmuz, and all other captains of fortresses in India, were instructed to observe this, as one would hope from good Christians zealous in the faith.[44]

Religious specialists on both sides led the antipathy, and tried to keep their secular colleagues up to the correctly intolerant mark. In return, religious leaders could suffer for their prominence. In a case not without an element of farce, two Jesuits were captured in 1589 and held at Dofar by the local Muslim chief for ransom. A sum of 900 ducats had been agreed on, but then a *caciz* (in another version a Turk) who had been captured by the Portuguese and subsequently ransomed in Diu for 5,000 pardaus (in another version 4,000) reached the town. He pointed out to the ruler that the Jesuits were the Christian version of *cacizes* and if he had been worth so much then the two of them would fetch much more. This held up the exchange, and subsequently the priests were taken to Sana, where there were another 28 Christian captives (in another version 18) whose faith was strengthened by the intrepid Jesuits. They remained imprisoned while haggling over their value went on at least until the end of 1594.[45] It is possible that it was these people who finally returned to Goa in 1596 on ships coming from the Red Sea; certainly in this year some Portuguese who had been captured by the Turks on the Melinde coast in east Africa were freed.[46]

The attitude of the secular authorities was generally a little more relaxed, though at times they could be pressured by the religious to be as strict and intolerant as they were. While the Provincial Council opposed any importation of Muslim religious books or relics, the secular authorities were less strict. When Albuquerque exchanged presents with a local Muslim ruler, one of his offerings was a copy of the *Qur'an* worth 200 pardaus.[47] The book had presumably been captured from some hostile trader. Certainly on other occasions the Portuguese were not averse to recycling items they had captured. In 1511 Albuquerque sent off an expedition east of Malacca, which he had just captured. Presents for local kings were sent too, and they included some of the highly prized Mecca velvet, which the Portuguese had taken off a hostile ship of Calicut.[48] On another occasion however this sort of recycling redounded on the Portuguese. In 1533 they had captured several ships trading with the Red Sea and taken off most of their cargoes. Among the cargo were highly valued velvet and brocade from Mecca and casks of rose water. Subsequently, when a Portuguese ambassador was ordered to Bengal for negotiations, these same captured items were sent along as presents for the ruler. All went well until a Muslim at the court in Bengal recognized the marks on these items. He had himself been a witness to the capture of the Muslim ships in question. He told the king of this, pointing out that not only was this robbery, but worse still the items had been taken from people on pilgrimage to Mecca. The embassy failed, and the Portuguese ambassador was held captive for a time.[49]

Despite, then, what the religious might think about this traffic in idolatry, the secular authorities always had to temper religious opposition to Muslims with economic realities. In 1514 Albuquerque decided to attack Hurmuz, rather than cruise in the Red Sea. He was well aware that it would be excellent to go as far as Suez and battle with the fleet of the sultan of Egypt, and also to hinder the pilgrimage to Mecca, and to concert his efforts with the ruler of Abyssinia, and finally if the Muslim Red Sea trade was blocked, then the goods which came from Portugal, often the same sorts of goods, would sell much better in India. But the costs of the expedition would be high, and on balance it appeared, despite its general desirability, to be financially impossible. So the fleet headed for Hurmuz instead.[50] More generally, financial officials often pointed out that strict anti-Muslim policies were all very well, and no doubt well-intended by the clergy, but the fact was that they hindered trade and lowered customs revenues. In 1559 an official wrote that where once Goa's customs had yielded 800 pardaus, more recently thanks to nondiscriminatory policies this had risen to 80,000 pardaus. Now this was being threatened by a new wave of discrimination.[51]

The records are unclear on the vital matter of the degree to which Portuguese secular authorities followed the advice of the religious and prohibited Muslims from going on *hajj*. Our records from later in the century show that the pilgrim traffic continued, and we can then assume that after their first burst of enthusiastic intolerance the secular authorities either did not hinder pilgrims, turned a blind eye to their presence, or simply were unable to tell a pilgrim from any other passenger on a ship going to the Red Sea. What is clear is that Portuguese policy on trade and travel to the Red Sea varied over the sixteenth century and was by no means one of total prohibition for the whole of the century.[52]

The Portuguese started off in the Indian Ocean in a very hardnosed undiscriminating way, attacking Muslim ships on sight. Records are rife with accounts of bloody massacres of all passengers and crew on ships going to or coming from the Red Sea, and the confiscation of their cargoes. The royal instructions to the second Portuguese voyage of 1500, commanded by Cabral, told him to make open war on Muslim shipping, for these were people with whom the Portuguese had a very ancient hostility.[53] Very soon, however, this policy became more discriminating, though no less bloody. The Portuguese began to separate ships from Mecca, that is the Red Sea, from local Muslim ships. Arabs and Turks were forbidden, but local Indian Muslims were treated rather differently. They could trade, but only under strict conditions. They were not to carry people belonging to these two Muslim groups, for they were considered to be inherently and irremediably opposed to the Portuguese. Nor were they to carry armaments capable of being used against the Portuguese. Much more important, they were not to carry spices. This was the key requirement of the Portuguese. The whole economic object of the exercise was to interdict the trade in spices through the Red Sea to Europe, and instead gain for themselves a monopoly of this valuable trade by using the route via the Cape of Good Hope.

Thus Portuguese policy mixed service to God and to Mammon, but it seems clear that Mammon, the monopoly of the spice trade, was the main ingredient. As early as 1502 a Portuguese fleet awaited ships from the Red Sea, "and they wished to destroy them in order that the king of Portugal be the only lord of the spices of India."[54] In 1505 the new viceroy, d'Almeida, pointed out that he had tried to be friends with the ruler of Calicut, but he preferred to stay friends with the Moors of Mecca. So d'Almeida was going to make clear to him the price of this choice, by blocking completely the spice trade to the Red Sea.[55] Putting this into effect, in 1506 a fleet patrolled the entrance to the Red Sea, stopped all ships, and imprisoned those which did not have a pass or *cartaz* from a competent Portuguese authority.[56]

This policy continued through the century.[57] On one successful patrol in 1525 a Portuguese fleet cruised in the "straits of Mecca," that is the entrance to the Red Sea, and burned 26 ships, killed many people, captured others, and took ships loaded with spices.[58] In 1528 the Portuguese defeated and sank a huge armada of 130 sail from Calicut, sixty of them guard ships and the rest cargo.[59] Not, however that the patrolling was always successful. A crucial gap was the failure to take Aden. Instead it was controlled by the Ottoman Turks from 1538, thanks to Sulaiman Basha, and definitively taken over by Piri Reis in 1549, after a period of quasi-independence.[60] This denied the Portuguese a base which would have made more effective their patrolling at the entrance to the Red Sea more effective. Sometimes illicit Muslim traders were able to slip past the Portuguese fleets, and sometimes the fleets got there too late and missed the spice ships.[61]

It is important to stress that the Portuguese soon forgot about trying to block *all* trade to the Red Sea. In general, if a ship took a *cartaz*, and paid customs duties to the Portuguese at one of their forts, they were free to trade. And obviously the Portuguese could not control the passengers, nor indeed did the *cartazes* ever forbid the passage of pilgrims, despite the demands of the religious authorities. Trade thus continued from India, and especially from Gujarat, to the Red Sea, and the pilgrim traffic was not affected. In the case of Gujarat, this policy was clearly laid out in peace treaties of the 1530s. In 1534 it was specified that all Gujarati ships going to the Red Sea must call first at Bassein and get a *cartaz*; the point is that they were allowed to go there.[62] We have plenty of evidence of actual *cartazes* being given to Gujarati ships for trade to the Red Sea from this time on.[63] Indeed, it seems clear that Gujarati trade with the Red Sea expanded greatly during this century.

Late in 1537 the Portuguese governor, Nuno da Cunha, wrote complacently to the king that the trade from Diu to the Red Sea was going well. Many Indian ships had left Diu for the Red Sea, and 35 had arrived from the Arabian coast, Aden and Jiddah.[64] In 1538 a Portuguese ship inspected a Muslim ship which had a *cartaz* from the captain of Diu "which said that that ship might navigate from Surat to Mocha and back to Diu, but was not to carry forbidden merchandise [essentially meaning spices] or Rumes or Turks . . . "[65] Three years later a Portuguese fleet off the entrance of the Red Sea inspected two ships, one large and one small. One had a *cartaz* from the Portuguese captain of Diu to go to Suez, and one from the captain of Bassein to go to Jiddah "and our ships honoured them."[66] In 1548 the municipal council of Goa wrote to the king that in the last year alone some fifty or sixty ships had come from the Red Sea to the Indian coast.[67] Even the Jesuit records routinely record the arrival of ships from the Red Sea, apparently unaffected and unbothered by the fact that these ships came from the heartland of Islam.[68] Couto has a curious story of a Muslim merchant who had some especially fine cloths ["bofatás, os mais ricos que podiam ser"] made in Broach which were destined for "the Pashas of the Turk" (presumably a Turkish governor somewhere in the Red Sea area). He had trouble with a Portuguese customs official over their valuation, but the point is that the Portuguese officials saw even this trade to the heartland of Islam as quite routine and unexceptional.[69]

In a particularly interesting case of 1609, a Portuguese fleet stopped an Arab ship on its way from Diu to the Red Sea. Most of its 700 passengers were pilgrims. It had a *cartaz* from no less a person than the Archbishop of Goa, who was acting governor of Portuguese India at the time.[70] In wartime, such as in the build up to the second siege of Diu in 1546, this trade was blocked to enemies of the Portuguese.[71] Other times *cartazes* were taken by most Indian traders, and honored by most Portuguese captains. In 1555 a fleet took four ships carrying spices, one of them being a Turkish vessel and so doubly forbidden, but 21 ships from Gujarat were inspected. All had *cartazes*, were allowed to proceed, except for one with eight Turks on board whose was confiscated and sold in Hurmuz.[72]

These incidents show is that the Portuguese were not acting in a vacuum. They had to conciliate powerful Indian rulers and traders and think not just of ideological hatred of Muslims but also of the way these Muslim traders could increase Portuguese customs revenues. While in theory the Portuguese exercised a total monopoly of the spice trades, in other areas they sometimes had to give a little. In the late 1580s the sultan of Golconda made an agreement with the Portuguese. He was to send a ship with 300 *candis* of rice to a Portuguese fort, at first in Sri Lanka, later in Melaka. In return he, like the sultan of Bijapur, got *cartazes* for ships bound for Jiddah and Mocha.[73] In 1543 the two *talukas* to the north and south of the small Portuguese territory of Goa, that is Bardes and Salcette, were ceded to them by the ruler of Bijapur. In return the Portuguese had to allow him to trade to the Red Sea. Duties had to be paid in Goa but the trade was allowed, and we must assume that many pilgrims were on board. [74] In the early seventeenth century the powerful de facto ruler of Ahmadnager, Malik Ambar, had two *cartazes* each year for the Red Sea.[75]

Similarly in Malabar, where again in the 1540s the Portuguese were dependent on local traders and rulers for a host of services. Again they had to be conciliated by being allowed to trade to the Red Sea, with *cartazes*.[76] In 1546 and 1547 a Cannanor notable wrote to the Portuguese governor, mentioning among other things that his ships had arrived from Jiddah and Mocha.[77] As K.S. Mathew notes, this licensed trade presumably led to much smuggling of illegal pepper, and so this Portuguese tolerance of trade to the Red Sea inevitably contributed to the revival of the spice trade via the Middle East to Europe.[78] The smuggling was made easier by the fact that the patrol to the Red Sea seems to have been given up around 1570.[79] In 1605 the king complained to the viceroy that the king of Cochin, and other Malabar and Kanara rulers, were using the concession of the *cartazes* to send pepper and other prohibited items to the Red Sea.[80]

The necessity for the Portuguese to conciliate local rulers was seen most clearly in their relations with the most powerful ruler of sixteenth-century India, Akbar, the ruler of the great Mughal empire. They were well aware of his formidable military capacity. Once he took Gujarat, in 1572, he became a neighbor of the vital Portuguese forts in Diu and Daman; Gujarat was also the most important area for Portuguese trade. The Portuguese rightly feared that if Akbar could stop their trade if he wanted to, and probably also take their forts, which would be unable to receive help by the sea during the three months (June to September) of the southwest monsoon. And even if they could have held out, they were still vulnerable, as a Jesuit letter of 1600 gloomily noted: "we remain surrounded by him, and although it is not possible for him to take our cities and forts by arms, nevertheless if he takes the places from where we get our provisions it would be our certain end, which God not permit, because then we would have no other refuge except Ceylon . . . "[81]

There had been a temporary problem in 1572-3 as Akbar conquered Gujarat. He seemed to be inclined to conquer the Portuguese territory of Daman also, but then he drew back. According to the Portuguese he did not want a rupture, but rather wanted peace so that his ships could trade freely to the Red Sea, and so that his mother and other élite women could visit "the tomb of Muhammad [sic]." So peace was restored, and he was given one *cartaz* a year on which he did not have to pay duties for a voyage to the Red Sea.[82] This turned out to be a very expensive Portuguese concession, for the merchants of Gujarat seized the opportunity and loaded all their most valuable goods on this ship in Jiddah, thus avoiding paying duties to the Portuguese on them. On their own ships they sent back less valuable commodities.[83] Nevertheless, the Portuguese felt they had no choice but to accept this unsatisfactory state of affairs, for Akbar was too threatening to risk alienating.

For his part, Akbar at times complained of the Portuguese and their depredations and their control over the pilgrim traffic, but these complaints seem to have been designed mostly to paint him as a valiant defender of Islam; certainly they led to no effective action from him. In 1580 he put it about that he was determined to capture the Portuguese ports, "in order to remove the Faringis who were a stumbling-block in the way of pilgrims to the Hijaz," and six years later he floridly informed the ruler of Uzbekistan that he wanted to "undertake the destruction of the Feringhi infidels who have come to the islands of the ocean, and have lifted up the head of turbulence and stretched out the hand of oppression upon the pilgrims to the holy places. May God increase their glory! They have become a great number and are stumbling blocks to the pilgrims and traders."[84]

The political results of the Portuguese presence in the Arabian Sea in the sixteenth century were then variable and certainly, never got near to blocking either trade to the Red Sea or the pilgrim traffic. Their weakness made it impossible for them to enforce fully the more hotheaded recommendations of the clerics. All this makes something of a contrast with another political influence on the *hajj*, that is, the attitudes of the Mughal emperors to this traffic.

# CHAPTER 5

# The Mughals and the *Hajj*

Mughal emperors varied greatly in their attitude toward Islam, but all of them, whether for reasons of piety or policy, found it valuable to have the reputation of being a staunch defender of Islam, and a patron of the Holy Places. Copying the *Qur'an* in one's own hand and sending the copy off to Mecca was a popular practice. An ancestor of the dynasty, who ruled in Ghazni in the mid-eleventh century, "was a just and devout king, and used to write each year a Quran with his own hand and despatch it to the holy city of Mekka."[1] Babur, first of the Mughals, devised his own (quickly forgotten) script, copied the *Qur'an* in it, and presented the manuscript to the rulers of Mecca. It does not seem that Babur was especially pious, however. After his victory in 1526 he engaged in routine giving of presents to all and sundry. His relatives did very well indeed, including those back home in Samarqand, and in a rather offhand way the chronicle also records that "To holy men belonging to Samarkand and Khurasan went offerings vowed to God; so too to Makka and Medina . . . "[2]

The ultra-pious Sultan Muzaffar II (r. 1511-26) transcribed the *Qur'an* every year and sent copies to Mecca and Medina. According to another account, he sent two copies of the *Qur'an* transcribed by his own hand in gold water to Mecca and Medina, and made a special annual grant to provide for the upkeep of the books and the maintenance of those who used the copies for recitation. Every day he transcribed a passage from the *Qur'an* in the *nashkh* style.[3] In the second half of the seventeenth century the long-lived Mughal emperor Aurangzeb emulated this practice.⁴ Muzaffar also constructed a hospice in Mecca, that consisted of a school, a place for the distributing water to pilgrims and other buildings, and set aside endowments for the maintenance of teachers and students. He provided a vessel to carry poor pilgrims to Mecca free of charge and covered all their expenses on the voyage, so that they could spend all their own money on charity for the poor of the Holy Cities.⁵ A variant on this contemporary Persian text claims that the giving of land grants to religious specialists had a political purpose too. The neighboring, and hostile, sultan of Malwa said it would be difficult to conquer Gujarat for there "much land is held on religious tenures. There is no district nor village in which there is not land endowed on religious institutions or as pensions to religious men or officers, and this constitutes an army without horses and riders that like the stars is ever wakeful."⁶ A successor of Muzaffar as ruler of Gujarat, Sultan Mahmud II (r. 1537-54), was similarly pious and generous. He reserved the revenues of some villages near Cambay as *waqf*, to be distributed in the Holy Cities, and in Mecca built various religious buildings.⁷ In the early fifteenth century rulers of Bengal did exactly the same.⁸ So too the ruler of Golconda, where in the 1620s "the King sends yeerely a proportion of rice as an almes to be distributed amongst the pilgrimes which resort to Mecha and Medina, where their prophet Mahomet's shrine is visited with much devotion."⁹

The centrality of Mecca for Muslim rulers in India is then easy to demonstrate. It can be seen also in the way in which the main port through which pilgrims passed, the great Gujarati port of Surat, was identified by various epithets which indicated the port's symbolic importance to India's Muslims. It was the Bab-ul-Mecca, the Gateway of Mecca, or the Bandar-i mubarak, the blessed port, or the "auspicious harbor" of Surat, or, most significantly, "the door to the House of God."

We noted in the last chapter that Akbar was anxious to

avoid a break with the Portuguese in part so that he could send off some of his women on pilgrimage. A surprisingly large number of élite Muslim women made the pilgrimage from India in our period, and in all cases they were copiously supported and helped by their male relatives. One of the first was Bega Begam, wife of one of Humayun's nobles, who later became Humayun's widow, and was known appropriately as Haji Begam.

More famous was Gulbadan Begam, a daughter of Babur. Akbar began to make arrangements for his aunt's *hajj* in 1575. In 1576 he heard that rumor had it that the journey was no longer a safe one because of Portuguese depredation. A top noble was sent to reassure the intending *hajjis*; finally, two ships set off with Gulbadan Begam, ten other ladies, and various royal officials.[10] Akbar gave her lavish expenses and also provided expenses and provisions "to all pious men and faqirs and soldiers that had the intention of making the pilgrimage."[11] Arriving in Mecca after an adventurous voyage, the party stayed some years, doing four *hajjs* and numerous *umrahs*. So lavishly were they provided with alms that indigents from the Hijaz, Syria, and Asia Minor all swarmed to Mecca to get a share of the bounty.[12] Badaoni claims they went to the important *shia* shrines of Karbala, Qum, and Mashhad, as well as Mecca.[13] They returned with various curiosities and some Arab servants after an adventurous journey which in total lasted seven years, from 1576 to 1582.[14]

Deccani Muslim rulers also made it possible for their women to make the pilgrimage. In 1640 the ruler of Golconda sent the ladies of his court to Iran to see the *shia* shrines, and then go on to Mecca. They traveled by sea from Golconda to Bandar Abbas, and in Persia were given all assistance by the Shah, their fellow *shia*. They got to Najaf and the tomb of Ali, and Karbala and the tombs of Hasan and Hussein, but the road to Mecca was blocked by war.[15] Twenty years later the Dowager Queen of Bijapur undertook a series of *hajjs*; four in all according to Manucci.[16] English records tell us that she went off to the Red Sea on a small Dutch vessel in 1661, reaching Mocha in March.[17] They must then have cooled their heels for some months, as Dhu al-Hijja this year began only at the end of July. Portuguese records, however, note the sale in March 1663 of a ship to the Queen Mother of Bijapur, who wanted to go to Mecca in it.[18] It was probably during the *hajj* journey on this occasion that she was sighted by Tavernier in Ispahan, where she was visiting the *shia* shrines.[19]

As we would expect, the majority of Muslim Indian *hajjis* in our period were men. Among the élite, the pilgrimage was undertaken for a variety of reasons. Piety was no doubt often a motive, or at least one of several. But many Indian Muslim rulers found that sending nobles and others off on *hajj* was an acceptable way to get rid of people whose presence was no longer desired at court, and to punish those who had failed. Given the centrality of the *hajj,* it was difficult for a noble to refuse the "opportunity" to make such a pilgrimage; on the other hand, a request to be allowed to go on *hajj* was one that a ruler would normally not want to refuse. Yet apparently few wanted to go except perhaps the very pious. In these very personalized courts, access to the centre, to the emperor, was crucial. Indeed, how close one got physically was important, a very public affirmation of one's standing or lack of it. And to be denied access to court was a humiliation. To go off to Mecca, on a journey lasting probably at least a year, and often longer, was in political terms at least a grave punishment, and one from which it was difficult to recoup one's fortunes.

All sorts of misbehavior could lead to this sort of exile disguised as an opportunity to fulfill a religious obligation. In Akbar's reign a rather turbulent noble, Mozaffar Khan, fell out of favor after he lost his temper playing a game at court. He "behaved in a savage and rustic manner," and as a result Akbar "cast him off from the pinnacle of confidence and sent him on pilgrimage in order that by playing the game of unimportance and exile, his unsound condition might be amend-ed."[20] In this case the threat was enough. His behavior pre-sumably became less rustic and he was pardoned and not required to go.[21] Around this same time, two important reli-gious leaders at court had been quarreling publicly for some time. Finally, Akbar sent them off on *hajj* in 986AH (1578-9); apparently while they became reconciled during the journey. Soon after another noble was so tactless as to oppose the influence of the rising star Abul Fazl and his defeat was pub-licly revealed when he was sent off to Mecca.[22]

Indeed going off on *hajj* was often the choice offered to the vanquished. For a new ruler, it was much more accept-able merely to exile defeated opponents to Mecca, rather than risk public opprobrium by killing them. In the late fourteenth century a puppet sultan in the Bahmani kingdom became vulnerable when his controller was killed. The ex-sultan, however, was merely allowed to move off to Mecca.[23] Humayun had constant trouble with his relatives and sent them off to Mecca as he consolidated his power. Askari, after a final display of disloyalty, was allowed to go to Mecca, but he died on the way. Kamran, after several false starts, final-ly was blinded and sent off in 1553. He did four *hajjs* and died in Mecca in 1557.[24] Akbar's guide Bairam Khan was involved in two similar incidents. In 1556, as he consolidated his influ-ence over the young emperor, an opponent, Mir Asghar Munshi, was exiled to Mecca and returned only in 1560.[25] Once Akbar became exasperated with his teacher's overbear-ing behavior. This time Bairam Khan himself was given money and allowed to go off to Mecca, but he was killed as a result of a private quarrel in Gujarat before he could embark. A Gujarati *sufi* associated with the ruler of independent Gujarat, Bahadur, discreetly moved off to Mecca after his patron was defeated by the Mughals in 1536.[26] Another reli-gious leader similarly was rusticated for his opinions. An important qazi under Aurangzeb, the Qazi ul-Quzzat, often clashed with the emperor. The last straw came when he

111

declared the invasion of Bijapur and Golconda to be illegal. He was allowed to resign and go to Mecca. [27]

There are then numerous examples of both religious and political figures at court losing favor and, going off on *hajj* voluntarily or otherwise. Nobles who did badly could be sent off. A noble asked to be allowed to go to Mecca after losing a battle in 1563. He wrote to Akbar that "he had not the face to come to the sublime threshold. He hoped that he would be allowed to go to Mecca, in order that he might in that holy land cleanse himself of his offences, and then come and kiss the threshold." Akbar, however, refused to let him leave.[28] In 1102 AH (1690-91) Abu al-Khayr performed poorly against the Marathas, and finally was relieved of his *mansab* and *jagir* and sent off to Mecca.[29] Around this same time another noble fell out with Aurangzeb, and similarly lost all his property and entitlements and was sent off on *hajj*; subsequently, however, he was pardoned.[30] As another variant, a noble would ask permission to go on *hajj* merely as a subterfuge, in order to escape the confines of the court, and once away either join a rebel or himself raise a rebellion. Such a request was, of course, very difficult to refuse, for it would mean a noble's right to undertake a prime obligation of his religion was being denied him.[31]

In Jahangir's reign a famous Persian doctor at court, Hakim Sadra Masihu-z-zaman, had the misfortune to fall out with the emperor. Jahangir records in his *Memoirs* that although he was very ill, "That ungrateful man, in spite of the claims which I had on him, though he saw me in such a state, did not give me medicines or treat me. Notwithstanding that I distinguished him beyond all the physicians who were waiting on me, he would not undertake my cure . . . . As there was no help for it, I gave them all up, and weaning my heart from all visible remedies, gave myself up to the Supreme Physician. As drinking alleviated my sufferings, I took to it in the daytime, contrary to my habit, and gradually I carried this to excess."[32] Apparently the hakim realized the emperor was displeased, for suddenly "he asked for leave to undertake a journey to the Hijaz, and make a pilgrimage to the holy house. Inasmuch as at all times and under all circumstances the reliance of this suppliant is on the Lord, that needs no return, and the gracious Creator, I gave him leave with an open brow. Though he had all kinds of things [for the journey] I made him a present of Rs.20,000 in aid of his expenses . . . "[33] So he moved off on pilgrimage, but on the way back in 1623 had the misfortune to be captured by the English.[34] He must have done another *hajj*, in 1632, returning four years later. He came back via Basra, where he acquired forty high quality Arab horses.[35]

The Hijaz was also a popular place of refuge for defeated nobles and aspirants to the throne. In 1535 the ruler of Gujarat, Bahadur Shah, was hard pressed by Humayun, and so he sent off a noble called Asaf Khan with his treasury and harem to Mecca. They remained there after Bahadur's death in 1537. Asaf Khan returned home only in 1548; the fate of the women and treasure seems to be unrecorded.[36] Similarly, in 1587, a rebel against Akbar moved off to Mecca after being defeated.[37] In 1659 Shah Shuja lost the struggle for the succession to Aurangzeb, and decided to try and escape from Arakan and take refuge in Mecca;[38] he was killed before he could leave.

There was often an implication that a *hajj* would bring a man to his senses or cure his evil behavior. In fact, however, the actual experience had diverse results. In Shah Jahan's reign Sayyid Mansur Khan Barah behaved very erratically, and was several times imprisoned; he was considered to have an "evil" nature. Finally, he was sent off to Gujarat "in order that he might proceed from there to holy Mecca and offer retribution for his ill deeds, in the hope that this might change his unbecoming habits into praiseworthy actions." In fact, this noble did do better, subsequently.[39]

But sometimes the experience had a strictly non-uplifting effect. Several Mughal pilgrims were so extensively fleeced by the people and rulers of Mecca that they lost their faith, or, at least, tended towards less orthodox Islam. The sharifs did very well as rulers of the Hijaz. In the first half of the fifteenth century their very wide claims were accepted, and apparently continued to be observed thereafter. They received one-quarter of the value of all ships wrecked on their coast, one-quarter of the value of all gifts sent from abroad "for the people of Mecca," and one-tenth of all imported goods, including one-tenth of all cargo on all Indian ships bound for Jiddah.[40] Despite this, they greedily continued to accept bribes and fleece pilgrims. In the 1580s Sultan Khwaja had been made Mir Hajj, the official in charge of the state-sponsored *hajj* party. He took with him a numerous party of courtiers, and also Rs.600,000 and 12,000 robes of honor to distribute to the people of Mecca. But he was mercilessly fleeced in Mecca and on his return joined the Divine Faith, that is, Akbar's mildly unorthodox syncretic sect.[41] The case of Akbar's foster brother, Mirza Aziz Koka, is quite well known. In the 1590s he fell out with the emperor, and set off on *hajj*, accompanied by six sons, six daughters, and about 100 attendants.[42] His intention was to stay in the Holy Cities indefinitely, but he soon became fed up with Mecca. It seems that his life there was made difficult by the sharifs. These men were in receipt of a regular pension from Akbar, and were instigated to harass the Mirza. Badaoni records the result: he returned from Mecca "where he had suffered much harm at the hands of the Sharifs, and throwing away the blessing which he had derived from the pilgrimage, joined immediately on his return the Divine Faith."[43]

Aurangzeb may have been the most lavish of the Mughals in terms of this patronage, and indeed he has a considerable reputation for being the most pious and orthodox of the dynasty. He complained bitterly of the way European pirates attacked merchants and pilgrims as they proceeded to the Red Sea, concluding firmly that "Moderation will not work. Severity and harshness are required."[44] He tried to get help from the European trading companies and also the Arabs of Mascat, but with very little success.[45] And, just as we saw in the last chapter the secular Portuguese sometimes were not as anti-Muslim as the clerics wanted, so also at times all the Mughals were forced to moderate their concern for the *hajj* by considerations of *realpolitik*. Orthodox theologians at court complained of the *shia* Safavids blocking the *hajj* from India, and even said a pilgrimage which involved travel through Persia was invalid. But the Mughals never brought up this matter in their many embassies and letters to the Safavids. According to Farooqi, the reason was that the Mughals needed to keep Persia strong so it would block the main threat to India from the northwest, the Uzbeks. This took priority over complaining of Safavid harassment of pilgrims.[46]

In any case, even Aurangzeb was not entirely captive to the prestige of Mecca. Early in his reign he was concerned, no doubt for both political and religious reasons, to stand out as a champion of the faith. He was well aware that many considered him to be a usurper and were disgusted by his treatment of his father and brothers. He was anxious then to get recognition of his position from the very prestigious sharif of Mecca, and late in 1659 sent to the Holy Cities presents worth the considerable sum of Rs.6,60,000. However, according to Manucci the authorities at Mecca stood on their dignity and refused these presents, pointing out more or less correctly that Aurangzeb could not be the legitimate ruler of Mughal India while his father was still alive.[47] However, not too much should be made either of the size of the presents or their rejection in Mecca. In order to gain recognition, Aurangzeb, spent a total of Rs.70,00,000 in 1661-7 on presents to various foreign kings,[48] so that the sum sent to Mecca in 1659 was actually quite small.[49] As to the second point, Manucci claimed that the sharifs soon regretted their hasty rejection of valuable presents, for Indian Muslims had always been major milk cows for them. Soon they tried to revive their previous practice, which was to send small, but very holy, presents, some apparently of dubious authenticity, and to expect major and valuable cash gifts in return. "The Sharif of Mecca in particular used to send his agents to the Delhi court every year with the object of levying contributions in the name of the Prophet . . . ."[50]

Disillusionment seems to have set in quite early. According to Manucci, in 1665 an envoy from Mecca, Sidi Yahya, brought 14 Arab horses and "a broom that had been used to sweep the tomb of Muhammad [sc. for the Ka'ba] and with it a little of the dust . . . Aurangzeb received these ambassadors and their presents with great consideration," but did not reciprocate very fully, so that they returned with "more in the nature of honour than of presents."[51] It was apparently this embassy which Bernier described in the following unflattering terms. He noted that an embassy came from the "Cherif of Meca, and the presents that accompanied this embassage consisted of a small number of Arabian horses, and a besom [small broom] which had been used for sweeping out the small chapel [sc. for the Ka'ba] situated in the centre of the great Mosque at Meca . . . Little or no respect was paid to . . . these diplomatists. Their equipage was so miserable that every one suspected they came merely for the sake of obtaining money in return for their presents, and of gaining still more considerable sums by means of the numerous horses, and different articles of merchandise, which they introduced into the kingdom free of all duty, as property belonging to ambassadors." They also were entitled to take Indian goods out of India duty free.[52]

Despite this lack of respect, the sharifs seem to have decided to keep up this profitable (for them) exchange. In 1668 another Meccan envoy was given permission to leave and took with him a robe, Rs.9,000, and a horse with silver trappings. Three years later a Meccan envoy brought two Arab horses, and a silver sword belt, and got in return a jeweled dagger, Rs.10,000, two valuable coins, and Rs.20,000 for the sharif. In 1674 yet another envoy took with him Rs.5,000, in 1685 a robe and Rs.2,000, and a year later a robe, a dagger, a horse and Rs.3,000.[53] What we notice is that the presents were getting smaller and smaller. Aurangzeb became increasingly fed up with the unequal exchange, especially as his presents were meant to be allocated as charity in Mecca, but were being kept by the sharifs for themselves. Aurangzeb circumvented them, and sent his gifts to mendicants and scholars in the Holy Cities through his own agents, rather than trusting the sharifs to do this distribution. He wrote to his *wazir* late in his reign that "The Sharif of Mecca, having heard of the great wealth of India, sends an envoy every year for making his own gain. The money that I send there is meant for the poor and not for him."[54] The most obvious sign of his disillusionment was the way in which in the early 1680s he kept a Meccan embassy waiting for some years. Failing to get an audience, it "proceeded in despair and dudgeon to Achin [Aceh], whence it returned home laden with rich booty."[55] We may note also that the successor states to the Mughals in the eighteenth century continued this patronage, in part no doubt to establish their legitimacy. Thus the ruler of Bengal in 1737, Shuja ud-din Khan, received a representative of "the Meccan *ulama*" and he and his courtiers gave him at least Rs.162,000. This envoy also received donations from the Muslim community in Bengal.[56]

So much for the élite and their various experiences with Mecca and the pilgrimage. It is a pity that our sources tell us so much about them, and so little about the vast majority of pilgrims, who were poor devout people, and for whom the *hajj* was the experience, often the culmination, of a lifetime. Many of these pilgrims were helped on their way by the state. While we have no records of either Babur or Humayun doing this, Sher Shah apparently did provide passage both ways and support for pilgrims, as one would expect from a newly established ruler.[57] He also hoped that once he had completed his conquest of north India he would then be able to get the Ottomans to ally with him in an attack on the Safavids, who

117

were hindering the *hajj*.⁵⁸ In the early sixteenth century Muzaffar II of Gujarat provided both ships and sustenance, so that the pilgrims could use all their own money for charitable giving in Mecca.⁵⁹ In the 1580s the ruler of Golconda also did this. Indeed, like the Mughals and the rulers of Bijapur he was prepared to conciliate the Portuguese in order to be allowed to do this. The agreement was that Golconda was to send a ship with 300 *candis* of rice to a Portuguese area, and in return get *cartazes* for the Red Sea.⁶⁰ But as with all these other state-sponsored ships, the motive was not only religious. Subrahmanyam tells us that in the case of Golconda the decision was to "send every year a large ship from Masulipatnam to the Red Sea, which would fly the Sultan's flag. These ships, constructed at the Godavari yard of Narsapur Pattai, were frequently of 600 tons burthen, if not larger still. They were to perform three roles: first, to exploit the Middle East market for north Coromandel textiles, while at the same time enabling gold and silver to be imported direct from the Red Sea ports; second, of permitting the Sultan to have alms distributed annually in his name at Mecca; and third, of ensuring the easy passage not only of pilgrims on the Hajj, but of immigrants from the Middle East to Golconda."⁶¹

Akbar's role was more complex. He has often been presented by Westerners as an apostate from Islam, or at least as a very free-thinking Muslim. These critics seem to ignore the considerable degree of flexibility in Islam; far from being totally rigid and intolerant, as they would like us to believe, there was and is quite large scope for diversity and heterodox opinion. It seems that Akbar never did anything which could be considered unIslamic, except perhaps by the ultra-orthodox. Certainly he inquired into all religions, but he also stood out often as a patron of Islam, and of the *hajj*. In 1576 when he heard that pilgrims were being put off by stories of Portuguese depredations, he took steps to reassure intending *hajjis*, and more generally he fulminated against the

Portuguese because he claimed they were blocking the pilgrimage.[62]

It seems that the acquisition of Gujarat in 1572-3 made possible a much more direct and important Mughal concern for and patronage of the pilgrimage. Local officials in Gujarat were often given jobs designed to help pilgrims. The father of the author of the *Arabic History of Gujarat* was appointed by Akbar to administer the *waqfs* in Gujarat which were dedicated to Mecca and Medina, and his son's job was to carry the money from there to the Holy Cities.[63] In the seventeenth century the job of the *sadr* in Surat was to distribute state endowments to places of worship, to Islamic educational institutions, and to finance indigent but pious pilgrims so that they could do the *hajj*.[64] Early in the eighteenth century we hear of the Surat official whose job it was to supervise the annual gifts which the Mughal emperor sent to Mecca. In 1704 a Dutch ship returned from the Red Sea, and among the passengers was "Nurul Haq, the censor of public morals at Ahmadabad, who had carried the annual Mughal donations to Mecca . . . "[65]

More directly important was the way Akbar and his successors financed the *hajj* for poor pilgrims. This began in earnest in the 1570s, after the acquisition of Gujarat, and despite the now discredited orthodox objections that the *hajj* was no longer binding as it could only be done through *shia* Persia or by sea with the permission of the infidel Portuguese.[66] As the chronicler-cum-panegyrist tells us, Akbar now decided that "every year one of the attendants of the threshold should be appointed to the post of Mir Haji; and a caravan should be sent from Hindustan like the caravans of Egypt and Syria. This resolution was carried into effect, and every year, a number of men of enlightened minds . . . received provisions and the expenses of the journey, from the public treasury, and went with the Mir Haj by way of the ports of Gujarat, and reached that sacred land. Up to the time of the rising of the Sun of this Sovereign, no other monarch had attained to such an honour and grandeur, that he should send a caravan from Hindustan to Mecca the revered, and should remove the custom of need from the poor of that honoured place."[67] An alternative, and slightly less positive, version is given by the more orthodox Badaoni. In 982 AH (1574-5) "it became an established practice for five or six years that one of the nobles of the Court was made Leader of the pilgrims, and a general permission was given to the people, so that at great public expense, with gold and goods and rich presents, the Emperor sent them on a pilgrimage to Mecca, but this was afterwards abandoned."[68]

While it lasted this was a major enterprise. In 984 AH (1576-7) the Mir Hajj was given Rs.600,000 in money and goods to distribute to the people of Mecca and Medina, and the expenses of all who wanted to do the *hajj* were met by the state.[69] Next year, in 985 AH (1577-8), Mir Abu Turab Wali was made Mir Hajj, and he got Rs.500,000 and 10,000 *khilats* [robes of honor] to distribute. Again many people were subsidized to make the pilgrimage, and Akbar also sent presents to the sharifs: "To the sharifs of that land—who had always sent presentations, and the rarities of the country—there were sent a lac of rupees and splendid goods."[70] Here certainly there was a political admixture, for we noted that these subsidies to the rulers of the Holy Cities meant that they kept an eye on, and if requested harassed, nobles from India who were in Mecca. It was this party of 1577 which brought back from Mecca a stone purportedly bearing an impression of the foot of the Prophet; Akbar treated this relic with ostentatious veneration. We have records of this lavish patronage continuing for at least another four years, for as late as 989 AH (1581-2) a noble was sent to Mecca with Rs.500,000 for presents.[71] Nor was it only Akbar who engaged in this support. At least one of his top nobles, the pious Abdur-Rahim, set aside three of his own ships, the "Rahimi," the "Karimi," and the "Salari" to transport pilgrims; he paid the crew himself, and provided maintenance for the pilgrims.

The "Rahimi" and the "Salari" both weighed in at a very large 1500 tons, according to a detailed survey by the English merchant Saris.[72]

This sort of state support was continued in the seventeenth century. Jahangir tells us nothing in his *Memoirs* of any general support, though we noted above an instance where he helped an individual noble. Shah Jahan, however, perhaps regularly sent charity to Mecca, appointing a Mir Hajj to convey the money and act as leader of the pilgrims.[73] This support seems to have increased under Aurangzeb. Early in his reign Manucci wrote of two royal ships in the Red Sea, with faqirs and lords and ladies of Hindustan on board. They returned to India with these passengers and a valuable cargo.[74] Tavernier also noted these two ships, which traveled to the Red Sea each year, and carried passengers free of charge. Fakirs came from all over India to sail on them. Trade items were also sent on them, and the profits were given in charity to poor pilgrims. All the main members of Aurangzeb's harem, and other notables, sent considerable donations to Mecca.[75] The *nakhoda* on these great ships was a *mansabdar*, and a person of considerable importance and self-esteem.[76] It appears that later in his reign Aurangzeb decided to send more. John Fryer, commenting sourly as usual and in an "Orientalist" mode, wrote that "The Emperor also has four great Ships in Pay always, to carry Pilgrims to Moecha on free Cost and bring them back from Hodge, where they prove a Crew of sanctified Varlets."[77] Finally, we must note that, as with most human endeavors, motives could be mixed. Qazvini, the author of our best account of a contemporary Mughal pilgrimage, was paid to go on *hajj* by his patroness, Zaibunnisa [Zeb un-Nisa], the daughter of Aurangzeb. In return he dedicated his account, the "Anis ul hujjaj," to her.[78] Similarly, profit both for patron and pilgrim was sometimes involved, and we must now turn to a discussion of the vexed matter of the "*hajj* market."

# Economic Dimensions of the *Hajj*: the Land Routes

The next three chapters will investigate the connection between the *hajj* and economic activity in our period. We will first look at the received wisdom on this matter, which sees a close connection between the two; it is claimed that Mecca was a great market place, that most pilgrims went to Mecca as much to trade as to observe the rituals of the *hajj,* and that the economy of large parts of India was dominated by the requirements of something called the "hajj market". Contemporary evidence from the Middle East tends to show that the matter is not as clear as the standard accounts claim. To anticipate the main finding, what we have are two major markets in the Hijaz in the early modern period. One was a "normal" market at the great port of Jiddah, its timing largely dictated by sailing seasons and in commercial terms by standard supply and demand factors. The other was at Mecca. Economically, this was a "freak" market. It lasted only a few days, and involved a range of unusual and specific goods. Its whole existence was a result not of commercial factors but of Mecca's role as the focus of the annual pilgrimage.

These three interlinked chapters then are to be seen as making contributions in three areas. First, they deal with the obvious matter of motivations for the pilgrimage. What role did economic factors play in encouraging people to go on *hajj*? Second, they seek to counter the mildly defamatory, or even blatantly hostile, tone of both contemporary and modern accounts, which in effect deny the religiosity of the pilgrims, and instead say, or at least imply, that they were only in it for the money. Third, these chapters will, it is hoped, contribute to a better understanding of the location of markets, and of the organization and direction of a major trade route in early modern times, namely the one that connected the Indian Ocean area, more narrowly the Arabian Sea and especially India, with the Middle East, to the Mediterranean, and the burgeoning markets of early modern western Europe. These markets were part of an economy which by the end of our period was beginning to engulf the trades we are describing.

The claim of a link between trade and religion, which in its extreme form finds that trade, not pilgrimage, was the motivation, has a long history. Godinho quoted a contemporary saying that the Cairo caravan went to Mecca "for absolution and for trade."[1] Even the authority of the *Encyclopedia of Islam* can be enlisted. Its second edition (s.v. Hadjdj) said "To the religious, social and even political significance which such a gathering [that is, the *hajj*] has today, was added, until the eighteenth century, an economic aspect; then, at this time of the year, Mecca was the site of one of the greatest commercial fairs of the world in which were found the products of Europe, Arabia and the Indies."

Contemporary accounts seem to modify this depiction in quite important ways. First, however, we must establish that Islamic tradition does not in any way see a mixture of piety and profit as being negative. Quite the contrary; the two are usually linked, and this is not seen as detrimental nor in any way remarkable. As is well known, the Prophet himself was a trader, and a successful one, while standard accounts present Mecca in his time as an important center of trade. The nexus, and sometimes the tension, between trade and religion is shown well in a crucial passage in the *Qur'an*: "O ye who believe! When the call is heard for the prayer of the day of congregation, haste unto remembrance of Allah and leave your trading. That is better for you if ye did but know. And when the prayer is ended, then disperse in the land and seek of Allah's bounty, and *remember Allah much, that ye may be successful.* But when they spy some merchandise or pastime they break away to it and leave thee [*sc.* the Prophet] standing. Say: That which Allah hath is better than pastime and than merchandise, and Allah is the best of providers."[2] More specifically, and very importantly for our discussion, Martin notes that "The intention to engage in business with other pilgrims is lawful, especially if it is meant to help defray the costs of the journey."[3] The modern anthropologist Clifford Geertz notes nicely that "Mosque and market have been a natural pair over much of the Islamic world, paving one another's way in the spread of a civilization interested equally in this world and the next."[4]

Even more relevant to our discussion, the *Qur'an* has several passages which speak approvingly of sea trade and maritime matters. The Prophet probably never himself traveled by sea, but the *Qur'an* is far from depicting an exclusively land-based society, let alone the old canard of "the religion of the desert." As the Holy Book says, "And of His signs is this: He sendeth herald winds to make you taste His mercy, and that the ships may sail at His command, and that ye may seek His favour, and that haply ye may be thankful." And again: "your Lord is He who driveth for you the ship upon the sea that ye may seek of His bounty." or "Allah it is Who hath made the sea of service unto you that the ships may run thereon by His command, and that ye may seek of His bounty."[5]

As for any specific tie with the *hajj*, Serjeant wrote that pilgrims carried goods, "hadjdj wa-hadjah," "pilgrimage and business," as the Arab says.[6] The great Islamicist S.D. Goitein similarly claimed that "Commerce and *hajj* became so intimately associated that a pilgrim was normally blessed with the formula: 'May God accept your *hajj*, condone your sins and let you find a good market for your wares.'"[7] In this matter, as in many others, preIslamic practice continued to be influential. Goitein notes that "the *Qur'an* and popular belief regard the yearly pilgrimage to the Holy Places in the environment of Mecca as an appropriate occasion for prosperous business—again in conformity with the fact that in pagan times the yearly pilgrimages were also the season of the yearly fair."[8]

But to accept that a connection between trade and religion was acceptable to the normative values of Islam, and that trade was not considered detrimental on the major religious event of the pilgrimmage is not to say that Hijaz trade all went through Mecca. Our evidence shows that places other than Mecca were the major markets, and this is not surprising, for Jiddah and Mocha in particular offered better facilities and more amenable locations for trade. We will turn to this matter shortly, but first we must look at what actually occurred as the vast *hajj* caravans from Cairo and Damascus made their way to Mecca. Here we are discussing primarily the land caravans which proceeded to the Hijaz each Muslim year. Their timings were very different from those governing the seaborne passage from India. This latter topic, our main concern, will be discussed fully in Chapter 7.

Barbir in his exemplary study of Ottoman Damascus provides a useful enumeration of trade connected with the *hajj*. After noting that the subject has been very little studied so far, he suggests four kinds of trade: goods shipped with the *hajj* caravan; goods sold to pilgrims along the way by villagers and beduin; goods sold to pilgrims by merchants who accompanied the caravan; and goods sold by the governor of Damascus in the Holy Cities for his own profit.[9] Our concern is with Mecca, but it should be noted that these *hajj* caravans were also important for the economies of the two cities whence they started, Cairo and Damascus. A Portuguese traveler confirmed in the 1520s in Cairothat the pilgrims bought all their provisions for the whole, one-hundred-day, journey there, and indeed spent a lot on show also.[10] Modern accounts agree. Peters notes that "for the merchants of Damascus, Cairo, and all the stops along the way, the *hajj* was nothing short of a bonanza, as it would be later for their counterparts in Mecca." Gibb and Bowen wrote of how in Damascus and its surrounds "The furnishing of the multitude of pilgrims with the quantities of provisions required for a three month's journey to and from Mecca, and of thousands of them with means of transport and camping materials, was, indeed, the foundation of the economic prosperity of Damascus during the Ottoman period."[11]

What we find in many of the contemporary accounts of the actual caravans is a clear distinction between merchants and pilgrims. As was frequently noted, "the merchants join themselves to those [pilgrim] caravans." In 1503 Varthema traveled on the pilgrim caravan from Damascus, and at one town the caravan had to delay three days, "that the merchants might provide themselves, by purchase, with as many horses as they required."[12] Much later a Kashmiri pilgrim on the same route noted that some of the camels were "richly laden."[13] A letter from 1781 from the Red Sea noticed "Large fleets of Arabian vessels are daily passing full of pilgrims going to Mecca, and merchandise . . . bound for Mocha and Juddah . . . "[14] Puey Monçon around 1600 wrote how his party left Djerba, both *hajjis* and many merchants, to go to Alexandria. Just after they set sail they were struck by a storm, and "jettisoned in the sea many of the rich goods of the merchants, and also part of the provisions of the *hajjis*."[15] An account from the 1580s similarly made a distinction concerning the members of the caravans: "some mooved by devotion, and some for traffiques sake, and some to passe away the time."[16] Varthema in Mecca itself described the people entering as "some had come for the purposes of trade, and some on pilgrimage for their pardon . . ."[17]

A French account from the eighteenth century noted "A proverbial Turkish expression is, 'both pilgrimage and religion.' In other words, the pilgrimage to Mecca serves two purposes at the same time, religion and business. One is often used as a pretext for the other because many people go to Mecca only to do business with the Persians, Indians and

Africans present there in great numbers at the time of Bairam (the day of Arafat) and spend part of their life making these journeys."[18] In the twelfth century Ibn Jubayr, in his detailed account, distinguished clearly between travelers, wayfarers, pilgrims and merchants.[19] Even the Portuguese in the sixteenth century tended to make clear that their presence in the Arabian Sea constituted both economic and religious threats to the Muslim powers. Thus Barros noted how within five years of the Portuguese arrival the rulers of the Middle East had had their trade severely disrupted, but even more important, the Portuguese were already at the entrance to the Red Sea and were threatening the passage of pilgrims.[20] And the Dutch also made a distinction. In 1649 they intended to seize some Mughal ships in order to get redress for their grievances. The captains were told that once the Indian ships had been taken, they were to "take the *Nachodas*, merchants and seamen over in their [Dutch] ships, and keep them under good guard . . . . After we have got all, or most of the *Moorish* vessels into our hands, you shall take care to embark all the *Facquiers*, and other loose people [that is, pilgrims] in one ship, and to let them sail their ways where they please, they being not worth our keeping."[21]

Merchants usually attached themselves to pilgrim caravans because they were more secure. The Ottomans saw it as a pious obligation to protect the caravans, so by joining them merchants got free protection from roving beduin and other robbers. Again the contemporary accounts make this quite clear. A well-informed Danish account noted in the caravans many "merchants, who think this the safest opportunity for the conveyance of their goods, and the most favourable for the sale of them;—purveyors of all sorts, who furnish the pilgrims with necessaries; and soldiers, paid by the caravan for escorting them. From this it happens, that many persons have seen Mecca several times, without ever visiting it upon any but views of interest." Also included in the caravans, he claimed, were some who had been paid to do the *hajj* on behalf of someone else, the benefit of which would accrue to the wealthy stay-at-homes.[22] Modave in the 1770s described how Indian cloths were traded in the Red Sea, and added "The pilgrims of Mecca and especially the merchants and the agents who follow the caravans, also pay in silver . . . "[23]

A modern account claims that merchants accompanied the caravans from both Cairo and Damascus, but that apparently they bought their trade goods to sell to the pilgrims in Jiddah.[24]   Similarly, an account from around 1580 of the Cairo caravan of 40,000 mules and camels and 50,000 people wrote of "The marchants which *followe* the Caravan, some carry for marchandise cloth of silke, some Corall, some tinne, others wheat, rise, and all sorts of graine. Some sell by the way, some at Mecca, so that every one bringeth something to gaine by, because all marchandise that goeth by land payeth no custome, but that which goeth by sea is bound to pay tenne in the hundred." The reference to "every one" is clearly to "every merchant," for later he distinguishes between pilgrims, "which have little to loose" to robbers, and merchants who do.[25]   In 1727 another eye-witness noted how "With Hadge [caravan from Mecca] to Suez go dusts [?] of Cattel, Bakers and Botiques, so never want Provisions . . . "[26]

A century later Poncet agreed: "There come every year caravans from the Indies and from Turkey, in pilgrimage to Mecca. There are some very rich ones, for the merchants join themselves to those caravans, to convey their merchandice from the Indies into Europe and from Europe into the Indies."[27] And it must have been the presence of these merchants which made the pilgrim caravans so subject to attack by robbers, as is noted in virtually every account for our period. Often, of course, merchants would also do the *hajj*. That is, they would do their trade either in Mecca, or more likely on the way at some bigger market, and then take the opportunity to do the pilgrimage as well. In 1640 the English in Surat noted that cloths were dear this year, in part because

131

of the "large investments made in the severall places for divers great persons which this yeare voiage first to Mocha to vend theire goods and thence to Mecha to visit Mahometts shrine [*sic*]."[28] Another contemporary account differentiated between exchange in Mecca and commerce in Jiddah: "Besides the cities of Mecca and Medina, to which the caravans annually bring the produce of distant countries, his [the sharif's] revenues are considerably augmented by the commerce, that is carried on with his ports of Yambo and Judda, by the vessels of Africa and India." Nor indeed was the sharif only after gain, for "Whatever sanctity he may pretend to, or indifference to the concerns of this world, like other hypocrites in religion, he prefers his own interest to that of his Maker; and uses his name as an instrument, to advance his own dignity and riches. The caravans, which professedly set out on a pious journey to Mecca, are more encouraged by this Pontiff for the sake of his own glory, than that of the Prophet; as the valuable goods they convey, and the high duties imposed upon the deluded merchants, sufficiently attest."[29]

Thus there clearly were merchants in the caravans, or more likely traveling just behind the hosts of pilgrims. But the pilgrims also sometimes traded; that is, people who are to be seen as more pilgrim than merchant still sometimes peddled goods on the way. The *Encyclopedia of Islam* refers to this as an early version of a traveler's check, and indeed this is an apt analogy. Gibb and Bowen noted "The connexion between the Pilgrimage to Mecca and petty commerce has always been very close in Islam. Practically all pilgrims chaffered their way to and from the Hijaz. Starting out with the merchandise of their native countries, they sold most of these on the journey and with the proceeds they purchased at Mecca the spices, pearls, and coffee of Arabia and the muslins, shawls and pepper imported from India, and disposed of these on their way home."[30] As food was needed, or taxes or transport charges were to be paid, pilgrims would sell some item they had brought with them, and so pay this expense and continue their journey. It seems that the 109 pilgrims attacked by the Portuguese in the Red Sea in 1650 were mostly carrying goods designed to pay their expenses.[31] English records give a precise account of this sort of trade. A letter from Bantam in 1641 reported "At the request of the king of Bantam they have allowed nine of his people to embark in the *Swan* for Surat, on their way to Mecca, and to carry some cloves etc to provide for their expenses."[32] Similarly, the royally-sponsored ships from Golconda were "crowded with numerous pilgrims, and their small bundles of merchandise with which they hoped to finance their voyage."[33] Richards and Moreland have also noted this sort of trade, but the former seems to see it as far more extensive and expensive than was really the case.[34] No matter, the point is that this was a trade which was designed to make possible a religious experience, not a trade undertaken for its own sake and in order to make a profit.

It is likely that a majority of people on the caravans, and indeed the ships, devoted to the *hajj* carried no goods at all, and had no economic motivations, not even those merely designed to make the journey possible. Many apparently brought with them their modest savings in order to finance their voyage and make an offering in Mecca. Niebuhr in 1763 noticed in Jiddah a vast amount of small-denomination coins: "Pilgrims bring this abundance of small money into the country, to defray their travelling expences, and the alms which they are obliged to bestow on their journey, and in the Holy City."[35] Terry observed on the great ship from Surat to Mocha 1700 passengers, "the most of which number goe not for profit but out of devotion to visite the sepulchre of Mahomet at Medina neare Mecha [*sic*] . . . "[36] Later in the seventeenth century Ovington described the flourishing trade of Jiddah, and the many visiting merchants there, but he also noted the pilgrims, who far from trading set off at once to Mecca.[37]

Late in the twelfth century Ibn Jubayr arrived in Alexandria in a caravan en route to Cairo and Mecca. The sultan insisted on being paid customs duties on any goods, but "Most of them were on their way to discharge a religious duty and had nothing but the bare provisions for the journey."[38] His subsequent detailed account of the caravan makes no mention of trade; rather we get an overwhelming sense of devotion and piety. Nor does Ibn Battuta's equally detailed description from the fourteenth century, apart from occasional mentions of the purchase of provisions.[39] Even this was apparently a bit unusual, for several accounts make it clear that many pilgrims in fact tried to take with them from their starting point all the provisions they would need for the entire journey; a remarkable aim indeed given that many of them would be traveling for months, but one which apparently could be achieved. Ibn Jubayr again described the vast Iraqi caravan, traveling as a self-sufficient assemblage.[40] Late in the seventeenth century Pitts said pilgrims from North Africa "toucheth at Egypt, where they take in what provision will serve to Mecca and back again to Egypt." "As to provision, they all bring sufficient with them, except it be of flesh, which they may have at Mecca; but as for all other provisions, as butter, honey, oil, olives, rice, bisket, etc., they bring with them as much as will last through the wilderness, forward and backward, as well as the time they stay at Mecca. As so for their camels they bring store of provender, etc., with them, for they meet with very little, if any, refreshment on the road." In the Holy City pilgrims worked out if they had too much food for the return trip, and if they did they sold the excess in Mecca.[41] A modern scholar similarly notes north African pilgrims stocking up in Cairo, with both food and goods, before setting off toward the Hijaz.[42] And our Indian pilgrim, Qazvini, advised his readers to take their own food supplies, not only for the voyage to the Red Sea, but also enough to cover the stay in Mecca and Medina, and ideally also enough for the return voyage. This should be done in order to avoid scarcity and price fluctuations in the Holy Cities. He then appended a long list of suitable food and

134

drink.[43]

We can now summarize this matter of land trade. What we find is an extensive caravan trade all over the Middle East. Some of this trade went via Mecca though, as we noted, the merchants in the pilgrim caravans must be clearly distinguished from the pilgrims. This caravan trade was the sector of the early modern economy of the Middle East most severely affected by the Europeans; not the Portuguese in the sixteenth century, but the Dutch and English in the seventeenth. This applies especially to the trade in spices to Europe, which from early in the seventeenth century was controlled by the Dutch East India Company in a much more effective way than had ever been achieved by the Portuguese in the previous century.[44]

The final general point to be made is that it was at least possible for these caravans to time their journeys to coincide with the *hajj*, for the camel caravans were of course not governed, circumscribed, by the monsoons. Indeed, those caravans, in economic terms probably the least important ones, which were primarily *hajj* caravans, with a few merchants tagging along, did rigorously time their departure, whether from Damascus or Cairo, their journey, and their arrival in Mecca to ensure that the Holy City was reached early in Dhu al-Hijja. They left again later in this month.[45]

There were of course many other caravans traveling in the Middle East, and these can be distinguished from the *hajj* ones by the much smaller number of people involved. In 1771 a caravan proceeding from Aleppo to Basra "consisted of thirty-three Christians, merchants and passengers, seven Jews [none of these of course would be found on a *hajj* caravan], and about twenty Turks, with Sheik Mahauson, our conductor, and an escort of 240 Arab soldiers under his command. Fifty horses, thirty mules, and about twelve hundred camels, six hundred of which were laden with merchandize, chiefly belonging to the Christians and Jews; amounting in value to near three hundred thousand pounds sterling; the remainder were either ridden, or loaded with provisions."[46]

We have some data on the caravan trade from the Persian/Arabian Gulf to the eastern Mediterranean. A priest who traveled overland from India in the 1520s noted in Hurmuz a large number of Jews, Armenians, Turks and Venetians who took goods overland to Turkey and Europe, including spices and Christian slaves. Goods from India were carried in caravans of 6,000 and more camels to the Mediterranean.[47] This trade continued through the sixteenth century. A report from Venice in 1566 noted that they had heard from Aleppo that the road to Basra was open, and they awaited the arrival of 1,500 quintals of spices.[48] Even in the 1620s Basra was described as a place of great trade because of the large caravans which came from Aleppo.[49] We must assume, following Steensgaard, that this was the Indian summer of this trade.

Other caravans passed into or through the Hijaz region. Late in the seventeenth century a traveler was at a small town five or six days south of Jiddah. He noted many Muslim merchants, and a large camel caravan traffic carrying goods from there to Jiddah.[50] In 1611 an English trader in Mocha saw the arrival of a large number of ships in the monsoon period of March to May. In the middle of this time, that is on April 17, "came into the Towne a great many Cammels and divers Merchants, which came from Damasco, Sues, and Mecca, to trade with the Merchants of India."[51] As usual, this caravan was not tied to the time of the *hajj*, but rather to the time of the arrival of the ships at Mocha on the monsoon; the *hajj* period in this year was in the middle of February. These caravans then, like most of the others, traveled according to a solar calendar tied in to the arrival of major fleets from major trading areas. This is quite a different matter to the pilgrim caravans. Other overland caravans operated within the Hijaz, for example along the shores of the Red Sea, especially the eastern one, from Mocha and even Aden in the south to Suez and further north. In the 1770s Modave

136

described a large trade in Indian cloth from Jiddah to Turkey and Cairo, which trade was done in caravans of 50,000 camels.[52]

To return to the pilgrim caravans bound for Mecca, what we can see so far is a sort of continuum among their participants. At one end are pure merchants, professionals who accompanied the pilgrims for reasons of security or in order to supply any wants the pilgrims might have while traveling. These men would do their trade in Mecca, or in one of the larger market towns through which the caravan passed. Next on the scale would be merchants who also took the occasion to make a *hajj*. Then we have people past the middle point of the continuum, that is pilgrims who also traded, mostly in order to provide for themselves, but some no doubt also to make a small profit. And finally we have what appears to be the majority, that is humble devout people who hoped to carry with them all they would need, and who had no thought at all of commerce. This sort of disaggregation seems to be more useful, and more accurate, when we talk of the general matter of a connection between the *hajj* and trade. In Chapter 7, the notion of a *"hajj* market" based on goods arriving by sea will be subjected to close scrutiny.

# CHAPTER 7

# Economic Dimensions of the *Hajj*: The Sea Routes

The historian Ashin Das Gupta puts forward an extreme version of the purported link between the pilgrimage and trade. He finds a close nexus between the trade from India, especially Gujarat, and the *hajj*. In an early piece he claimed gross profits of around 50 percent could be made on Gujarati trade to the Red Sea, "if the hajj turned out a clement one," and added in a footnote "It is possible that as much as two-thirds of the Gujarati exports to the Red Sea were sold at Mecca."[1] In the same piece, in a way reminiscent of Braudel, he seems to confuse Jiddah and Mecca. He claims that "The major attraction for the Gujaratis was the annual pilgrim market at Mecca where merchants from the far-flung cities of the Ottoman empire came to buy coffee and textiles . . . " then talks of the "failure of the hajj," that is a poor market for Indian goods in the Hijaz, and then describes the Muslim merchants who "came every year to Jedda with the hajj caravans."[2] Similarly, Gujarati textiles brought to the Red Sea mostly sold "to the annual market at Mecca . . . " "It was stated repeatedly that trade at Mocha depended upon the market at Jedda—that is, the market of the hajj. The pilgrim caravans which came to Hejaz [sic] via Cairo [sic] brought money for those Yemeni merchants who sold coffee and for the Gujaratis who sold cloth. It was a complex and delicate network which reached Mecca through and from many another city of western Asia and northern Africa."[3] In a later piece, in the standard *Cambridge Economic History of India*, he wrote "The international market of the hajj continued to be the principal draw for the trade in the Indian Ocean . . . "⁴ Similarly, the "Islamic peace" of the sixteenth and seventeenth centuries "promoted a new prosperity for the annual market at Mecca." ⁵

On other occasions Das Gupta ties in the *hajj* and the seasons, and this should have given him, a maritime historian, pause. He notes of Gujarat that the weavers did their basic work during the wet season, but got their orders after this, when shipping returned to Gujarat from overseas. "The expectation of a good *hajj*, for instance, would make for frantic buying in the months of September to January . . . "⁶ Note in this fuller account how the pilgrimage and the seasons are linked: he points out that travel and trade were governed by the winds and the monsoon rains, and then says

> "The major consideration in any season at Surat was the market of the *haj*. A major part of the city's shipping was engaged in the Red Sea run, and they took their textiles to the port of Mocha which was the principal trading centre in the Red Sea at the time. Some of the ships would sail past Mocha and make for Jedda further up the coast, but this was probably because of the proximity of Jedda to Mecca. Indian cloths which were thus carried to the Red Sea went to two rather different kinds of markets. For one, there was what may be called a local market, comprising the demands of Yemen, Hejaz, the African coast of the Red Sea and the coast of Hadramaut. Considerably more important than this, there was the market at Mecca which functioned every year as pilgrims from all over the Ottoman empire and the Islamic world assembled at this city. It was this demand, usually described in the documents as that of 'the Turkish merchants,' which was crucial for Surat. A poor *haj* or the expectation of one would create a profound depression from Jedda to the farthest points of Surat's hinterland."⁷

Most recently, and a little more cautiously, he has written that "The annual pilgrimage of the *hajj* [*sic*] helped the growth of the largest market for the Indian Ocean merchant." "The Islamic pilgrimage of the *hajj* [*sic*] of which we still await a proper study drew together the Muslim network of the ocean and connected it with the diaspora further to the west."[8]

This argument has been put forward cogently and influentially by Das Gupta, which is why I have quoted him at such length. There is, however, as I hinted above, an immediate problem, which has to do with seasons and calendars. The basic point is obvious enough. The *hajj*, as we have noted, is done in the Islamic month of Dhu al-Hijja, on set days in a set month. But this set time is according to the Islamic calendar, which is based on the moon, not the sun. As a result, the lunar Muslim year is ten or eleven days shorter than the solar Christian year. Although some modern authors have trouble with this, it was recognized by Pyrard of Laval, to an extent, in the first decade of the seventeenth century.[9] While he failed to grasp the full implications of the lunar versus solar matter, he did say "In the month of December, about the new moon, they observe a fast, called in Arabic *Ramedan* . . . I say about the month of December, for I cannot with certainty designate the time, seeing that their month and year are lunar, and are not fixed as ours are."[10]  In the 1750s a French writer also got it right: he noted that Muslim festivals "are movable festivals which, in a thirty-three year period, fall in every season and every month of the year because the Muslim calendar is lunar and advances eleven days each year."[11] Set Christian festivals are observed at the same time each year, and at the same season, except for Easter, whose time is governed by the moon to some extent and so is a movable date. Set Muslim festivals move through the seasons, so that the *hajj* could be at the hottest season, but then would slowly, ten or eleven days each year, move towards cooler weather.

So much is obvious. The second point is that trade by sea at this time was totally dependent on the monsoon winds, and these, crucially and obviously, are based on a solar, not lunar calendar. We will establish this point, and then look at the implications. Poncet in the late seventeenth century noted that merchants from Ethiopia had a great trade within and outside the Red Sea, this being governed by the monsoons.[12] In 1541 a Portuguese marauding fleet in the Red Sea set sail to return to India on the 10th of July. The headstrong captain refused to listen to the advice of his Muslim pilots, who, basing themselves on centuries of experience, told him that by leaving at this time he would have no trouble getting to the entrance to the Red Sea, but that once in the Arabian Sea weather of such vileness could be expected that no ship could navigate. And this advice, of course, turned out to be correct.[13] An English traveler in 1780 wrote of the pilgrimage, and noted that "As different winds prevail on the different sides of the Tropic in the Red Sea, ships may come to Gedda [Jiddah] from opposite points at the same season of the year; those which come from Suez at the above mentioned time [that is November to January], benefit by the N.W. wind, while those that come from India and Arabia Felix are assisted by the regular S.W. monsoon. The pilgrims . . . embark at Gedda time enough to avail themselves of the Khumseen [according to Capper this is Arabic for 50, which is the length of time this wind blows] wind, which blows southerly from the end of March to the middle of May, and conveys them in less than a month back again to Suez; the India vessels must also quit Gedda so as to be out of the straits of Babelmandel before the end of August."[14] Two years later another English traveler confirmed this as regards the voyage from Jiddah back to Suez. Jiddah had to be left before the end of May or the voyage would be aborted by head winds.[15] Even today within the Red Sea the monsoons act as a governing factor for traditional navigators, as a modern account of the sea's routes, winds and sailing times makes clear.[16]

This situation, of course pertained even more strongly in the Indian Ocean, and Arabian Sea. Mme. Bouchon has described how the great fifteenth-century trade between Calicut and the Red Sea was timed. Ships left Calicut in January, and vessels from the Red Sea arrived there between August and November.[17] The Portuguese described the military significance of this on the Malabar coast. The west coast of India, then and now, is unnavigable for sailing ships between roughly June and September. In the 1530s the Portuguese were concerned at the way ships from the hostile port of Calicut could sail just before or just after this, before their blockading fleets could arrive. The solution seemed to be to build a fort very near to Calicut. Thus they could patrol right up to the end of May, just before navigation became impossible, and resume the blockade early in September as soon as the slackening of the southwest monsoon made seafaring possible again.[18]

As for Gujarat, Terry noted how the great ship going from Surat to Mocha "beginnes her voyage about the twentieth of March, and finisheth it towards the end of September following. The voyage is but short and might easily bee made in two months; but in the long season of raine, and a little before and after it, the winds are commonly so violent that there is no coming but with great hazard, into the Indian Seas."[19] Mandelslo echoed him in his account of the trade from Surat to Aden and Mecca: "They sometimes carry above a thousand persons together, who for the most part go upon Pilgrimage to *Meca*, that at their return they may be put into the number of their *Hoggoi*, or Saints [*sic*]. They set saile at the beginning of the *March-Moon*, and return in *September*, for the tempests, which reign from *June* till that time upon those Coasts, make them spend six months in a Voyage which might be performed in two."[20] Baldaeus also said "These [Surat] ships set sail in *March* and *April* for the Red Sea, and return in *September* or *October*; they seldom spend above twenty-five days in their passage."[21] And Ovington also knew all this: "The Ships from *Suratt* that Sail for the *Red Sea* take their departure generally about *March*, and Arrive at *Mocha* towards the latter end of *April*, or before the 20th of *May*; at which time . . . the Winds vary, and prevent any more Ships entring into the Sea that Year."[22] Similarly, a Dutch merchant noted that Indian ships bring many pilgrims to Mocha, "These ships come every year in April and half of March and leave for home in the other monsoon, in August . . . "[23] There was however an alternative season for Surat, for ships could leave late in the year also, as did Qazvini in 1676.[24]

With Diu also the seasons were rigid indeed. From the start of September the winds were variable, and this was a good time for going and coming to Diu. The easterlies started in November, during the period from midnight to midday, and for the other twelve hours the prevailing wind was from the sea, from southwest to northwest. In February and March and until May the former easterlies became north and northeast, and in the afternoons northwest, so large ships could no longer approach Diu from the south. At the end of May the winter started, but at the beginning of it some ships got to Diu, riskily, from the north. As for the Red Sea voyage, the ships left Diu in November or December, and some returned in May, but most in early September.[25] And again, from Golconda: "To Mocha they set sayle in January, and returne in September or October following."[26] The matter was most pithily expressed by an Arab author, who wrote that "He who leaves India on the 100th day [2nd March] is a sound man, he who leaves on the 110th will be all right. However, he who leaves on the 120th is stretching the bounds of possibility and he who leaves on the 130th is inexperienced and an ignorant gambler."[27] The point of this rather excessive compilation of evidence is merely to make clear that everyone, whether European or Asian, in western India in our period knew all about the monsoons and what the implications were; what a pity some modern authors have not profitted from this age-old wisdom!

The problem with writing about a *hajj* market is now I hope clear. It is true that the overland pilgrim caravans did not have this problem, so that they could leave, as they did, at the correct time to reach Mecca early in Dhu al-Hijja, and govern their movements by the lunar, not the solar, calendar. We showed in the last chapter, however, that there was little trade done by these pilgrim caravans. But for trade and travel by sea there is an unresolvable contradiction. The arrival in say Jiddah or Mocha was governed by one calendar, the *hajj* by a different one. Thus for Indian markets in say Gujarat to be controlled by the *hajj*, we are asked to believe that merchants would load their goods and take them to the Red Sea, arriving at a time dictated by a solar calendar. Then they would wait for the correct time in the lunar calendar to go to Mecca to catch the so-called *hajj* market. The very notion is ridiculous; it means that on some occasions these merchants would sit in Jiddah for eleven months or even more waiting for the time of the *hajj*, and only then would set off to Mecca with their goods.

As we will see, most Red Sea trade focused on Jiddah, and was controlled by the monsoons. However, if goods were destined for the great fair at Mecca during the time of the *hajj*, precisely this situation did pertain. A Dutch report, written at second hand but based on accounts by French and English who had been in Jiddah, noted that profits in Jiddah depend "principally on a successful voyage, for if the ships were to arrive there after the aforementioned Hagie the cargos would have to lay over there for one entire year. This means that the transporter has in effect suffered a lost voyage like happened to the French last year [that is, 1736]."[28] A second qualification is to suggest that traders from the Indian Ocean into the Red Sea could well have had agents permanently resident in Jiddah, who could hold goods until the market was high. This of course was commonly done in this period all over the Indian Ocean trading area precisely in order to avoid the "dictatorship of the monsoons."

Unfortunately we have no direct evidence of this being done in Jiddah.[29] We must assume then that trade in Jiddah was very largely regulated, and its times governed, by the sailing seasons which dictated the arrival and departure of ships to and from this port.

Pilgrims coming by sea had no choice but to be governed by these sailing seaons. They could pass away the time by traveling in the Hijaz, by visiting Medina, or by spending time in Mecca doing *umrahs*, study, or just sight-seeing at the numerous sanctified places we noticed at the beginning of Chapter 2. Pyrard commented on the centrality of the festival on the 10th of Dhu al-Hijja when he wrote: "and sometimes when they have arrived too late, and it is over, they have to await the return of the festival for ten or eleven months."[30] Only in the nineteenth century did this change. As Xavier de Planhol noted perceptively, "the advent of steamship travel simplified the pilgrimage of the Indians, many of whom during the age of the sailing ships had had to wait at Medina or Mecca for the coming of the summer monsoons in order to get back home."[31] But merchants did have a choice, and this was to do most of their trade in the ports of the Red Sea, Jiddah and Mocha, at times dictated by the solar monsoon calendar which had nothing to do with the lunar *hajj* one. As one concrete contemporary example, in Jiddah in June 1727 the Muslim sailors on an English ship wanted to wait and undertake a *hajj*. In this year the *hajj* was soon due, for 20 July 1727 was the start of Dhu al-Hijja. Unfortunately, to delay the departure for the Arabian Sea by six weeks would be hazardous, precisely because of the dictatorship of the monsoons, so permission was denied.[32]

What I have done so far is to describe in some detail the constraints which affected sailing ships in this early modern period. In a sense this is negative support for my contention that there were two major markets in the Hijaz at this time, one a routine commercial exchange in Jiddah or other Red Sea ports, and one an atypical one in Mecca. Fortunately we have a mass of empirical evidence which shows convincingly that there was indeed very substantial trade in these Red Sea ports, and especially in Jiddah. More important, we can show clearly that this trade had no connection at all with the quite different matter of the pilgrimage to Mecca and the fair in Mecca associated with this religious event. We will first present evidence to show the importance of the great ports of the Red Sea.

At first sight it would seem more obvious for ships carrying Asian, and especially Indian, goods destined for the Mediterranean and the Middle East to sail directly from the Arabian Sea into the Red Sea past Aden, and then proceed up to Suez. Here goods could be transhipped and taken overland to Cairo, and so to Alexandria and the Mediterranean, or to Damascus and so to Syria and Turkey. But there are three problems with this. There was first a political objection. Under the Ottomans the sharifs of Mecca continued to be influential. In particular, they continued to have a virtual monopoly on trade north of Jiddah to Suez, in conjunction with a group of Cairo merchants. The general pattern is of Indian ships unloading either at Mocha, or more likely Jiddah, where their goods were transferred, either to Egyptian vessels which then made the voyage to Suez, or to the camel caravans we discussed in Chapter 6.[33] But this monopoly on trade past Jiddah seems not to have been as rigid as Das Gupta would have us believe, for we do have one record from the 1540s of a Gujarati ship which had a *cartaz* from the Portuguese to enable it to sail to Suez.[34] Nevertheless, this political factor no doubt contributed to make Jiddah a great market and great transhipment centre.

A second, and very basic, factor which militated against any direct passage to Suez was merely the fact that while historians have often stressed the trade between Asia and Europe, in fact much Asian trade was with the Middle East, not with Europe. Most of this trade went inland from Jiddah or Mocha more or less due north along the coast to Palestine,

Syria and Turkey.

The difficulty of navigating in the Red Sea was probably the most important problem. We have noted already how the monsoons acted here also as a strait jacket, but apart from this the Red Sea in general was notoriously hazardous. The voyage from Mocha to Jiddah, usually considered to be relatively routine, turned into a horror for Henry Rooke in 1782. The voyage usually took eight to ten days, but his passage in a local craft took 28.[35] The passage north of Jiddah was very much worse, being full of shoals and reefs. Thus large ships from the Arabian Sea could not safely sail past Jiddah anyway; their cargoes had to be transferred to smaller local ships which had more chance of making the passage safely. Sometimes also their cargoes would be taken overland from Jiddah on caravans to Suez, or on to Damascus.

An Arabic account from the ninth century will begin to make clear the dangers. Ships from the Persian/Arabian Gulf port of Siraf "put into *Judda*, where they remain; for their Cargo is thence transported to *Kahira* [Cairo] by Ships of *Kolzum*, who are acquainted with the Navigation of the Red Sea, which those of *Siraf* dare not attempt, because of the extreme Danger, and because this Sea is full of Rocks at the Water's Edge; because also upon the whole Coast there are no Kings, or scarce any inhabited Place; and, in fine, because Ships are every Night obliged to put into some Place of Safety, for Fear of striking upon the Rocks; they sail in the Day time only, and all the Night ride fast at Anchor. This Sea, moreover, is subject to very thick Fogs, and to violent Gales of Wind, and so has nothing to recommend it, either within or without."[36]

A millennium later, nineteenth-century accounts by Burton and Ali Bey make clear the hazards of navigation in the upper reaches of the Red Sea, and these are supported by Tibbetts' modern survey of navigation in the whole of the Red Sea.[37] Henry Rooke, who in 1782 had had such a bad trip from Mocha to Jiddah, had a much worse time going from there to Suez. He traveled on a boat full of *hajjis*, and has left us a day-by-day log of his hazardous six week voyage.[38] Daniel's account in 1700 similarly clearly describes the hazards, in this case on a voyage from Suez to Yanbo, the port of Medina. His ship anchored each night in order to avoid reefs, rocks and shoals, and this short voyage took from July 12th to August 10th. Jiddah was reached only on August 29th. The difficulties experienced included repairs to the ship, having to bribe local coastal rulers, and the intrinsic hazards of the voyage.[39] In 1777 an even shorter voyage of less than 500 kilometres from Yanbo to Cosire [Quseir], took Eyles Irwin from June 10 to July 9.[40] One of our most graphic accounts comes from Tomé Pires in the early sixteenth century. In the Red Sea "there are many rocky banks and they are difficult to navigate. Men do not navigate except by day; they can always anchor. The best sailing is from the entrance to the strait as far as Kamaran. It is worse from Kamaran to Jiddah and much worse from Jiddah to Tor. From Tor to Suez is a route for small boats even by day, because it is all dirty ['cujo'] and bad."[41]

Frederic Lane years ago gave us a good description of trade routes in our period. Spices were in demand in Europe and the Middle East. Pepper was the nearest there was to a bulk spice trade, but mace, nutmeg, cloves, ginger and cinnamon were also important. The Italians were the middlemen for this trade once the goods reached the Mediterranean. Spices were very valuable by weight, though not quite as "splendid and trifling" as Gibbon told us. Their routes were determined according to taxes, protection costs, and social conditions, to which should be added geographical hazards and advantages, such as navigation problems and the existence of oases to service camel caravans. Ships with spices entered the Red Sea and stopped at Jiddah, where the cargoes were divided, especially because of the navigation problems north of there. Some spices went on camels up the eastern Red Sea coast, and so on to Damascus, and the eastern

Mediterranean. Others went further by sea, to Suez and so to Cairo and Alexandria. Still other goods on this route went by sea only as far as Quseir, west and a little north of Medina. Yanbo, the nearest port to Medina, was also important. From there the goods went overland to the Nile, and so to Cairo, and on to Alexandria, where Venetians took over.[42]

At different times different ports in the Red Sea are noted as important. Ibn Jubayr late in the twelfth century described a large caravan, carrying mostly pepper, leaving Aydhab, on the coast opposite Jiddah and northwest of it, and proceeding overland up the Nile to Cairo and Alexandria.[43] The port of Yanbo was affected in the late fifteenth century by political disputes between the sharifs and the Mamluks. In the early sixteenth century the presence of the Portuguese also made a difference; their activities meant that Aden now became an important port of call. Prior to this the merchants had gone directly from Jiddah to the Arabian Sea, with the usual first port of call being Calicut. Once the Portuguese began to blockade the Red Sea the Muslim ships had to go slowly and carefully. They stopped at Aden to get news of the Portuguese armadas, and indeed sometimes did trade in Aden. This port thus became an important transhipment center, with Jiddah merchants exchanging goods with merchants from Malabar, and also from east Africa, Cambay and Hurmuz. There was an additional reason for this. In order to avoid the Portuguese, ships from India now often got to the entrance to the Red Sea late in the season. Consequently, they were unable to sail in the Red Sea, having lost the right monsoon, and so again they were forced to trade in Aden. In the first few decades of the sixteenth century there were in Aden merchants from Jiddah with copper, mercury, vermilion, coral, and silk and wool cloths, East African traders with gold and ivory, Malabar merchants with spices and drugs, and people from Cambay with cotton cloths and rich other goods.[44]

It appears that this fortuitous situation did not last long.

As is well known, the Portuguese blockade of the Red Sea decreased in effectiveness later in the century, and beginning in the 1540s it is clear that large amounts of spices were again safely passing into the Red Sea and so to markets in the Middle East and the Mediterranean. The effects of the establishment of Turkish control over Aden in 1538 are unclear, but there is no doubt that the boom of the early sixteenth century was transitory. An English merchant, Robert Coverte, noted, in a little-known account of 1608, that "we met with a Guzarat ship, laden with Cotton woolls, Callicoes, and Pentathoes [?], beeing bound for Adden, whether wee kept her company, in regard they told us it was a Towne of great trading, but wee found it quite contrary: for it was only a Towne of Garison, and many Souldiers in it . . . "[45]

In the seventeenth century the port of Mocha seems to have expanded greatly, so that it began to rival Jiddah. The reasons for this are unclear. It is at least possible that because larger ships were being used now and they were afraid of the dangerous waters of the Red Sea, so instead goods were transhipped to smaller vessels in Mocha for the passage further north. Coverte, who had just complained of Aden, went on to Mocha and was very impressed: "It is a place that is neuer without shipping, for it is a Towne of great trade of merchandize, and hath Carauans or Conuoies that come from Seena, from Mecha, from grand Cairo, and Alexandria, and all those places." Mocha, despite its barren inland, was not an expensive place, for he very usefully left us lists of prices for Mocha and for Agra a year later. In both places a goat or a sheep cost two shillings, but in Mocha one ox cost 12 shillings, while in Agra two could be bought for 16 shillings. In the former, three pence bought enough fish for a meal for ten men, while at inland Agra the same amount bought only enough for five men.[46]

In 1610 a European observer recorded the arrival at Mocha of three "great ships" from Dabul, owned by the Persian who was governor of this Konkan port. Soon after they arrived there "came into the Towne a great many Cammels and divers Merchants, which came from Damasco, Sues, and Mecca, to trade with the Merchants of India."[47] Six years later we have a much-quoted account from the Dutch factor van den Broeke. He claimed the town had risen only in the last 40 or 50 years after it was taken by the Turks.[48] Aden was now eclipsed, as it was safer for the great ship of the Turks from Suez to call at Mocha rather than go on to the entrance of the Red Sea, to Aden. He saw "in the roadstead more than thirty Indian, Persian, and Arab ships, large and small . . . " He noted that "These ships come every year in April and half of March and leave for home in the other monsoon, in August, richly laden with cash and European wares." While some of these Indian goods were taken on by sea, van den Broeke also noted that "a caffel [qafila] or caravan arrived here from Aleppo and Suwees, about 1,000 camels strong, laden with the following merchandise—about 200,000 rials of eight and 100,000 ducats, Hungarian, Venetian and Moorish, excluding what was not declared, besides velvets, satins, damasks, sarsenents, Turkish gold, brocades, camelots, cloth, saffron, quicksilver, vermilion, and Nuremburg wares. They are usually two months on their way. These goods mentioned above are mostly traded by the Indians, Persians, and Arabs against fine and coarse cotton clothing, indigo, pepper, cloves, nutmeg, mace and Chinese wares."[49]

English factors a little later similarly noted how a great "junk" came down from Cairo [sic] each year to Mocha, was freighted and then returned. There was also an annual caravan of 800 or even 1,000 camels which traveled from Cairo to Mocha. It mostly brought merchants and their money, and returned via Jiddah with Indian goods, few of which however were sold in Arabia.[50] At this same time Terry wrote that "The ship that usually goeth from Surat to Moha [Mocha] is of exceeding great burthen. Some of them, I beleeve, at the least fourteene or sixteene hundred tunnes; but ill built, and, though they have good ordinance, cannot well defend them-

154

selves." After noting many passengers, mostly pilgrims, and the way in which the voyage was governed by the monsoons, he concluded that "The ship returning is usually worth two hundred thousand pounds sterling; most of it in gold and silver."[51] In 1622 a similar ship was estimated to have a cargo worth 250,000 rupees on its return to Surat.[52]

As coffee rose in importance as a trade item in the late seventeenth century, Mocha continued to flourish.[53] Baldaeus, in 1672, wrote of the trade there between March and September each year, and of the big ship which came down from Suez. In March a land caravan arrived from Aleppo and Alexandria (the latter seems doubtful). Both ship and caravan left again around the turn of the year, laden with Indian goods.[54] In 1709 a French exploratory expedition found out that "every year the Dutch send a seven hundred ton vessel from Batavia to Mocha to load coffee and other merchandise from Arabia. "[55]

Turning now to Jiddah, we will present a mass of evidence which shows that regardless of the rise and fall of Aden, or the later rise of Mocha, Jiddah, not Mecca, was the great commercial center in the Red Sea for most of our period, and that this important role had a religious input only in a very peripheral way. Jiddah acted as the great hinge, or nodal point, for all trade in the Red Sea. This is not to say that Jiddah was in any sense an adequate roadstead; the point is simply that transhipment was a necessity, so that even so unsatisfactory a port as Jiddah had to do. Ibn Jubayr described how difficult it was to enter Jiddah, "because of the many reefs and the windings."[56] Stripling says the port was wretched, being full of rocks and sand, so that ships had to anchor two miles away and use lighters to get their goods to the port.[57] Nevertheless, there was always a great trade at Jiddah at the times when the monsoons allowed ships to come to it both from the south and the north. Sometimes this trade would be expanded by the fortuitous addition of thousands of pilgrims, that is when the time for the *hajj* coincided with the monsoon-determined time for trade. But most of the time these two did not coincide, and Jiddah's vast trade was a strictly economic one having nothing to do with religion.

The occasional transit of masses of pilgrims, most of them anxious to get to Mecca quickly was, in economic terms, a peripheral event in the life of the port. In this Jiddah was like a host of other cities associated with the pilgrimage. For Jiddah, and for such other cities as Damascus, Cairo, Surat and Aceh, the pilgrimmage was not the focus, the raison d'être. It was merely a bonus, a supplement. In this important matter Mecca must be very clearly differentiated, because for the Holy City (and also for Medina) the reverse is true. For Mecca the pilgrimage was the central fact, the very reason for its existence. One other related factor should be mentioned here. Mecca's trade, as we will see, was not helped by the ban on non-Muslims approaching the city. Mecca was isolated and insular economically, but non-Muslims could trade with ease in Jiddah.[58]

Before the sixteenth century Jiddah was already a major port, occasionally helped by government policy. In 1429 the Mamluk sultan even decreed that spices from the east could only be sold in Jiddah, and only to his agents.[59] In that century the port was known to the Arabs as the "Bride of the Red Sea."[60] Portuguese accounts of trade before their arrival make clear Jiddah's central role. Barros noted how it was the major focus of the spice trade, saying that Jiddah, with its buildings, trade and commerce, and because almost all the ships that come from India call at it, "is the most celebrated and noble settlement of all this Arabian coast inside the entrance," and added that "most of the residents of that city [Jiddah] were merchants, because of the merchandise that flowed through it, both entering and leaving . . . "[61] Elsewhere he described how the goods came down from Cairo, and the ships called at Jiddah. From there the goods went off to the Arabian Sea directly, not calling at Aden, with their times of sailing determined by the monsoons. Thus they left the Red Sea "in the months of navigation, when the westerlies prevail," and came back with the easterlies.[62] Not however that this was the only route. In his detailed description of Asian trade in 1500 he noted how the alternative route to the Middle East and to Europe was via Hurmuz and so to Basra, and then overland to Armenia and the Black Sea, or to Aleppo, Damascus and Beirut, where the spices were brought by Venetians, Genoese and Spanish merchants.[63] Albuquerque's son confirmed some of this, describing how before the Portuguese arrived merchants used to come to Cairo from all over the Maghreb, "and from Cairo they used to make their way to Juda and from Juda to Calicut, with ready money, and there they used to build new ships, and load them with spiceries, and so returned to their own lands." This was a valuable trade indeed, "for, for every cruzado laid out in Calicut, they used to make twelve or thirteen in Juda and in all the places that stood within the mouth of the Straits," that is within the Red Sea.[64]

Castanheda confirms and amplifies our knowledge of this trade. He said that before the arrival of the Portuguese the Muslims of Mecca and Egypt and the Venetians made huge profits from spices: "It was like this. These Muslim merchants lived in Mecca and Jiddah and they had their factors in Calicut, from whom they ordered spices, drugs, precious stones and fine cotton cloths, in the huge ships that they made in Malabar, because there was no wood in the Red Sea to make ships." Gold and goods were sent to pay for the spices, "And all these things they took from Alexandria to Cairo by the upper Nile, and from Cairo they were taken overland on camels to the city of Suez which is at the head of the strait of the Red Sea on the coast of Arabia, a matter of three days travel from Cairo. In Suez they loaded these goods on small ships called Gelbas, and took them to Jiddah ["Iuda"], 160 leagues from Suez, and they used these gelbas because they were safer, because in big ships they would be endangered by the many shallows that there are from Suez to Jiddah, where they load them in the large ships ["naus"] and take them to Calicut . . . " More soberly than Albuquerque, he estimated that the profits were such that from one they would make eight. The Mamluk state played an active role in this trade, and the state role both demonstrates, and perhaps helped cause, the central role of Jiddah in the whole trade. The Mamluk rulers decreed that one-third of all cargoes carried between Calicut and Jiddah had to be pepper, and sold to the ruler at Calicut prices. Indeed, if a merchant arrived in Jiddah with goods worth 3,000 cruzados and no pepper, goods worth 1,000 cruzados had to be sold and the proceeds used to buy pepper, and this at the high Jiddah price rather than the cheap Calicut one.[65]

Other sixteenth century accounts continue this refrain. A patrol in 1506 noted how most of the ships entering the Red Sea were bound for Jiddah.[66] A more detailed description of the trade of the Indian Ocean at this time again makes the point that Jiddah, here erroneously called Mecca, was the center. Correa mentioned a brush between a very powerful Cambay ship and the Portuguese, and added "These are the large ships which they arm in Cambay, and load with much merchandise, and they sail out past the island of Ceylon and enter the Bay of Bengal, and go to Pegu and Tennasarim, where they load rich goods, and then they go to Pacem and load pepper, and go via the Maldives to Mecca [sic]; these ships are so powerful and well armed and have so many men on board that they dare to do their voyages without fear of our ships . . . "[67] By contrast, a later letter from a Muslim trader in Malabar said correctly, as we would hope, that he had ships trading to Jiddah and Mocha.[68]

Much other data shows the continuing role of Jiddah. In 1517 the Portuguese governor Lopo Soares cruised in the Red Sea, and even got as far as Jiddah. The contemporary accounts by both Correa and Castanheda stress the difficulties of the anchorage, and the aridity and infertility of the

area around the town. The size of the population was vari-
ously estimated at 1000, and 1500, "vezinhos" or "visinhos,"
that is, neighborhoods. Both stressed the large trade there,
Castanheda saying the port was "Well provided with food
that came from outside, and with much merchandise because
there are joined all those that come from India with those
from Cairo and Alexandria." Both accounts also noted Mecca
at seven leagues distance, and described how this was where
the Muslims made their pilgrimage, just as Christians did to
Jerusalem, to the body of Muhammad, a very common error
at this time.[69] A letter to the Portuguese king of 1538 said the
Portuguese should build a fort at the mouth of the Red Sea,
for thus "India would be sealed off, and the key in the hands
of your highness." In particular, this would mean the
Malabaris would be checked, "for they have no life outside of
their trade with Jiddah ["Judaa"]"[70]

Accounts from later in the sixteenth century from other
Europeans continue to confirm the centrality of Jiddah. An
anonymous account from around 1580 gives a long description of the caravan from Cairo to Mecca and the *hajj*, but has
only one fleeting reference to trade and two to merchants
accompanying the pilgrim caravan. But of Jiddah he noted
specifically that 40 or 50 great ships called each year with
spices and merchandise, and paid customs of 150,000
ducats.[71] English accounts from the early seventeenth century again expatiate on the large trade of Jiddah; thus Saris
in 1612 noted eleven Indian ships in the Red Sea, all bound
for Jiddah. These were very large ships indeed. Three of
them, as we noted in Chapter 5, were pilgrim ships belonging
to the great noble Abdur-Rahim. Saris had two of them mea-
sured. The "Rahimi" was 153 feet from stem to stern post,
and her rake from the post aft was 17 feet. From the top of
her sides in breadth was 42 feet, and her depth 31 feet. The
"Muhammadi" was 136 feet long, with a rake of 20 feet,
breadth of 41, and depth of 29 and a half. Her main mast was
108 feet, and her main yard 132 feet. The other nine were, he

said, not much smaller.[72] A few years later Lobo wrote generally of Jiddah, "which has been made so famous in these times in all of the East by the great number of ships that go there and the rich trade the merchants find there, and the superstitious custom of pilgrimages to Mecca made by those who follow the infamous Koran . . . . since the ships which sailed to Juda made excellent business profits, because of the great wealth of the universal market of people and merchandise carried on in that city, they became so famous in India that when people wanted to indicate that something was very costly and valuable they would call it a ship from Mecca or Juda."[73] Faroqhi's modern account, based on Ottoman sources, similarly notes how Jiddah was the main port for the masses of Indian spices and cloths carried up the Red Sea.[74]

Our Indian pilgrim Qazvini described a large trade, and numerous pilgrims, in Jiddah.[75] John Fryer in the 1670s in Surat saw the great fleets from Jiddah and their huge trade and values. He wrote how this Jiddah fleet exported "vast quantities of Indico, Cotton, Cotton-Yarn, and Silks; and vend them to the Caphalay [cafila, caravan] waiting on them [in Jiddah] over-land; so that returning they are forced to ballast their Ships with Dates, Persian and Arabian Drugs; and freight with Horses from each Place: But the main is brought back in Gold, Silver and Pearl, which does in a manner center here [in Gujarat]."[76] An observer from the later seventeenth century had noted the large fleet from Suez, supplied by the government. Ovington thought it was about 20 or 25 strong, and carried supplies and money. Also at this time Daniel saw at Suez 40 sails, which traded to Jiddah, taking coin and provisions and bringing back spices, cloths, precious stones, musk, coffee and other products which came from India to Mocha and Jiddah and were transported by land on camels to Cairo and Alexandria.[77] The experienced Captain Hamilton belittled Jiddah's trade, but the bulk of the evidence counters him. A French report of his time depicted Jiddah as the great entrepot for coffee, which was taken to

160

Jiddah from the south by small boats, and then loaded on Turkish vessels which took the crop to Suez and so to the Ottoman Empire and the Mediterranean.[78] Ovington similarly noted that "*Judda* flourishes in a constant Traffick from *India*, *Persia*, other parts of *Arabia*, and the *Abasseen* shore."[79]

Jiddah's trade seems to have been important for some decades of the eighteenth century. The Dane Niebuhr wrote in 1763 that "Although the trade of Jidda is so considerable, yet this city is no more than a mart between Egypt and India. The ships from Suez seldom proceed further than this port; and those from India are not suffered to advance to Suez." Jiddah still acted as a link in the great trade between the Indian Ocean and especially India, and Egypt, and hence the Mediterranean and the Ottoman Empire. Its imports were large "because both Mecca and Medina are supplied from this [Egyptian] market. Large quantities of corn, rice, lentiles, sugar, oil, etc are imported from Egypt, without which this part of Arabia could not possibly be inhabited. All goods from Europe come also by the way of Egypt; and, on the other hand, those which are brought hither from India pass generally into Egypt."[80] A decade later a French observer wrote of the large trade of Jiddah, especially in fine shawls from Kashmir, and cloths from Gujarat and Bengal. Modave also noted how the Egyptian government sent 20 ships each year to provision Jiddah. Eight of these were large, being of 1000 or 1500 tons, and the others only 200-500 tons. These ships left Suez at the end of February with the monsoon, and got to Jiddah in ten or twelve days laden with foodstuffs, but also carrying gold and silver to pay for goods in Jiddah. Most of this was sold in Jiddah, and some in Mecca. The fleet stayed in Jiddah three months discharging and waiting for the arrival of Mocha coffee, by this time an important trade item, to arrive. The return cargo was coffee and fine cloths from India; some also went overland on camel caravans. Modave claimed that large amounts of Indian cloth were traded from

Jiddah to Turkey and Cairo by merchants who formed caravans of 50,000 camels.[81] Even in the 1780s two English travelers still found the port's trade impressive. Rooke traveled
from Jiddah to Suez on a ship of 500 tons, in a fleet of 25 of
varying sizes, but one was 1200 tons. He was scornful of the
town, describing it as "an old and ill-built town, surrounded
by a broken and ruinous wall, having no fort, nor any guns
mounted" yet it was also "a place of the greatest trade" in the
Red Sea.[82]

These last accounts, from the 1770s and 1780s, seem to be
describing the end of the heyday of Jiddah. As navigation
techniques improved and Western dominance was extended
the port finally began to decline. A description of 1807 seems
to show the beginnings of this decline. Ali Bey wrote of
Jiddah that "There are about 5,000 inhabitants in the town,
which may be considered as the mart of the *interior* commerce of the Red Sea. The ships from Mokha bring to it coffee, and the products of the East, which are unloaded here,
re-shipped in other vessels, and transported to Suez, Janboa,
Kossier and all other points of the Arabian and African
coasts."[83] In other words, the port was now of only regional
importance, and much trade between Asia and Europe
bypassed the Red Sea altogether by using the Cape of Good
Hope route. Thirty years later a French observer wrote of
"Jidda, that old concierge of the Holy City . . . "[84] and indeed
by then this was all it was.

To close this discussion of Jiddah and the Red Sea trade,
all of which supports our contention that this trade, quite
exclusive of Mecca, was the main one, we can very relevantly
note what information we have on the numbers of ships
involved, and their values. It is clear that very large numbers
of ships traded from the Arabian Sea into the Red Sea, mostly to Jiddah, and that these could carry very wealthy cargoes
indeed. As for numbers, from Calicut early in the sixteenth
century we have Portuguese complaints of 23 large ships, or
alternatively between 10 and 15 ships, leaving for the Red

Sea each year.[85]  In the 1560s it was claimed that 11 or 12 ships made this voyage.[86] Also at this time a Portuguese complained that lots of pepper had got to Cairo recently, carried to Jiddah on a total of 23 ships from Aceh and Baticala.[87] Trade from Diu was even greater; a retrospective account spoke of 40 or 50 ships doing this voyage each year.[88]

As to hard data on values, too often we merely have awed expressions of the huge value of some of these ships. Two Surat ships came back, we are told in a Persian chronicle, very richly laden as they were full of "one kind of ashrafis."[89] Portuguese accounts similarly sometimes just talk of "rich merchandise" and "much money."[90] But sometimes we have better estimates. We have data on how much the king of Portugal got as prize money from various ships captured by his fleets and confiscated because they did not have *cartazes*. We also know that the king got a "quinto," or fifth, of the total value.[91]  Given that his share tended to be underestimated so that the Portuguese on the spot could keep more for themselves, the following estimates of values are undoubtedly low. In 1519 a fleet off Diu took six ships "of Mecca" and from them the king got over 200,000 cruzados, making then a total value of 1,000,000 cruzados.[92] Five years later three "naus de Meca" yielded 60,000 pardaus for the king.[93] Two years later a similar capture, again of three such ships, yielded another 60,000 pardaus, while two years later again one large ship from Mecca yielded 60,000 pardaus, and this excluded chests of gold and silver which had been lost, and which were worth even more than this.[94] In the 1530s a Portuguese fleet in the Persian/Arabian Gulf took a Mecca ship "so rich, that even leaving aside what was robbed from it, it yielded for the king 60,000 pardaus of gold, and 200 slaves for the galleys."[95] In the 1550s a ship sailing from the Red Sea to Dabul, owned by the ruler of Bijapur, produced 30,000 cruzados for the king of Portugal.[96] On all of these occasions the total value on board is to be taken as five times that reserved for the king.

On other occasions we have estimates of the total value of

these ships. In 1524 a captured ship from Mecca had in goods alone 60,000 cruzados.[97] A similar prize in 1532 was worth close to 200,000 pardaus.[98] Details from customs payments can also be informative. Thus a ship heading for Surat from the Red Sea in 1556 paid duties of 3,000 pardaus, and nothing on the gold and silver it carried. At a rate of 5 percent, the goods alone were worth 60,000 pardaus.[99] Five years later a ship from Aceh reputedly had on board more than a million of gold, and a palanquin being taken to give to the sultan of Turkey which was so richly decorated as to be worth alone 200,000 cruzados.[100] We noted that it was estimated that 40 or 50 ships left from Diu bound for the Red Sea each year in the sixteenth century, loaded with Gujarati products such as cloths, saltpeter and opium. The Diu customs house as a result yielded 230,000 xerafins a year, making then a total value of trade between there and the Red Sea of over 4.5 million xerafins.[101] Nor is this necessarily an extravagant figure, for one ship alone could pay duties of 18,000 pardaus, which gives a cargo value of about 432,000 xerafins.[102]

Another estimate of a rich royal ship from 1618 provides further confirmation, for it was claimed to carry a cargo of Rs.2,500,000, that being equal to a truly fabulous value of over 1,500,000 xerafins.[103] Other ships from the Red Sea in the 1630s were worth up to 500,000 xerafins.[104] Later in the century Fryer noted the arrival of the Jiddah fleet at Surat, carrying (in the whole fleet) Rs.5,000,000.[105] This figure is confirmed by Martin at the same time.[106] Finally, in 1695 the largest of the state pilgrim ships was captured by English pirates, and this one ship had on board in cash alone Rs.5,200,000.[107] From the context, it is clear that this ship, like many of the others which sailed back from the Red Sea, was loaded mostly with cash, for at this time India basically exchanged goods for bullion, either coined or not. In any case, all this data may at least tend to show that trade from the Arabian Sea, especially from India, to the Red Sea, and especially to Jiddah, was an extremely large and valuable.

The total picture of long-distance trade in the Hijaz, and the vast distant areas trading with and through this region, is complex. If we were to summarize, we would write of the totally land route from the Persian/Arabian Gulf and so all the way to the shores of the eastern Mediterranean. This route declined in the seventeenth century. In the Red Sea area the situation was much more complex. It is clear that both land and sea routes, or a combination of both, were used. It was possible to go by land all the way from say Cairo to Mocha, with numerous stops on the way. Damascus to Mecca or Jiddah was usually done entirely by land, though sometimes the sea would be used for the last sector, from say Yanbo to Jiddah. The route from Cairo was, similarly, usually done by a combination of land and sea, and Suez was the usual place of transhipment and transfer. As we stressed, Jiddah was the major mart, where goods arrived both by land and sea, but mostly the latter, and were then transferred to more suitable conveyances. In the case of goods going north, to either Damascus or Cairo, this meant a transfer to smaller boats for goods going on by sea, or to camel caravans for goods going by land. For goods going south towards Mocha and the Arabian Sea, the transfer was most often to larger ships, though some goods did continue by land as far as Mocha.

What is most clear in all this is that very little of this trade had anything to do with religion or specifically with the *hajj*. The sea trade simply could not fit the times of the *hajj*. Land trade could, but given the way so many goods travelled part of the way by sea, much land trade also was circumscribed by the monsoons, and was timed to arrive at a particular port when ships could also reach it on the relevant monsoon. The exceptions were the pilgrim caravans which, of necessity, were governed by the lunar calendar. As we have seen, their economic role was small,. We can now turn to an investigation of the economy of Mecca itself, and conclusively put to rest the whole notion of a link between trade and religion, or anything which could be described as a *"hajj* market" dominating the whole trade and economy of the Middle East and western India.

# CHAPTER 8

# The Economy of Mecca

When we look at economic activity in Mecca in the early modern period we find substantial trade, especially at the time of the pilgrimage, in provisions and other goods connected with the *hajj* and the needs of the pilgrims. What we do not find is significant trade through Mecca in which the town was used as a market or a transhipment center. There was some trade to be sure, but in the context of total Middle East trade, and the trade of the Hijaz, it was minor. Most people on the *hajj* caravans did not trade, except in souvenirs and provisions. The so-called *hajj* market was a market to meet the needs of the pilgrims. As such, in economic terms it was quite atypical, and in sum was of much less economic importance than more routine markets in such port cities as Jiddah.

But there were, of course, connnections between Mecca and Jiddah. Part of Jiddah's trade was related to the *hajj*. Those pilgrims who came by sea passed through the port, and a proportion of the products sold during the *hajj* obviously were imported through Jiddah. Thus we could say that Mecca was to considerable extent dependent on Jiddah, but that the reverse does not apply, for as we saw Jiddah had a large trade from its role as a hinge or nodal point in the Red Sea and this had nothing to do with Mecca. For Jiddah, trade with Mecca was only one of many links.

The trouble with Mecca was that it was unable to feed itself, and was not located so as to be a natural trade center. It has long been believed that, at the time of the Prophet, Mecca was an important trade center, and that the flux and change caused by this, notably the way new economic élites were undermining traditional kin-oriented allegiances, created conditions sympathetic to the message of the Prophet. Recent research has begun to question this, in particular to say that Mecca was in fact not an important trade center at this time. In any case, it seems clear that soon after the time of the Prophet whatever role the town may have had in trade entered a period of decline which continues today.[1] As an early nineteenth-century pilgrim noted, Mecca "is not placed in any direct line of passage . . . . Its centre, therefore, cannot be in any direct line of communication with the neighbouring countries to which access may be had by sea. Its ports at most will only serve as sea-port towns to trading vessels, as is the case with Djedda and Mokka upon the Red Sea, and Muscat near the mouth of the Persian Gulph. Mecca not being situated in the route to any country of consequence, nature has not designed it as a place of commerce, placed as it is in the middle of an extremely barren desert, which prevents its inhabitants from being either husbandmen or shepherds. What resources then remain to them for subsistence?"[2]

What resources indeed, for the surrounding area was and is notoriously infertile. As Varthema said, "You must know that, in my opinion, the curse of God has been laid upon the said city, for the country produces neither grass nor trees, nor any one thing. And they suffer from so great a dearth of water . . . "[3] As a result the town was almost totally dependent on imported food, which came from as far away as Cairo, via Jiddah, and Arabia and Ethiopia.[4] A mid-fifteenth-century pilgrim noted that the inhabitants of Mecca "have no food-stuffs or other supplies apart from what is brought to them by pilgrims and by Indian and Egyptian ships, for as God has said, Mecca is barren and has no tillage."[5] Such was the lack of productivity of the Hijaz that not only food, but even teak to repair the Great Mosque had to be imported, from India, and iron from southern Bulgaria via Egypt.[6] The early Portuguese noted that Mecca was dependent for food on sup-

170

plies from Jiddah, which itself imported most of its food from other areas on the shores of the Red Sea.[7] It was in fact a pious and meritorious act to send food to Mecca and Medina. Several travelers noticed how the Ottomans did this so lavishly. Ovington found each year 20 or 25 ships coming from Egypt, financed by the government and laden with provisions and money.[8] Sixty years later Niebuhr noticed very large patronage from the Ottomans to the whole area and its rulers. The sharifs and their numerous families were given pensions, and "With these pensions, and the freight of four or five large vessels, which he sends every year to Jidda, laden with provisions, he supports almost all the inhabitants of Mecca and Medina. During the whole time, while the pilgrims remain in the city of Mecca, as much water as two thousand camels can bear is daily distributed gratis; not to speak of the vast number of presents with which he adorns the *Kaba*, and gratifies the descendants of Mahomet."[9]

The result was that the towns were usually well supplied with provisions. A late twelfth century pilgrim said that wheat was cheap when he was in Mecca, and typically attributed this to divine intervention: "This price in a land that has no farms, and no source of sustenance for its people save the provisions imported to it, is one in which the aid and favour of God is manifest."[10] As we noted, many pilgrims tried to overcome this problem by bringing with them all the supplies they would need both for the journey to and from Mecca, and for their stay in the Holy City. Obviously not everyone could do this, and in any case for fresh provisions, such as meat and fruit, recourse had to be made to the very inflated monopolistic Mecca markets.

Contemporary accounts make it all too clear that the residents of Mecca were totally dependent for their livelihood on the annual pilgrimage. A pilgrim wrote that "Mecca is so poor by nature, that if the house of God ceased to exist, it would be inevitably deserted in two years, or at least reduced to a simple douar, or hamlet; for the inhabitants in general subsist

171

for the rest of the year upon what they accumulate during the time of the pilgrimage, at which period the place puts on a lively appearance, commerce is animated, and the half of the people are transformed into hosts, merchants, porters, servants, etc; and the other, attached entirely to the service of the temple [*sc.* for Ka'ba], live upon the alms and gifts of the pilgrims."[11] All this was recognized in popular sayings. An old Meccan one ran: "We sow no wheat or sorghum, the pilgrims are our crops," and another said that the *hajj* was "the bread of the Hijaz."[12] The economy in fact was purely an exchange one. Nothing was produced, there were not even any factories except small ones producing goods oriented to the pilgrimage.[13] This applied beyond our period too, and indeed until today. Hurgronje in the late nineteenth century noted that the residents made all their money from supplying, and cheating, the pilgrims, as the town offered no other source of livelihood.[14] Burton noted disapprovingly, "It is common practice for the citizen to anticipate the pilgrimage season by falling into the hands of the usurer. If he be in luck, he catches and 'skins' one or more of the richest Hajis." If not he was in trouble, as interest rates were high.[15] An account of the *hajj* of 1991 noted that "Saudi merchants do more business in a few days than in the entire year outside the Haj."[16]

It is sometimes claimed that while Jiddah, Mecca and Medina were all almost totally dependent on imported food, Mecca was unique in that its main need for food was when its population was grossly inflated at the time of the *hajj*. The other two cities were different in that visitors came all through the year, to Jiddah for trade, and to Medina to visit the tomb of the Prophet, something which could be done at any time. However, while there is no doubt that the great concentration was at the time of the pilgrimage, we noted earlier that it was always meritorious to visit Mecca, to circumambulate the Ka'ba, to study there, and to engage in a series of *umrahs*. There was in fact a mini-version of the *hajj* on the occasions when especially important times for an *umrah* occurred, for while these can be done at any time there are nevertheless certain times when it is better than usual to do them. Ibn Jubayr noted that the month of Rajab had associated with it an important lesser pilgrimage and many people came to Mecca for it. In a minor version of what happened during the great pilgrimage, a tribe from the Yemen "prepare themselves to arrive at this Blessed City ten days before the festival combining the aims of performing the lesser pilgrimage, and of provisioning the land with various kinds of food . . . They arrive in thousands, men and camels, laden with the goods we have described, and bringing an abundance of viands to the people of the City and to the pilgrims who have settled there."[17]

The *hajj*, and generally the esteemed position of Mecca in the Muslim world, had another economic significance also. As we noted, many Indian Muslim rulers saw it as a pious obligation to send charity, and build hospices, in the Holy City. So also some sent charitable supplies of food. Aurangzeb, it will be remembered, sent quite large sums, as also did several of Gujarat's more pious rulers. We also have evidence of charity and alms being sent from Muslims in India via the merchant fleet trading, in the period before the Portuguese disrupted this, from Calicut.[18] The famous raconteur and dubiously veracious traveler Fernão Mendes Pinto, while a slave in Mocha, was nearly sent off as an offering to the ruler of Mecca.[19] The powerful Muslim ruler of Aceh, in Sumatra, also maintained close ties with Mecca and sent expensive gifts to the rulers, receiving in return titles and recognition.[20] Nearly three centuries later, in the 1770s, we have a full, denigrating, and grossly overwritten account of this from an Englishman: "The remotest corners of the East pay homage to his [the sharif's] title. The way-worn pilgrim ceaseless toils from Teflis' towers or Mesopotamia's waste, to add his little mite to the treasure of Medina's people; while Asiatic princes, subahs of Ind, and sultans of the Spicy Isles, which westward bound the Southern ocean, enrich the Prophet's shrine with gems and gold. The large sum of money which our vessel brought for the service of the Mosque, as a peace-offering from the nabob of Arcot, on the decease of his daughter, is a corroborating evidence of the enthusiasm of Mussulmen. It amounted to one lack and a half of rupees, which is near £20,000 sterling, and was the gift of a prince, whom the world need not be told is so involved in debt, as not to require this drain to exhaust his mortgaged revenues."[21]

The *hajj* also produced economic benefits of dubious legality for local rulers and bandits. A Portuguese report from the early sixteenth century tells us that the sharif made large sums from taxing all of the pilgrim caravans. It appears that from the Cairo caravan alone he made from this head tax 12,000 cruzados.[22] We presumably should at least double this to cover all the other caravans coming from Damascus, and from the south. The pilgrims complained about this, but much worse were the local beduin, who specialized in robbing the pilgrim caravans. It was for this reason that the relative law and order provided by the Ottomans from the early sixteenth century resulted in an increase in the number of pilgrims.

As we have noted, merchants often accompanied these caravans, and it is also to be remembered that they were all Muslims. While this monopoly was nice for them, this fact alone militated against major trade at Mecca, for many merchants in the early modern Middle East were Christians or Jews. It is clear that in Mecca there was a major market during the time of the *hajj*, as indeed one would expect given the numbers of people involved. It will be remembered that perhaps 200,000 people would be present for the *hajj*. Pitts noted Indian pilgrims bringing "many rich and choice goods, which are sold to all sorts of persons who resort to Mecca."[23] Ibn Jubayr similarly wrote that in Mecca in 1183

"From all parts produce is brought to it, and it is the most prosperous of countries in its fruits, useful

174

requisites, commodities and commerce. And although
there is no commerce save in the pilgrim period, nevertheless, since people gather in it from east and west,
there will be sold in one day, apart from those that follow, precious objects such as pearls, sapphires, and
other stones, various kinds of perfumes such as musk,
camphor, amber and aloes, Indian drugs and other
articles brought from India and Ethiopia, the products
of the industries of Iraq and Yemen, as well as the
merchandise of Khurasan, the goods of the Maghrib,
and other wares such as it is impossible to enumerate
or correctly assess. Even if they were spread over all
lands, brisk markets could be set up with them and all
would be filled with the useful effects of commerce. All
this is within the eight days that follow the pilgrimage, and exclusive of what might suddenly arrive
throughout the year from the Yemen and other countries. Not on the the face of the world are there any
goods or products but that some of them are in Mecca
at this meeting of the pilgrims." [24]

Varthema in the early sixteenth century said "in this city
there is carried on a very extensive traffic of merchandise,
that is, of jewels, spices of every kind in abundance, cotton in
large quantities, wax and odoriferous substances in the
greatest abundance."[25] And as we would expect, we have
records of goods, including spices, entering places like Egypt,
Iran, Iraq and Damascus on caravans which had come via
Mecca.[26] This trade was mostly done by the merchants who
came with the caravans. Our Indian pilgrim noted an
Egyptian, "who had frequently visited Mecca for trade and
had also performed the Hajj many times."[27] Some trade also
was done by pilgrims, who sold goods in Mecca and so
financed their return home. Another variant was the sale of
goods from which the proceeds were given as alms in Mecca.
The point to stress about this trade in Mecca of costly but not

specifically religious goods is that it was a trade in "rarities" —pearls, carpets, fine cloths—and precisely because they were being bought in Mecca (they were of course imports, not local products) they sold at double their usual price. In other words, some of Mecca's sanctity rubbed off on these mundane, though costly, goods.[28]

We also have descriptions of markets in Mecca itself during the *hajj* period and immediately after it. Faroqhi has produced by far the best modern account of this matter.[29] She notes that Mecca lived from pilgrims, and subsidies from the Ottomans. There were few artisans, and no mention of guilds, nor of local agriculture or manufactures. The main time for trade was after the restraints were lifted following the end of the rites at Mina. At this huge market there may have been 6,000 shops, or more, though most of them were small affairs, stalls rather than shops. Many of those who traded were not professional traders at home; some sold goods in order to cover their costs, and others bought goods in a speculative fashion, hoping to sell them for a profit back home. The whole complex made up a very large, if atypical, fair.

The contemporary sources are a little confused on this matter. Our Indian pilgrim saw perfume sellers and other shops in the town.[30] Ibn Battuta did the running between al-Safa and al-Marwa, and found there "an immense bazaar, in which are sold grain of various kinds, meat, dates, clarified butter, and other varieties of fruits . . . . There is at Mecca no organized market beyond this, except the cloth-merchants and druggists at the Gate of the Banu Shaiba."[31] Other accounts, however, describe a large market just after the *hajj*, at Mina on Dhu al-Hijja 11 to 13, that is, when the *ihram* was no longer being worn.[32] A contemporary account says the pilgrims stayed five days at Mina, "because at that time there is a faire free and franke of al custome."[33] In the late seventeenth century it was claimed that pilgrims stayed in Mecca for 10 or 12 days after their *return* from Arafat and Mina, and that *this* was the great fair time, and was permissible because now the rites were completed and the newly-titled *hajjis* could engage in purchasing. Available were "all manner of East India goods, and abundance of fine stones for rings and Bracelets etc., brought from Yeamane [Yemen]; also of China ware and musk, and variety of other curiosities."[34]

A Danish traveler, who wrote at second hand, claimed that the Ka'ba was surrounded by arcades "designed to protect the pilgrims from the torrid heat of the day. They answer likewise another purpose; for the merchants, of whom great numbers accompany the caravans, expose their wares for sale under those arcades."[35] But at least by the mid-nineteenth century the Mina market was hardly impressive. Burton said "I could not see the principal lines of shops, and, having been led to expect a grand display of merchandise, was surprised to find only mat-booths and sheds, stocked chiefly with provisions." He mentions no other markets in Mecca. We should however, be wary of using nineteenth century evidence at all. We have noted that the whole economic picture of the Middle East had been changed by the increasing dominance of western Europe. Furthermore, from late in the eighteenth century Wahhabi influence was important in Mecca. These puritans were bitterly opposed to what they saw as innovations, and acted forcefully to clean up religious observance in general, and especially the corruption of the *hajj* by too much pelf as opposed to piety.[36] Today commerce again is given free reign, but apparently more often now before the pilgrimage starts. An account of the 1991 *hajj* noted that "Although Islamic teaching disapproves, the pre-Haj period is also a time of non-stop shopping."[37]

Some pilgrims were offended by trading activities during the *hajj* period at least. Ibn Jubayr in 1183 noted disapprovingly that "Throughout all the days of the festival, the sacred Mosque . . . became a great market in which were sold commodities ranging from flour to agates, and from wheat to pearls, and including many other things of merchandise . . . .

That this is forbidden by divine law is known."[38] In the late seventeenth century our Indian pilgrim also found this to be inappropriate. "It was also observed that many of them [pilgrims] were frequently busy in worldly things particularly in purchasing goods and valuables." He also complained of disorder at the time of the *hajj*. "In the season of pilgrimage the market of cutpurses becomes more brisk. The violence and disturbance of the wicked persons from Egypt and western countries [that is, the Maghreb] generate much heat during the mercantile activities in the market . . . "[39] Even in the nineteenth century we get these sorts of complaints; note how in this one merchants are clearly distinguished from pilgrims. "At the Mina market large quantities of goods are sold, and pilgrims say that the merchants are so absorbed in business that they have no leisure for devotion, and that with the view of protecting their goods, they remain in their shops and omit to perform the rites."[40]

The crucial point then is that Mecca was not an "ordinary" center of exchange. A perceptive English traveler in the late seventeenth century put it as well as anyone ever has: "Its buildings are . . . very ordinary, insomuch that it would be a place of no tolerable entertainment, were it not for the anniversary resort of so many thousand *hagges*, or pilgrims, on whose coming the whole dependence of the town (in a manner) is; for many shops are scarcely open all the year besides."[41] The modern French savant Jean Aubin is similarly perceptive: "Situated in the precarious environment of a desert city threatened by Beduin incursions, Mecca is a great commercial and intellectual crossroads teeming with the faithful from all countries during the pilgrimmage season; the rest of the year the city is alive with cargo arrivals, merchants bound for India or returning from a dangerous crossing, the celebrations they give for marriages, etc."[42]

By far the best analysis of this matter comes in the work of the urban geographer F.E. Peters. Any possibility of normal trade in Mecca was ended early in the Islamic period

because the town "found a new and extraordinarily successful export item of its own manufacture," that is, religion.
Commerce in the town was all oriented to the *hajj*. Beduin
sold sheep and goats for the sacrifice. Barbers plied their
trade, camel brokers provided transport to Arafat, others
flourished as loan sharks, pawnbrokers and prostitutes.
Nearly everyone rented out rooms during the season. Some
even made a living acting as bridegrooms for temporary marriages so that single women could engage in the rituals.
Peters notes that one of the many specialist functions to service pilgrims were the guides, *dalil*, or more correctly
*mutawwif*, whom we have described previously. They were
"Mecca's largest and most important guild industry." They
arranged everything, and were indispensable as guides to the
complicated ritual. They were very tightly organized, and
acted generally as agents and facilitators for the pilgrims.

"Though it had no share in the great international spice
trade, Mecca was from beginning to end a community of
entrepreneurs, eager if occasionally amateur practitioners of
a highly seasonal occupation that engaged the energies of
everyone from sharif to beggar." Before the *hajj* caravans
arrived all the inhabitants went to Jiddah to buy Indian
goods, took them back to Mecca, and sold them to pilgrims at
a markup of at least 50 percent. Once the *hajj* was over the
merchants closed their shops and went off to al-Ta'if, in the
mountains, or to Jiddah, where most of them had their
homes. Peters makes a very useful comparison between this
sort of commerce and more usual activity: "Mecca was
undoubtedly one of the great trading centers of the Islamic
Middle Age, not in the familiar manner of Cairo or Istanbul
or Damascus, however, where commerce was part of an intri-
cate network of wholesale and retail trade, of import and
manufacture, credit and banking, and where merchant
princes stored their goods in monumental khans and did
their business in elegant bazaars. There were wealthy
Meccan merchants, to be sure, and healthy profits to be

made, but the trade there was overwhelmingly retail as well as occasional and so necessarily opportunistic, and there was little in Mecca that resembled a commercial network or even a permanent economic establishment."[43]

Thus most of the trade of Mecca was designed to cater to the needs of the pilgrims, perhaps 200,000 of them. Among the goods sold were provisions most obviously, but also souvenirs which the more wealthy at least could take home and use to impress their neighbors. While anything bought in Mecca, even if it was not a local product, would still have a certain aura about it, items closely associated with the Ka'ba, the Great Mosque, and the religion in general were especially valued and especially esteemed as things to take home.

We may note first several rather less important "pious souvenirs." It will be remembered that Aurangzeb was meant to be impressed by small brooms which had been used to sweep out the interior of the Ka'ba; these indeed were important items. Peters calls them "souvenir whisks made from the brooms used to sweep out the *Bayt Allah*."[44] A contemporary described how the sharif himself swept out the interior of the Ka'ba, using water, and people even tried to get some of this. "And the besoms wherewith the *Beat* is cleansed are broken in pieces and thrown out amongst the mob; and he that gets a small stick or twig of it keeps it as a sacred relique."[45] A Danish visitor in 1763 bought, in Jiddah, a drawing of the Ka'ba. "This painter gained his livelihood by making such draughts of the Kaba, and selling them to pilgrims."[46] A generally well-informed European traveler described a more bloody souvenir, one for which I can find no other supporting evidence. After Arafat, back in Mecca "their *Hetzas*, or High-Priest, makes a Procession, conducting through the chief streets a Camel which is appointed for the Sacrifice. The Hair of this Camel is a very precious Relick among them; whence it comes, that the Pilgrims throng, to get as near as they can to the Beast, and to snatch off some of his Hair, which they fasten to their arms, as a very sacred thing. The *Hetzas*, after he hath walk'd the Beast sufficiently, leads him to the *Meydan*, that is the great Market-place, and puts him into the hands of the Baily, or Judge of the City, whom they call *Daroga*, who, attended by some other Officers, kills him with an Axe, giving him many blows in the Head, Neck, and Breast. As soon as the Camel is dead, all the pilgrims endeavour to get a piece of him, and throng with such earnestnesse and so confusedly, with Knives in their hands, that their Devotions are never concluded, but there are many Pilgrims kill'd and hurt, who are afterwards allow'd a place in their Martyrologies."[47]

Two items were most valued. One was the highly ornate covering of the Ka'ba, which each year was replaced by the ruler of Egypt, at first the Mamluks and later the Ottoman sultan, who indeed also provided annually a new covering for the tomb of the Prophet in Medina. Each year the new covering of the Ka'ba took six months to make. The cost was met from *waqfs* and other state support. The Cairo caravan was distinguished by the fact that it took with it this *kiswa*, or covering for the Ka'ba, which was carried in the *Mahmal-i Sharif*, a richly adorned litter which accompanied the caravan to the Holy Places and back again. E.W. Lane in 1835 left us a famous description of this, which gives some impression of the general opulence and prestige of the whole caravan:

It is a square skeleton-frame of wood, with a pyramidal top; and has a covering of black brocade, richly worked with inscriptions and ornamental embroidery in gold, in some parts upon a ground of green and red silk, and bordered with a fringe of silk, with tassels surmounted by silver bells. Its covering is not always made after the same pattern with regard to the decorations, but in every cover that I have seen, I have remarked, on the upper part of the front, a view of the Temple of Mekkeh [*sc.* for the Ka'ba], worked in gold; and, over it, the Sultan's cypher. It contains nothing;

but has two *mushafs* (or copies of the Koran), one on a scroll, and the other in the usual form of a little book, and each enclosed in a case of gilt silver, attached, externally, at the very top . . . . The Mahmal is borne by a fine tall camel, which is generally indulged with exemption from every kind of labor during the remainder of its life.[48]

The actual covering was called the *kiswa*, the "curtain" of the Ka'ba. A European pilgrim in about 1580 noted that before the Cairo caravan left, the Pasha handed over to the leader of the caravan "ye Chisva Talnabi, which signifieth in the Arabian tongue, The garment of the Prophet: this vesture is of silke, wrought in the midst with letters of gold, which signifie: La illa ill'alla Mahumet Resullala: that is to say, There are no gods but God, and his ambassadour Mahumet. This garment is made of purpose to cover from top to botome a litle house in Mecca standing in the midst of the Mesquita [i.e. the Ka'ba]"[49] Once the new one arrived in Mecca, the old one was taken off "and the olde vesture is [given to] the eunuches which serve in the sayde Mosquita, who after sell it unto the pilgrimes at foure or five serafines the pike, and happy doth that man thinke himselfe, which can get never so little a piece thereof, to conserve ever after as a most holy relique: and they say, that putting the same under the head of a man at the houre of his death, through vertue thereof all his sinnes are forgiven."[50]

There appears to have been a substantial trade in the pieces of this covering, for our Indian pilgrim also noted "It is lawful to purchase the cover of the Khana Ka'ba from the servants and poor among whom it has been distributed, and it is also disallowed to sell it."[51] We have an extended description of the whole matter from a European traveler of the late seventeenth century. The sharif takes off the old covering, "and cuts it into pieces and sells it to the *hagges*, who care not (almost) how much they give for a piece of it. They being so eager after these shreds, a piece of the bigness of a sheet of paper will cost a *sultane*, i.e. nine or ten shillings. Yea, the very cotton rope (to which the lower part of the covering was fastened) is also cut into pieces, untwisted, and sold. Many buy a piece of the covering of the *Beat* [the *Bayt Allah*, that is the Ka'ba] on purpose to have it laid on their breast when they are dead and be buried with them. This they carry always with them, esteeming it as an excellent amulet to preserve them from all manner of danger. I am apt to believe that the Sultan Shirreef makes so much money of the old covering as the new may cost; although they say that the work that is in it is alone the employment of many people for the whole year's space." [52]

The other main religious souvenir or relic was the water of the famous well of Zamzam. As Qazvini noted, it was meritorious to drink this water, and to wash in it, and even to peer down into the well. And he added that "It is virtuous to take it to other parts of the world." [53] A European account conveys the whole matter well. Four men drew the water out, and were not paid for this task. The *hajjis* drank it, and washed in it. "The *hagges*, when they come first to Mecca, drink of it unreasonably; by which means they are not only much purged, but their flesh breaks out all in pimples; and this they call the purging of their spiritual corruptions." "Yes, such a high esteem they have for it, that many *hagges* carry it home to their respective countries, in little latten or tin pots (Peters notes that making these was just about the only domestic production of Mecca.) [54], and present it to their friends, half a spoonful, it may be, to each; who receive it in the hollow of their hand with great care and abundance of thanks, sipping a little of it and bestowing the rest on their faces and naked heads; at the same time holding up their hands and desiring of God that they also may be so happy and prosperous as to go on pilgrimage to Mecca." [55] At the time of the fair after the *hajj* "the dervises are wholly employ'd in distributing and selling that holy water to the ignorant people."[56] Some pilgrims simply took a small container of the water back home with them, but "Everyone almost now buys a *caffin*, or shroud, of fine linen to be buried in, for they never use coffins for that purpose; which might have been procured at Algier, or their other respective homes, at a much cheaper rate, but they choose to buy it here, because they have the advantage of dipping it in the holy water, *Zem Zem*. They are very careful to carry the said *caffin* with them wherever they travel, whether by sea or land, that they maybe sure to be buried therein."[57]

This practice in fact did have a profound secondary economic significance. A French observer from the 1770s noted the huge trade in Indian cloth at Mocha and Jiddah, and stressed that this was helped by religious factors. Pilgrims in Mecca, he said, always provided themselves with some shrouds, made of Bengal cotton. The majority of these pilgrims, however, were doing this on commission for those who themselves could not make the *hajj*. He claimed, in what seems to be a gross exaggeration, that there were always at least 500,000 *hajjis* each year, and they had each with them a minimum of three shrouds, so that, according to him, some 3,000,000 shrouds were traded, and blessed, each year.[58] Be this as it may, it is clear that this trade in holy souvenirs was an extensive one. We noted other relics being sent to Mughal emperors in what was really a thinly disguised form of trade, for the sharif expected to get back items more valuable even if less holy. In the early nineteenth century similarly Ali Bey acquired various souvenirs of his *hajj*; not only a bit of cloth from the Ka'ba, but also Zamzam water and several small brooms which had been used to sweep out the Ka'ba.[59]

To summarize this important matter, it seems clear that trade in Mecca was very largely restricted to the period of the pilgrimage; at other times there was only a minor market in provisions. At the time of the *hajj* there were variations in trade. On the one hand we have the vast majority of people in the town, who were visitors for the religious ceremonies, and who took no part in trade for profit. Indeed, many of these did not even do any shopping; forewarned of the expense of Mecca, and the profiteering propensities of its inhabitants, they took all they needed with them, and also had on hand food sufficient to get them back home again. If they did not, they would buy what food was absolutely essential; if they had overcalculated, they would sell the surplus to their less provident fellow pilgrims. These people might, at the most, buy some holy water and a piece of the covering if they could afford it, but this normally was the limit of their trade. We must remember that very many of the pilgrims were poor people, who had saved for years to make this great journey. Indeed many were subsidized by pious rulers and nobles. Such people obviously were not going to be buying jewels or spices.

Then there are the doubtless rather large numbers of pilgrims who not only did pious souvenir shopping but also had to buy food for the journey home. This group might also, if they could afford it, buy more secular souvenirs, or even take advantage of a good buy to pick up something they then would sell on the way home, in other words the early modern travelers' check phenomenon.

Finally we have merchants pure and simple, who took advantage of the vast concourse of people to sell their wares, and might also take the time to do the *hajj* themselves. The goods traded would be souvenirs for the pilgrims, and provisions for their return journey, and other normal trade goods which would be sold to other merchants or to the few more wealthy pilgrims. And finally we must remember that for the inhabitants of Mecca and its environs this was their great opportunity to provide for the rest of the year when the town would be more or less deserted. During the *hajj* they acted as guides, they leased rooms in their houses, they provided transport, porterage, and animals for the sacrifice, they engaged in commerce, and those of them attached to the Great Mosque sold pious souvenirs and controlled access to

185

Zamzam and other significant places. It is this sort of disaggregation of our data which enables us to see in its correct perspective the whole link between the *hajj* and economic activity, and which means we can say that the connection was tenuous, and that while Mecca was the site for a major, if economically atypical, fair during the *hajj* period, it then each year returned to a position of commercial insignificance.

# CHAPTER 9

# Conclusion

The whole subject of pilgrims and pilgrimages seems to be a vague one at present, even if the Islamic version has been by and large neglected. This is strange, for the *hajj* is the largest routine gathering of people for any purpose in world history, a status it has enjoyed for well over a millennium. This concluding chapter aims to describe pilgrimage as a more general phenomenon, which will compare accounts of pilgrimage in other religious traditions and look at more theoretical studies, especially those of Victor and Edith Turner.[1]

South Asian scholars, often geographers, have recently produced many studies of Hindu pilgrimages, among them Irawati Karve's brief but evocative article[2] and Bhardwaj's larger academic study.[3] Some accounts of Christian pilgrimages can be of use and interest. Sumption produced an excellent account of medieval Christianity which discusses saints, relics, miracles and finally pilgrims. His account is however very much social and religious description, with very little discussion of any economic or political implications.[4] Braudel provides a typically excellent brief account in his classic *The Mediterranean*.[5] An older study by Heath of medieval pilgrimages is full of curious information on, for example, flagellants, indulgences and actual routes, the "Pilgrims' Way" followed by his pilgrims.[6] Kendall's book is basically descriptive, profusely illustrated, and contains long quotations from documents, while the Davies' case study is full of interest.[7] Howard's study of Christian pilgrimages is a graceful account of the role of these in the wider religion, and again is short on economic and political implications. Yet his approach is not totally pious and religious.[8] An excellent comparative study has been produced by the urban geographer Peters, who compares Mecca and Jerusalem in the early modern period. This is a most distinguished work.[9]

Nevertheless, in general statements about pilgrimage, and in accounts of Christian pilgrimages, we begin to find problems. This applies particularly to the important anthropologist Victor Turner, whose work, while purportedly describing pilgrimage in general, in fact is based on his profound knowledge, and acute analysis, of Christian practice. What are some of his main insights?

The best short statement of Victor Turner's ideas came in a piece by his widow and collaborator, in the *Encyclopedia of Religion*. She wrote, "Pilgrimage has the classic three-stage form of a rite of passage: (1) separation (the start of the journey), (2) the liminal state (the journey itself, the sojourn at the shrine, and the encounter with the sacred), and (3) reaggregation (the homecoming). . . . The middle stage of a pilgrimage is marked by an awareness of temporary release from social ties and by a strong sense of *communitas* ('community, fellowship') . . . " For pilgrims *communitas* means "a special sense of bonding and of human kindness . . . . Yet, in each case, this *communitas* is channeled by the beliefs, values, and norms of a specific historical religion."[10]

The key terms are "liminal" and "communitas." These related terms are to be seen as part of Turner's distinction between "structure" and "anti-structure." "Man [*sic*] is both a structural and an anti-structural entity, who *grows* through anti-structure and *conserves* through structure." "Structure, or all that holds people apart, defines their differences, and constrains their actions, is one pole in a charged field, for which the opposite pole is communitas, or anti-structure." Communitas occurs during the liminal stage of a journey, that is after the departure but before the return, "when the subject is in spatial separation from the familiar and habitu-

al . . . . [it stresses] generic rather than particularistic rela-
tionships," it is "a threshold between more or less stable
phases of the social process" or again, it is any condition outside or on the peripheries of everyday life, and a time which,
because "the rules recognized as legitimate by the political
and intellectual elites at a given time" are less operable, is
often marked by cultural creativity. Despite the constraints
and obligations, pilgrimages at least in premodern times
"represented a higher level of freedom, choice, volition, struc-
turelessness, than did, say, the world of the manor, village, or
medieval town. It was *yin* to its *yang*, cosmopolitanism to its
local particularism, communitas to its numerous structures."[11]

There is no need to question the power and analytical
rigor of Turner's work, nor indeed the usefulness of some of
his insights for a study such as ours, but when he purports to
describe pilgrimage as a universal phenomenon he and his
followers often go astray. He once claimed that caste continues to differentiate Hindu pilgrims, just as Islam does not
allow non-Muslims to go to Mecca.[12] The comparison is non-
sense, for the first relates to divisions *within* a perceived religious group, while the second is a distinction *between* one
religious group and all others. Similar problems appear in his
discussions, and those of his followers, about the "orthodoxy"
of pilgrimages. Edith Turner sees them as "outside the
bounds of religious orthodoxy." They draw "the faithful away
from the center of organization."[13] Similarly, Peter Brown
notes that "As Victor Turner has pointed out, the abandon-
ment of known structures for a situation where such structures are absent, and the consequent release of spontaneous
fellow feeling, are part of the enduring appeal of the experience of pilgrimage in settled societies."[14]

Now most of this simply does not apply, or at least not
without serious qualifications, to the *hajj*. The *hajj* is central
and orthodox, indeed it exemplifies orthodoxy and what is
done is dictated by orthodox texts and guides. Certainly there

is *communitas*, but all constraint and control is not lost. Certainly it is an overwhelming experience, but within tightly circumscribed bounds. Those on the *hajj* were not free-floating, unbounded by any social norms; quite the reverse, for usual social structures were replaced by others which often were stricter than those of everyday life, such as the obligation for the *hajji* to wear special clothes (the *ihram*) and to abstain from cutting hair and sexual relations until the rituals were completed. Nor does this quotation from A. Dupront quite hit the mark for the *hajj*: "Pilgrimage society is a mixed and, therefore, to a high degree, a cohesive society in which persons of different ages, social standing, males and females and even clergymen and laymen take part in a vague communion."[15] True, the *hajj* is meant to be like this, so that for example everyone is meant to wear the same humble *ihram,* and women need not be veiled for no man would have impure thoughts on this most sanctified of occasions. Nevertheless, modern documentary films and books make it clear that distinctions of various sorts are in fact still observed.

Similarly, Brown, again basing himself on the Turners, seems to find Islam to be much more centralized than it really is: "if the translation of relics had not gained a major place in Christian piety, the spiritual landscape of the Christian Mediterranean might have been very different. It might have resembled that of the later Islamic world: the holy might have been permanently localized in a few privileged areas, such as the Holy Land, and in 'cities of the saints,' such as Rome. There might have been a Christian Mecca or a Christian Kerbela [*sic*], but not the decisive spread of the cult of major saints . . . "[16] But it is common knowledge that the Muslim world has a vast array of holy places, often tombs of holy people, and some of these are at least as widely known and revered as the great Christian saints Brown mentions. As just one example, Xavier de Planhol found in 1937 no less than 250,000 pilgrims at a shrine in Senegal,[17] while in recent times each year some millions of shias visit the tomb of the eighth Imam at Mashhad in Iran.

In some areas we find similarities, in some differences. Physical contact with a sacred object seems to have been more important for Christians, showing that Islam does not have the quasi-deification of saints that medieval Christianity had. Brown writes of what he happily calls "contact relics," for example cloths which had touched a tomb of a saint.[18] These could well be equated with the shrouds dipped in Zamzam water which we noted in Chapter 8. On the general matter of pious souvenirs, Peters notes more similarities, for he quotes an account of how in Jerusalem there was the sale of "a variety of souvenirs which the pilgrims take back with them to their homeland. There they give them to their families and friends who regard them as valuable and cherished presents since everything that comes from Jerusalem is believed to be holy and that possession of them confers a blessing."[19] Similarly with the very difficulty of doing a pilgrimage at all in a time before modern mass communications. We noted what a long journey the *hajj* was for many who undertook it, but similarly Braudel notes that Christian pilgrims to the Holy Land from Venice would spent on average 43 days on the journey there, and 93 for the return, all this for less than a month in Palestine![20]

Goitein provided a useful comparative perspective when he wrote that "Merchants, craftsmen and scholars alike would combine journeys undertaken in their personal interests with pilgrimages to holy places. The Muslim pilgrimage, of course, far outstripped in importance those of the other two religions. In the first place, pilgrimage was one of the main religious duties of a Muslim whereas in Christianity and Judaism it was only a meritorious deed."[21] However, this applies to Jews only after the destruction of the Second Temple in the year 70. Before this time Jewish males were obliged to visit the Temple on, according to various accounts, one or three festival days each year.[22] Islam differs in that it retains a compulsory pilgrimage and is happy to include women as well as men.

When scholars write of pilgrimage as a form of travel, or even as tourism, they can also often be led astray. Turner can lead us into an investigation of the meanings of travel. He tells us that "we can envisage the social process involving a particular group of pilgrims during their preparations for departure, their collective experiences on the journey, their arrival at the pilgrim center, their behavior and impressions at the center, and their return journey, as a sequence of social dramas and social enterprises and other processual units . . . "[23] Some indeed have evaluated pilgrimages precisely as a form of tourism.[24] Victor Turner once remarked casually that pilgrimages are booming nowadays, but many "should perhaps be considered as tourists rather than pilgrims per se."[25] But more recently his widow tells us that "The temporary release from social ties that characterizes a pilgrim's journey is shared by other travelers who have an affinity with pilgrims, especially tourists and mystics. Tourists may, at heart, be pilgrims . . . "[26]

Pilgrimage has been facilitated by the same developments, notably better and cheaper communications and means of travel, as has travel and tourism, but the purpose obviously is different. Travel and tourism are for fun, but the purpose of pilgrimage is at heart religious; to fulfil an obligation, or to gain a blessing. Here is where the degree of voluntariness, or conversely compulsion, is important. One can always chose not to travel this year, or indeed ever, if one cannot afford it, or if one chooses to spend discretionary income on other things. Pilgrims have less or no choice. Muslims going to Mecca are fulfilling a basic obligation of their faith, as were male Jews visiting the Temple before its destruction in 70CE. Others are slightly less obligatory, but still must be distinguished from travel and tourism. Sometimes the pilgrimage is undertaken after some boon has been granted, sometimes it is hoped that the pilgrim will be rewarded for her efforts. The pilgrim believes that if God or some divine agent does such and such, he or she will be obliged to fulfil her part of the bargain and go to Jerusalem, Varanasi, Canterbury. Alternatively, if a pilgrim goes to Lourdes he will be cured.

Thus while travel by definition is recreational and voluntary, pilgrimage is not, or at least not to the same extent. This is reflected in the vast numbers of poor people who have taken part in pilgrimages over the millennia, but who have never gone away on holiday. Chaucer reminds us of this, as do the many accounts of medieval pilgrimage to the Holy Land, and perhaps most powerfully in the case of the *hajj*, not surprising as this is the most compulsory of all.

More correctly, one would find a continuum of compulsion, and of religiosity, in pilgrimage. This sort of mixing, even confusion, can be illustrated by the popular use of the word "Mecca." The place is of course the focus of the Muslim *hajj*, so holy that non-Muslims are forbidden access, but in popular discourse it has been secularized, so that we talk of Nashville as a Mecca for country music fans, and Disneyland as a Mecca for visitors to the West coast. No doubt the aficionado does feel awe and wonder at these places, as does the *hajji* in Mecca, yet this pale secular imitation of the experience of the pilgrim is still voluntary. But to the extent that the tourist visiting a secular "Mecca" undergoes a religious or mystical experience, this points to the dangers of over schematization. A *hajji* will buy souvenirs, a visitor to Nashville will have a lump in the throat.

The point of course is obvious; "pure" travel, and especially "pure" pilgrimage, do not exist, except as heuristic devices. How to categorize a person hacking around in the Holy Land, visiting shrines and also buying trinkets? As we have noted, pilgrim shrines inevitably are neighbors to markets which sell vaguely sanctified goods, and on to mundane goods, and so to quite "unholy" products such as drugs and purchased sexual relations. Turner noted "Communion, marketing, the fair, all went together in a place set apart."[27] A study of medieval Christian pilgrimage noted that "While the pilgrimage was a metaphor for human life and a spiritual exercise, the thing itself was a trip to and back from Jerusalem, Rome, or a particular shrine; so it was travel, which meant danger, adventure and curiosity. Hence the carnival spirit that moralists frowned upon, and the startling abuses . . ." such as sexual escapades, graffiti writing on tombs and relics, and souveniring bits from shrines.[28]

Finally, what of the degree and nature of *communitas* to be found among pilgrims, and how are the adepts set off by the way they define themselves by distinguishing themselves from the non-adepts, that is the role of the "Other" in creating a bond among fellow pilgrims? At first sight it seems this may well be a useful insight for Christian or Hindu pilgrims, for they undertake their rituals surrounded by a mass of "Others" who are taking no part. What of Islam? On the face of it there is no comparison with any Other which can create solidarity, for only Muslims are allowed into Mecca. But in fact this seems to be an extreme version of what we have been saying. The Other is even more powerful, more defining by contrast, more given to create a feeling of community precisely because it is not there at all. It is a matter of Muslims set off against the whole world, all people and all places outside of Mecca. It is true that in Anderson's terms the Muslim pilgrims are an "imagined community," for one does not "know" all the other (maybe 2,000,000) pilgrims, yet the tie is no less strong, for all are bonded by undertaking common actions and austerities, and by a common at least minimal, knowledge of the requirement of the pilgrimage and the religion in general.[29]

Other structural imperatives also reinforce this separateness, the mirror image of *communitas*. It is not a matter of the traveler leaving behind all restraints, all baggage from his "normal" life. As Turner noted, "though pilgrimages strain, as it were, in the direction of universal *communitas*, they are still ultimately bounded by the structure of the religious systems within which they are generated and persist."[30] The Muslim pilgrim travels relatively free, but once in the sacred area of Mecca his every action is constrained and regimented, especially by his guide, the *mutawwif*. Such mediators have been called "cultural brokers," who guide and instruct the traveler, so that the "Other Place" is filtered through their eyes. In the case of the *hajj* each national group has its own broker who guides the pilgrim through the strictly defined rituals of the days of the pilgrimage, arranges accommodation and food. Anderson notes the horde of pilgrims at a sacred site, originating from all over the world, their imagined community being one created by a religious bond, but he goes on to distinguish between the vast horde of illiterate vernacular-speaking pilgrims and a small number of literate bilingual adepts drawn from each vernacular community, who perform the unifying rites and interpret to their followings the meanings of their actions.[31]

What we have been writing about is a major matter, for we have been describing the main reason why people moved in the early modern period. Far more people traveled for pilgrimage than for any other reason, even for war. Thus they acted powerfully to break down the particularism of premodern societies. Nor of course was pilgrimage only travel. The vitality of all the major religions is largely a result of pilgrimage. Pilgrimage creates *communitas* indeed, and also bestows powerful benefits on those who return, whether this be a cure, a sense of personal accomplishment, or a new role as an exemplar of the faith. Those who "guard" the holy place accrue considerable prestige and often also profit. It is my hope that the present modest and limited work will serve to introduce others to this fascinating topic, and encourage more research and more comparisons with other forms of pilgrimage and of travel in general.

# Notes

## Chapter 1  (Pages 1-34)

1.  Satish Chandra, ed., *The Indian Ocean: Explorations in History, Commerce and Politics*, New Delhi, 1987; K.N. Chaudhuri, *Trade and Civilization in the Indian Ocean. An Economic History from the Rise of Islam to 1750*, Cambridge, 1985; K.N. Chaudhuri, *Asia before Europe: Economy and Civilisation of the Indian Ocean from the Rise of Islam to 1750*, Cambridge, 1990. For a recent excellent discussion see S. Arasaratnam, "Recent Trends in the Historiography of the Indian Ocean, 1500 to 1800," *Journal of World History*, I, 2, Fall 1990, pp. 225-48.

2.  Kenneth McPherson, "Maritime Passenger Traffic in the Indian Ocean Region before the Nineteenth Century," *The Great Circle*, X, l, April 1988, pp. 49-61, and more recently some passages in his *The Indian Ocean: A History of the People and the Sea*, Delhi, 1993.

3.  On this last point Rooke in 1782 agreed: Henry Rooke, *Travels to the Coast of Arabia Felix and from thence by the Red-Sea and Egypt to Europe*, London, 1783, p. 58. Hamidullah claims the prohibition dates only from Ottoman times, but this has been contradicted authoritatively by Peters. See *Les Pèlerinages: Égypte Ancienne; Israel; Islam; Perse; Inde; Tibet; Indonésie; Madagascar; Chine; Japon* (Sources Orientales, III), Paris, 1960, p. 106, and F.E. Peters, *Jerusalem and Mecca: The Typology of the Holy city in the Near East*, New York, 1986, pp. 55, 70.

4.  William R. Roff, "The Meccan Pilgrimage: Its Meaning for Southeast Asian Islam," in R. Israeli and A.H. Johns, eds., *Islam in Asia*, vol. II, Southeast and East Asia, Boulder, 1984, pp. 239-40.

5. Ira M. Lapidus, *A History of Islamic Societies*, Cambridge, 1988.
6. *Hajj Studies*, ed. Ziauddin Sardar and M.A. Zaki Badawi, London, 1978-
7. William R. Roff, "Meccan Pilgrimage," p. 238. Unfortunately, Professor Roff tells me that he does not intend to proceed with his studies of the *hajj* from southeast Asia.
8. Ashin Das Gupta, "Introduction II: The Story," in Ashin Das Gupta and M.N. Pearson, eds., *India and the Indian Ocean, 1500-1800*, Calcutta, 1987, p. 27.
9. J.F. Richards, review of *India and the Indian Ocean, 1500-1800*, and *The Indian Ocean* in *Journal of Asian Studies*, XLVIII, 3, Aug. 1989, pp. 651-3.
10. Marc Gaborieau, ed., *Islam et société en asie du sud*, Paris, 1986.
11. Immanuel Wallerstein, *The Modern World-System*, 3 vols, New York, 1974-89; Eric R. Wolf, *Europe and the People without History*, Berkeley, 1982, and for a general discussion of these theories as applied to Asia, M.N. Pearson, *Before Colonialism: Theories on Asian-European Relations 1500-1750*, Delhi, 1988.
12. Naimur Rahman Farooqi, *Mughal-Ottoman Relations* (A Study of Political and Diplomatic Relations between Mughal India and the Ottoman Empire, 1556-1748), Delhi, 1989. Chapter 4, "The Problem of the Hajj Traffic: Mughal Response and Ottoman Reaction," pp. 144-72, is virtually identical to his article "Moguls, Ottomans, and Pilgrims: Protecting the Routes to Mecca in the Sixteenth and Seventeenth Centuries," *The International History Review*, X, 2, May 1988, pp. 198-220.
13. S.A.A. Rizvi, *A History of Sufism in India*, New Delhi, 1978-83, 2 vols; *Muslim Revivalist Movements in Northern India in the Sixteenth and Seventeenth Centuries*, Agra, 1965; *Religious and Intellectual History of the Muslims in Akbar's Reign*, New Delhi, 1975; *Shah 'Abd al-'Aziz: Puritanism, Sectarianism, Polemics and Jihad*, Canberra, 1982; *Shah Wali-Allah and his Times: a Study of Eighteenth-Century Islam*, Canberra, 1980.
14. Muhammad Mujeeb, *The Indian Muslims*, London, 1967; Aziz Ahmad, *Studies in Islamic Culture in the Indian Environment*, Oxford, 1964.
15. Peter Hardy, *The Muslims of British India*, Cambridge, 1972.

16. Annemarie Schimmel, *Islam in the Indian Subcontinent*, Leiden, 1980. See p. 119 for a short discussion of the role of the *hajj* and Mecca.
17. Marc Gaborieau, op. cit.
18. See R. Israeli and A.H. Johns, eds. *Islam in Asia*, 2 vols., Boulder, 1984.
19. D.S. Richards, ed., *Islam and the Trade of Asia,* Oxford, 1970. *Mouvements de populations dans l'océan Indien*, Paris, 1979.
20. William R. Roff, "Islamic Institutions in Muslim Southeast Asia and cognate phenomena in the Indian sub-continent," in D. Rothermund, ed., *Islam in Southern Asia; a Survey of Current Research*, Wiesbaden, 1975, pp. 10-12. See also William R. Roff, "Sanitation and Security: The Imperial Powers and the Nineteenth Century Hajj," *Arabian Studies,* VI, 1982, pp. 143-60; Roff, ed., *Islam and the Political Economy of Meaning: Comparative Studies of Muslim Discourse*, Berkeley, 1987; Roff, "Pilgrimage and the History of Religions: Theoretical Approaches to the Hajj," in Richard C. Martin, ed., *Approaches to Islam in Religious Studies*, Tucson, 1985, pp. 78-86 and William R. Roff, "The Meccan Pilgrimage," op. cit.
21. *Report of the Haj Inquiry Committee*, Calcutta, 1930. J.A. Rahim, *Report of the Special Hajj Inquiry*, c.1940. More recently, the Pakistan Central Haj Organization published a useful set of statistics for 1974: *Haj Statistics, December 1974*, Islamabad, 1975.
22. The only publication by Metcalf that I have seen is "The pilgrimage remembered: South Asian accounts of the *hajj*, " in Dale F. Eickelman and James Piscatori, eds., *Muslim Travellers: Pilgrimage, Migration and the Religious Imagination*, London, 1990, pp. 85-107.
23. It would obviously be more appropriate to use Muslim era dates for this study, but for the convenience of my non-Muslim readers I have chosen to use the more familiar Christian or Common Era system.
24. G.E. von Grunebaum, *Muhammadan Festivals*, London, 1976, pp. 39-40.
25. See an account of the *hajj* for 1991 in *The Independent*, [London], reprinted in the *Sydney Morning Herald*, June 20, 1991.

26. See Sadashiv Gorakshkar, "Anis al-Haj," in Karl Khandalavala, ed., *An Age of Splendour: Islamic Art in India*, Bombay, 1983, pp 132-5, and for the *mutawwif* generally see Gwyn Rowley and Soleiman A. El-Hamdan, "Once a Year in Mecca," *Geographical Magazine*, vol. 49, 1977, p. 753.

27. For example, A.H. Johns, "Sufism as a Category in Indonesian Literature and History," *Journal of Southeast Asian History*, II, 1961, pp. 10-23.

28. Virginia Matheson and A.C. Milner, *Perceptions of the Hajj. Five Malay Texts*, Singapore, 1984.

29. Mary Byrne McDonnell, "The Conduct of the Hajj from Malaysia and its Socio-Economic Impact on Malay Society: A Descriptive and Analytical Study, 1860-1981." Columbia University unpublished Ph.D. dissertation, 1986. [DAI XLVII, no. 7, Jan. 1987, p. 2701 A]; McDonnell, "Patterns of Muslim pilgrimage from Malaysia, 1885-1985," in Eickelman and Piscatori, eds., *Muslim Travellers*, pp. 111-130.

30. Harry J. Benda, *The Crescent and the Rising Sun: Indonesian Islam under the Japanese Occupation, 1942-5*, The Hague, 1958.

31. Jacob Vredenbregt, "The Haddj, some of its Features and Functions in Indonesia," *Bijdragen tot de Taal-Land-en Volkenkunde*, vol. 118, 1962, pp. 91-154; D. van der Meulen, "The Mecca Pilgrimage and its importance to the Netherlands East Indies," *Muslim World*, XXXI, 1941, pp. 48-60.

32. Patricia Crone, *Meccan Trade and the Rise of Islam*, Princeton, 1986, casts doubt on Mecca's importance as either a pilgrimage or trade center before the rise of Islam.

33. See W.R. Roff in Rothermund, ed.

34. See Abdul Kadir Haji Din, "Economic Implications of Moslem Pilgrimage from Malaysia," *Contemporary Southeast Asia*, IV, 1, 1982, pp. 58-75, and references there cited.

35. As two recent fine articles remind us. See Barbara Metcalf, and Mary McDonnell chapters in Eickelman and Piscatori, eds., *Muslim Travellers*.

36. See S.A. Arjomand, and P.M. Lubeck, in William R. Roff, ed., *Islam and the Political Economy of Meaning: Comparative Studies of Muslim Discourse*, Berkeley, 1987, pp. 125, 100.

37. G. Rowley, and S.A.S. El-Hamdan, "The Pilgrimage to Mecca:

an exploratory and predictive model," *Environment and Planning A*, 1978, X, pp. 1053-71; Ziauddin Sardar, "The Future of Hajj: Some Basic Considerations," *Islamic Culture,* vol. LVIII, no. 4, Oct. 1984, pp. 307-26.

38. Suraiya Faroqhi, *Herrscher über Mekka: Die Geschichte der Pilgerfahrt*, Munich, 1990.

39. See Dale F. Eickelman and James Piscatori, eds., *Muslim Travellers: Pilgrimage, Migration and the Religious Imagination*, London, 1990; Ian Richard Netton, ed., *Golden Roads: Migration, Pilgrimage and Travel in Medieval and Modern Islam*, London, 1993.

40. Albert Kammerer, *La Mer Rouge, l'Abyssinie et l'Arabie aux XVIe et XVIIe siècles et La Cartographie des Portulans du Monde oriental* (Mémoires de la Société Royale de Géographie d'Egypte, tome XVII), 3 vols, Cairo, 1947-52. [First part: Abyssins et Portugais devant Islam; Second part: Les Jésuites Portugais et l'ephémère triomphe du Catholicisme en Abyssinie (1603-32); Third part: La Cartographie du Monde Oriental, Mer Rouge, Océan Indien et Extrême-Orient jusqu'au XVIII siècle. Cartographes Portugais et Français.] Kammerer, *La Mer Rouge, l'Abyssinie et l'Arabie depuis l'Antiquité. Essai d'historique* (Mémoires de la Société Royale de Géographie d'Egypte, tomes XV-XVI), 2 vols in 5 parts, Cairo, 1929-35. [Tome I, Les pays de la Mer Erythrée jusqu'à la fin du Moyen Age; Tome II, Les Guerres du poivre. Les Portugais dans l'océan indien et la Mer Rouge au XVIe siècle. Histoire de la cartographie Orientale.] For an extended and quite well-informed contemporary (1620s or 1630s) account of the Red Sea, see Jerónimo Lobo, *The Itinerary of Jerónimo Lobo*, trans. Donald M. Lockhart, London, Hakluyt, 1984, pp. 87-109.

41. *Encyclopedia of Islam*, Leiden, 1960 - , 2nd. ed., s.v. "hadjdj."

42. *The Encyclopedia of Religion*, ed. Mircea Eliade, vol. XI, New York, 1987, s.v. "Pilgrimage," pp. 327-54. The section on the *hajj*, by Richard C. Martin, is on pp. 338-46.

43. *Encyclopedia of Asian History*, ed. Ainslie T. Embree, New York, 1988, 4 vols, III, 256-60; Richard Barber, *Pilgrimages*, Woodbridge, 1991.

44. *Les Pèlerinages: Égypte Ancienne; Israel; Islam; Perse; Inde; Tibet; Indonésie; Madagascar; Chine; Japon* (Sources

Orientales, III), Paris, 1960; the *hajj* is covered on pp. 89-138. Also Maurice Gaudefroy-Demombynes, *Le pèlerinage à la Mekke: Étude d'histoire religieuse*, Paris, 1923.

45. Abdullah Ankawi, "The Pilgrimage to Mecca in Mamluk Times," *Arabian Studies*, I, 1974, pp. 146-70.

46. Jacques Jomier, *Le Mahmal et la caravane Egyptienne des pèlerins de la Mecque (XIII-XX siècles)*, Cairo, 1953.

47. David E. Long, *The Hajj Today: a survey of the contemporary Makkah pilgrimage*, Albany, N.Y., 1979. J.S. Birks, *Across the Savannas to Mecca: the overland pilgrimage route from West Africa*, London, 1978.

48. Russel King, "The Pilgrimage to Mecca: Some Geographical and Historical Aspects," *Erdkunde*, 26, 1972, pp. 61-73.

49. G.E. von Grunebaum, *Muhammadan Festivals*, pp. 15-49.

50. Richard Burton, *Personal Narrative of a Pilgrimage to al-Madinah and Meccah*, London, 1898, 2 vols; C.M. Doughty, *Travels in Arabia Deserta*, London, 1926, 1 vol ed.; C. Snouck Hurgronje, *Mekka in the Latter Part of the Nineteenth Century*, Leiden, 1931; T.F. Keane, *Six Months in Meccah*, London, 1881; J.L. Burkhardt, *Travels in Arabia*, London, 1829; Ali Bey, *Travels of Ali Bey in Morocco, Tripoli, Cyprus, Egypt, Arabia, Syria and Turkey, 1803-1807,* London, 1816, 2 vols; H.T. Norris, trans. and ed., *The Pilgrimage of Ahmad, Son of the Little Bird of Paradise. An Account of a 19th Century Pilgrimage from Mauritania to Mecca*, Warminster, 1977.

51. Ezzedine Guellouz, *Pilgrimage to Mecca*, London, 1980; Mohamed Amin, *Pilgrimage to Mecca*, London, 1978.

52. Ahmad Kamal, *The Sacred Journey: being pilgrimage to Makkah*, New York, 1961.

53. Syed Muhammad Badre-i Alam, *How to Perform Hajj*, Lahore, 1971; S.A. Husain, *A Guide to Hajj*, Lahore, 1972; Julien Claude Galland, *Recueil des rites et cérémonies du pèlerinage de la Mecque; auquel on a joint divers écrits relatifs à la religion, aux sciences & aux moeurs des Turcs*, Amsterdam, 1754, pp. 3-47.

54. Eldon Rutter, *The Holy Cities of Arabia*, London, 1928, 2 vols; Saida Miller Khalifa, *The Fifth Pillar: The Story of a Pilgrimage to Mecca and Medina*, Hicksville, N.Y., 1977.

55. Winifred Stegar, *Always Bells,* Sydney, 1969.

56. M.R. Ali, *My Umra*, Dacca, n.d.; S.M. Zafar, *Haj: A Journey in Obedience*, Lahore, 1978; Sultan Jahan Begam, Nawab of Bhopal, *The Story of a Pilgrimage to Hijaz*, Calcutta, 1909.

57. Nawab Sir Nizamat Jung, "At the Haj," *Islamic Culture*, VII, 2, 1933, p. 195; "In the Kaaba," *Islamic Culture*, VII, 3, 1933, p. 379; "Round Mecca," *Islamic Culture*, VIII, 2, 1934, p. 178. Another piece of literary curiosity is Hugh Brackenridge and Philip Freneau, *Father Bombo's Pilgrimage to Mecca, 1770*, ed. Michael D. Bell, Princeton Library, 1975, a rather silly piece of juvenalia which could be the first American novel, and was part of an undergraduate "paper war" at Princeton in 1770-1. It has nothing to do with the *hajj*.

58. J.D. Pearson, *Index Islamicus*, London, 1958- .

59. A theme underlying several of the chapters in Eickelman and Piscatori, eds., *Muslim Travellers*,

60. Naimur Rahman Farooqi, *Mughal-Ottoman Relations*, Faroqhi, *Herrscher über Mekka*.

61. Ibn Battuta, *The Travels of Ibn Battuta*, trans. H.A.R. Gibb, Cambridge, Hakluyt, 1958-71, 3 vols, I, pp. 242-8.

62. Muhammad ibn Ahmad ibn Jubair, *The Travels of Ibn Jubayr (1183-1185 AC)*, trans. R.J.C. Broadhurst, London, 1952.

63. Henry Bigot, "Les strophes du pèlerin de Puey Monçon (Voyage à la Mecque à la fin du XVIe siècle) avec préface, traduction et commentaire," *Revue Tunisienne*, 1916, pp. 87-124.

64. Bernard Lewis, ed., *Islam: From the Prophet Muhammad to the Capture of Constantinople*, New York, 1974, 2 vols, II, pp. 22-32.

65. William Foster, ed., *The Red Sea and Adjacent Countries at the Close of the Seventeenth Century*, London, Hakluyt, 1949 (accounts by Joseph Pitts, William Daniel, and Charles Jacques Poncet). Pitts' account is on pp. 21-47, and the quotations from pp. 4 and 12.

66. Ludovico di Varthema, *The Itinerary of Ludovico di Varthema of Bologna from 1502-1508*, ed. Sir Richard Carnac Temple, London, 1928. Anon., "A Description of the yeerely voyage or pilgrimage of the Mahumitans, Turkes and Moores unto Mecca in Arabia," in Richard Hakluyt, *The Principal Navigations*, Glasgow, 1903-5, 12 vols, V, 329-65. See also for analysis of this account C.F. Beckingham, "Hakluyt's Description of the Hajj," *Arabian Studies*, IV, 1978, pp. 75-80, and G. Levi Della Vida, "A

Portuguese Pilgrim to Mecca in the Sixteenth Century," *Muslim World*, XXXII, 1942, pp. 283-97.

67. Albert Kammerer, *Antiquity*, I, p. 62.

68. Conde de Ficalho, *Viagens de Pedro de Covilhan*, Lisbon, 1898, p. 125 et seq; Albert Kammerer, *Antiquity*, II, pp. 14-15.

69. Arnold von Harff, *The Pilgrimage of Arnold von Harff, Knight ... in the Years 1496-99*, ed. and trans. Malcolm Letts, London, Hakluyt, 1946, pp. 153-4 and f.n. 2.

70. F. Eugene Roger, *La Terre Saincte ou Description topographique très particulière des saincts lieux & de la terre de promission ...*, Paris, 1646, pp. 220, 236-9.

71. Adam Olearius, *The Voyages & travels of the ambassaddors sent by Frederick, duke of Holstein, to the great Duke of Muscovy, and the King of Persia. Began in the year MDCXXXIII and finish'd in MDCXXXIX ...*, trans. John Davies, London, 1662.

72. Adrianus Reeland, *Four Treatises concerning the doctrine, discipline and worship of the Mahametans .. III. A treatise of Babovius (sometime first interpreter to Mahomet IV) concerning the liturgy of the Turks, their pilgrimage to Mecca, ...*, London, 1712, pp. 125-36; Carsten Niebuhr, *Travels through Arabia and other Countries in the East*, trans. Robert Heron, 2 vols, Edinburgh, 1792, vol. I, passim.

73. Gulbadan Begam, *The History of Humayun,* trans. A. Beveridge, Delhi, 1972.

74. Hajji ad-dabir, *An Arabic History of Gujarat*, trans. M.F. Lokhandwalla, Baroda, 1970-74, 2 vols, I, p. 503.

75. Francis Gladwin, trans, *The Memoirs of Khojeh Abdulkurreem (of Kashmir)*, Calcutta, 1788, pp. 137-9.

76. D.N. Marshall, *Mughals in India: A Bibliographical Survey*, London, 1967, nos 468 (xi); 1295.

77. For two short studies of this text, with splendid copies of some of its illustrations, many of which I have used in this book, see Sadashiv Gorakshkar, "An Illustrated *Anis al-Haj* in the Prince of Wales Museum, Bombay," in Robert Skelton, et al, eds, *Facets of Indian Art*, London, V and A Museum, 1986, pp. 158-67 and Gorakshkar, "Anis al-Haj," in Karl Khandalavala, ed., *An Age of Splendour*, pp 132-5.

78. A. Jan Qaisar, "From Port to Port: Life on Indian Ships in the sixteenth and seventeenth centuries," in Ashin Das Gupta and

M.N. Pearson, eds., *India and the Indian Ocean*, 1500-1800, Calcutta, 1987, pp. 331-49; John Correia-Afonso, ed., *Intrepid Itinerant: Manuel Godinho and his Journey from India to Portugal in 1663*, Bombay, 1990, espec. pp. 72-8, 86-90, 114-9, where the Jesuit traveller provides excellent detail of his voyage from Surat to Gombroon via Muscat, and then to Basra. Jean Aubin has recently supplemented these with an interesting account of an early sixteenth-century voyage: "Un voyage de Goa à Ormuz en 1520," *Modern Asian Studies*, XXII, 3, 1988, pp. 417-32. This account by Qazvini will be referred to as "Qazvini." I owe an enormous debt to Professor Qaisar for making available to me his translation of this very valuable document.

79. Metcalf in Eickelman and Piscatori, eds., *Muslim Travellers*, p. 86.
80. Qazvini, p. 23 of the manuscript translation.
81. Gulbadan, pp. 72-3.
82. See further on this matter my "Conversions in Southeast Asia: Evidence from the Portuguese Records," *Portuguese Studies*, VI, 1990, pp. 53-70.
83. Fernand Braudel, *The Mediterranean and the Mediterranean World in the Age of Philip II*, London, 1972, 2 vols., I, pp. 555, 564.
84. Fernand Braudel, *Civilization and Capitalism, 15th to 18th centuries*, London, 1981-84, 3 vols., II, p. 127.
85. *Ibid*, III, p. 478.
86. Braudel, *Mediterranean*, I, p. 550.
87. William Foster, ed., *The Red Sea and Adjacent Countries at the Close of the Seventeenth Century*, London, Hakluyt, 1949, pp. 78-9.
88. Thomas Wright, ed., *Early Travels in Palestine, comprising the narratives of Arculf, Willibald, Bernard, Saewulf, Sigurd, Benjamin of Tudela, Sir John Mandeville, de la Brocquière, and Maundrell*, London, 1848, p. 302; Harff, *The Pilgrimage of Arnold von Harff*, pp. 153-4 and f.n. 2; Roger, *La Terre Saincte*, pp. 236-9; Pieter van den Broecke, *Pieter van den Broecke in Azie*, ed. W. Ph. Coolhaas, The Hague, 1962-3, 2 vols, p. 96. Coolhaas corrects this and says Medina is meant.
89. Correia-Afonso, ed., *Intrepid Itinerant*, p. 82.

90. William Foster, ed., *The English Factories in India, 1618-1669*, Oxford, 1906-27, 13 vols, 1637-41, p. 99.
91. Georg Schurhammer, *Francis Xavier: His Life, His Times*, vol. II, India, Rome, 1977, p. 135.
92. Tomé Pires, *The Suma Oriental of Tomé Pires*, ed. A. Cortesão, London, Hakluyt, 1944, 2 vols, I, pp. 12-13; Daniel in W. Foster, ed., *The Red Sea*, p. 78.
93. Correia-Afonso, ed., *Intrepid Itinerant*, p. 81.
94. Nicolas Sanson, *L'Asie en plvsievrs cartes novvelles, et exactes; en divers traittes de geographie, et d'histoire* . . . Paris, 1652, p. 27.
95. Colonel James Capper, *Observations on the Passage to India through Egypt and across the Great Desert* . . . , 2nd ed., London, 1784, p. vi.
96. Norman Daniel, *Islam and the West; the making of an image*, Edinburgh, 1960; Edward Said, *Orientalism*, London, 1978.
97. Qazvini, pp. 30, 33.
98. See Bigot, ed., p. 113.
99. Abu al-Hasan Ali ibn Bakr al-Harawi, *Guide des Lieux de Pèlerinage*, trans. Janine Sourdel-Thomine, Damascus, 1957, p. 198; Gaudefroy-Demombynes, p. 85.
100. Anon., in Hakluyt, V, pp. 352, 355.
101. A splendid recent book claims that until the late eighteenth century the prime differentiator was religion. See Michael Adas, *Machines as the Measure of Men: Science, Technology and Ideologies of Western Dominance*, Ithaca, 1989.
102. Olearius, *The Voyages & travels of the ambassaddors* pp. 231-2. It is hardly necessary to gloss this account in detail. Suffice it to note that parts are astray, but much of the detail, and the corrupt versions of Arabic and Persian words, are near enough to true.
103. John Henry Grose, *A Voyage to the East Indies . . . to which is added A Journey from Aleppo to Busserah, over the Desert, by Mr. Charmichael* [lst French ed, 1758, lst English ed 1766, 2nd Eng ed 1772, which adds Charmichael] 2nd ed., 2 vols, London, 1772. I, pp. 175-6.
104. Henry Rooke, *Travels to the Coast of Arabia Felix and from thence by the Red-Sea and Egypt to Europe*, London, 1783, pp. 61-2.

105. Eyles Irwin, *A Series of Adventures in the Course of a Voyage up the Red Sea . . . in the Year MDCCLXXVII*, London, 1780, pp. 45-6.
106. See Roff's excellent overview: Roff, "Pilgrimage and the History of Religions" in Martin, ed., *Approaches to Islam in Religious Studies*, pp. 78-86.
107. G.R. Tibbetts, "Arab Navigation in the Red Sea," *Geographical Journal*, vol. 127, 1961, pp. 328, 344.
108. Niccolao Manucci, *Storia do Mogor*, trans. W. Irvine, London, 1905-7, 4 vols, II, pp. 101-2.
109. Fernão Lopes de Castanheda, *História do descobrimento e conquista da India pelos Portugueses*, 3rd. ed., Coímbra, 1924-33, 9 vols, II, pp. 381-2; Gaspar Correa, *Lendas de India*, Coímbra, 1921-31, Lisbon, 1969, 4 vols, I, pp. 745, 747, 748.
110. Correia-Afonso, ed., *Intrepid Itinerant*, pp. 81-2.
111. *Pieter van den Broecke in Azie*, ed. W. Ph. Coolhaas, pp. 85, 86. Coolhaas corrects this and says Jiddah must be meant.
112. Schurhammer, p. 268; Vitorino Magalhães Godinho, *Os descobrimentos e a economia mundial*, 2nd. ed., Lisbon, 1981-83, 4 vols, III, p. 113.
113. Kamal Salibi, *A History of Arabia,* Delmar, N.Y., 1980, pp. 128, 138-9, 149; R.B. Serjeant, *The Portuguese off the South Arabian Coast*, Oxford, 1963, p. 5; Ashin Das Gupta, "Introduction II: The Story," in Das Gupta and Pearson, eds, *India and the Indian Ocean*, pp. 28-31.
114. André Raymond, *The Great Arab Cities in the 16th-18th Centuries: An Introduction*, New York, 1984, pp. 8-9. For a detailed modern account see Faroqhi, passim. The theme of her book is about Ottoman concern for Mecca and the *hajj*.
115. Ashin Das Gupta, "Indian Merchants and the Trade in the Indian Ocean," *Cambridge Economic History of India*, vol. I, Cambridge, 1982, p. 426.
116. See Ali Bey, *Travels,* and generally for the Wahhabis in the Hijaz see Gerald de Gaury, *Rulers of Mecca*, London, 1951, pp. 181-242, and Edward Mortimer, *Faith and Power: the Politics of Islam*, New York, 1982, pp. 56-79.

## Chapter 2 (Pages 35-58)

1. Xavier de Planhol, *The World of Islam*, Ithaca, 1959, pp. 73-4.
2. Abu al-Hasan Ali ibn Bakr al-Harawi, *Guide des Lieux de Pèlerinage*, trans. Janine Sourdel-Thomine, Damascus, 1957.
3. Surinder Mohan Bhardwaj, "Non-Hajj Pilgrimage in Islam: a Neglected Dimension of Religious Circulation," typescript, 1989. My thanks to Prof. Bhardwaj for letting me see this excellent paper.
4. Sidi Ali Reis, *The Travels and Adventures of the Turkish Admiral Sidi Ali Reis in India, Afghanistan, Central Asia and Persia during the years 1553-1556*, trans. A. Vambéry, London, 1899, pp. 2-3, 5-7, 8, 9, 32, 35, and *passim*.
5. Henry Bigot, "Les strophes du pèlerin de Puey Monçon (Voyage à la Mecque à la fin du XVIe siècle) avec préface, traduction et commentaire," *Revue Tunisienne*, 1916, pp. 101-3.
6. Mulla Safi-ud din Qazwini, "Anis-ul hujjaj, "trans. A. Jan Qaisar and Z. Islam, 71 pp. typescript, cited as "Qazvini," c. II, p. 10. For longer lists for Mecca and Medina, see Harawi, pp. 197-217.
7. *The Voyage of François Pyrard of Laval to the East Indies, the Maldives, the Moluccas and Brazil*, trans and ed. Albert Gray, London, Hakluyt, 1887-90, 2 vols, I, pp. 134-5.
8. Qazvini, p. 57.
9. Mohamed Amin, *Pilgrimage to Mecca,* London, 1978, pp. 18-19, and *Encyclopedia of Islam*, Leiden, 1960, 2nd. ed., s.v. hadjdj.
10. Gwyn Rowley and Soleiman A. El-Hamdan, "Once a Year in Mecca," *Geographical Magazine*, vol. 49, 1977, pp. 755.
11. Muhammad ibn Ahmad ibn Jubair, *The Travels of Ibn Jubayr (1183-1185 AC),* trans. R.J.C. Broadhurst, London, 1952, pp. 127, 135-6.
12. Richard Burton, *Personal Narrative of a Pilgrimage to al-Madinah and Meccah*, London, 1898, 2 vols., II, pp. 241-6.
13. Ibn Battuta, *The Travels of Ibn Battuta,* trans. H.A.R. Gibb, Cambridge, Hakluyt, 1958-71, 3 vols., pp. 355-9.
14. Khwajah Nizamuddin Ahmad, *The Tabaqat-i-Akbari*, trans. B. De, Calcutta, 1911-40, 3 vols., II, p. 557.
15. Qazvini, pp. 23-4.
16. Bigot, p. 106.

17. C. Snouck Hurgronje, *Mekka in the Latter Part of the Nineteenth Century*, Leiden, 1931, pp. 39, 80.

18. Mohammed Marmaduke Pickthall, trans., *The Meaning of the Glorious Koran*, New York, n.d., II, p. 196; III, p. 97; XXII, p. 27.

19. G.E. von Grunebaum, *Muhammadan Festivals*, London, 1976, p. 39.

20. Dr. John Fryer, *A New Account of East India and Persia*, London, Hakluyt, 1909-15, 3 vols., III, 163. This printed edition of Fryer has "Pelf" instead of "Pestilence", but this is incorrect. K.N. Chaudhuri points out that the word "Pelf" was misread. The manuscript in fact reads "Pestilence." K.N. Chaudhuri, *Asia before Europe: Economy and Civilisation of the Indian Ocean from the Rise of Islam to 1750*, Cambridge, 1990, p. 399, f.n. 52.

21. For a fuller discussion of the motives of pilgrims from early modern India, see my "Pious Passengers: Motivations for the *Hajj* from Early Modern India," in K.S. Mathew, ed., *Studies in Maritime History*, Pondicherry, 1990, pp. 112-26.

22. For a useful sketch of the activities of *sufis* on the *hajj* see G.E. von Grunebaum, *Muhammadan Festivals*, London, 1976, pp. 47-9.

23. Dr. John Fryer, *A New Account of East India and Persia*, London, Hakluyt, 1909-15, 3 vols., III, p. 80.

24. Marshall G.S. Hodgson, *The Venture of Islam*, Chicago, 1974, 3 vols., II, p. 151.

25. William R. Roff, "Islamic Institutions in Muslim Southeast Asia and cognate phenomena in the Indian sub-continent," in D. Rothermund, ed., *Islam in Southern Asia*, Wiesbaden, 1975, p. 11.

26. Henry Rooke, *Travels to the Coast of Arabia Felix and from thence by the Red Sea and Egypt to Europe*, London, 1783, p. 77.

27. See Suraiya Faroqhi, *Herrscher über Mekka: Die Geschichte der Pilgerfahrt*, Munich, 1990, pp. 18-19 for an excellent map of land routes leading to Mecca.

28. I.M. Shair and P.P. Karan, "Geography of the Islamic Pilgrimage," *GeoJournal*, III, 6, 1979, p. 600.

29. Sadashiv Gorakshkar, "An Illustrated *Anis al-Haj* in the Prince of Wales Museum, Bombay," in Robert Skelton et al, eds, *Facets of Indian Art*, London, V and A Museum, 1986, p. 158. For Zeb-

un-nisa see Jadunath Sarkar, *Studies in Aurangzib's Reign*, 3rd ed. London, 1989, pp. 90-98.

30. Though Patricia Crone's excellent book casts some doubt on this; see *Meccan Trade and the Rise of Islam*, Princeton, 1986.

31. Pyrard, I, p. 143.

32. G. Levi Della Vida, "A Portuguese Pilgrim to Mecca in the Sixteenth Century," *Muslim World*, XXXII, 1942, pp. 288-9; see also Jacques Jomier, *Le Mahmal et la caravane Egyptienne des pèlerins de la Mecque (XIII-XX siècles)*, Cairo, 1953, for copious analysis. For an account of the Egyptian caravan in the 1920s, which shows very little change as compared with our period, see S. Bey Spiro, *The Moslem Pilgrimage*, Alexandria, 1932.

33. Francis Gladwin, trans, *The Memoirs of Khojeh Abdulkurreem* (of Kashmir), Calcutta, 1788, pp. 133-4.

34. Russel King, "The Pilgrimage to Mecca: Some Geographical and Historical Aspects," *Erdkunde*, 26, 1972, p. 63.

35. A. Jan Qaisar, "From Port to Port: Life on Indian Ships in the sixteenth and seventeenth centuries," in Ashin Das Gupta and M.N. Pearson, eds., *India and the Indian Ocean, 1500-1800*, Calcutta, 1987, pp. 331-49.

36. Qazvini, pp. 1-2, 55-6, 58. For detail on navigation, but not trade or passengers, in the Red Sea, see G.R. Tibbetts, "Arab Navigation in the Red Sea," *Geographical Journal*, vol. 127, 1961, pp. 322-34.

37. For an extended description of these two official caravans, see Faroqhi, pp. 44-74.

38. Rooke, op. cit., p. 76.

39. Ibn Jubayr, Bigot, and Burton, *ops. cit.*; Ali Bey, *Travels of Ali Bey in Morocco, Tripoli, Cyprus, Egypt, Arabia, Syria and Turkey, 1803-1807*, London, 1816, 2 vols.

40. Ali Bey, pp. 27-40.

41. See Jomier, *passim*.

42. See King, p. 65, and Abdullah Ankawi, "The Pilgrimage to Mecca in Mamluk Times," *Arabian Studies,* I, 1974, pp. 146-8.

43. Stanford J. Shaw, *The Financial and Administrative Organization and Development of Ottoman Egypt, 1517-1798*, Princeton, 1962, p. 239.

44. João de Barros, *Da Asia,* Lisbon, 1778-88, II, pp. viii, 1. For a discussion of the decline of the formerly important port of

'Aydhab, opposite Jiddah and a little north, see Yajima Hikoichi, "On the Date of Decline of 'Aydhab, An International Port of Trade on the Red Sea," *Journal of the East-West Maritime Relations*, I, 1989, pp. 167-72 (English summary), and for an excellent map of the Red Sea in our period see *ibid.*, p. 177.

45. André Raymond, *The Great Arab Cities in the 16th-18th Centuries: An Introduction*, New York, 1984, p. 105.

46. King, p. 64.

47. Ludovico di Varthema, *The Itinerary of Ludovico di Varthema of Bologna from 1502-1508*, ed. Sir Richard Carnac Temple, London, 1928, p. 13.

48. Gladwin, pp. 115-20.

49. Karl K. Barbir, *Ottoman Rule in Damascus, 1708-1758*, Princeton, 1980, p. 153.

50. Thomas Wright, ed., *Early Travels in Palestine, comprising the narratives of Arculf, Willibald, Bernard, Saewulf, Sigurd, Benjamin of Tudela, Sir John Mandeville, de la Brocquière, and Maundrell*, London, 1848, p. 301. Wright notes that this is a very early mention of portable firearms in the Muslim world, and that they were still novelties in Europe at this time.

51. Mohammed Marmaduke Pickthall, trans., *The Meaning of the Glorious Koran*, New York, n.d., IX, p. 97.

52. Affonso de Albuquerque, *Cartas,* Lisbon, 1884-1935, 7 vols., letter to king of 4 Dec. 1513, I, p. 229; and to Duarte Galvão, n.d., I, 398. I have been unable to indentify "benybraem" unless it is a very corrupt version of beduin; the word "cabilas" is used for tribe, and for this see S.R. Dalgado, *Glossário Luso-Asiático*, 2 vols, Coímbra, 1919-21, s.v.

53. Felix Fabri, quoted in F.E. Peters, *Jerusalem and Mecca: The Typology of the Holy city in the Near East* (New York University Studies in Near Eastern Civilization, Number XI), New York, 1986, p. 45. See also Barbir, pp. 174-7, for attacks in the sixteenth to eighteenth centuries on the Damascus caravans.

54. Captain Robert Coverte, *A True and Almost Incredible report of an Englishman, that (being cast away in the good Ship called the Assention in Cambaya the farthest part of the East Indies) Travelled by Land through many unknowne Kingdomes and great Cities . . .* , London, 1612, p. 63.

213

55. See Faroqhi, pp. 89-95 on this matter, and pp. 102-25 for an extended description of Ottoman patronage of the Holy Cities and pilgrims to them.

56. Gladwin, pp. 133-7.

57. *Ibid.*, pp. 130-2.

58. Barros, III, pp. vi, 3; I, pp. viii, 4; for "alarves" see Dalgado, *Glossário*, s.v. For other brief descriptions of various caravans see Carsten Niebuhr, *Travels through Arabia and other Countries in the East*, trans. Robert Heron, 2 vols, Edinburgh, 1792, II, pp. 37-8; and Xavier de Planhol, pp. 70-1.

59. *The Encyclopedia of Religion*, ed. Mircea Eliade, vol. XI, New York, 1987, p. 338. This number for total Muslims seems low, given a total of over one billion today. Esposito finds 854 million in 1985: John L. Esposito, ed., *Islam in Asia: Religion, Politics and Society*, New York, 1987, Appendix, "The Peoples of Islam."

60. Ezzedine Guellouz, *Pilgrimage to Mecca*, London, 1980, p. 199.

61. David Holden and Richard Johns, *The House of Saud*, London, 1981, p. 400.

62. Guellouz, p. 198.

63. Rowley and El-Hamdan, *Geographical Magazine*, p. 753.

64. Faroqhi, pp. 63-4, and cf. 117-8 where again she is reluctant to try and calculate the populations of Mecca and Medina in this early modern period.

65. King, pp. 65-6.

66. Varthema, p. 19.

67. Anon., "A Description of the yeerely voyage or pilgrimage of the Mahumitans, Turkes and Moores unto Mecca in Arabia," in Richard Hakluyt, *The Principal Navigations,* Glasgow, 1903-5, 12 vols, V, p. 356.

68. Joseph Pitts' account in William Foster, ed., *The Red Sea and Adjacent Countries at the Close of the Seventeenth Century*, London, Hakluyt, 1949, p. 35.

69. F. Eugene Roger, *La Terre Saincte ou Description topographique très particulière des saincts lieux & de la terre de promission* . . . , Paris, 1646, p. 234; Cheleby Evliya quoted in Gerald de Gaury, *Rulers of Mecca*, London, 1951, p. 152.

70. Nicolas Sanson, *L'Asie en plvsievrs cartes novvelles, et exactes; en divers traittes de geographie, et d'histoire* . . . Paris, 1652, p. 27.

71. Comte de Modave, *Voyage en Inde du Comte de Modave, 1773-1776*, ed. Jean Deloche, Paris, 1971, p. 342.

72. Raymond, p. 8.

73. Anon., in Hakluyt, V, p. 340.

74. Qazvini, pp. 51, 53, 57.

75. Rooke, p. 76.

76. Varthema, p. 13.

77. Roger, p. 234; Rooke, p. 76.

78. Barbir, p. 155.

79. B. Schrieke, *Indonesian Sociological Studies*, The Hague, 1955-57, 2 vols, I, p. 14, and repeated on p. 19.

80. William R. Roff, "Sanitation and Security: The Imperial Powers and the Nineteenth Century Hajj," *Arabian Studies,* VI, 1982, pp. 145, 148.

81. William Foster, ed., *Early Travels in India*, Delhi, 1968, p. 301.

82. Samuel Purchas, *Purchas, His Pilgrimes*, Glasgow, Hakluyt, 1905-7, 20 vols., III, p. 193.

83. John Jourdain, *The Journal of John Jourdain, 1608-17*, ed. William Foster, London, Hakluyt, 1935, pp. 208-9.

84. Ashin Das Gupta, "Indian Merchants and the Western Indian Ocean: The Early Seventeenth Century," *Modern Asian Studies*, XIX, 3, 1985, pp. 491.

85. Suraiya Faroqhi, *Herrscher über Mekka: Die Geschichtedes Pilgerfahst*, pp. 205-6.

86. Philip Baldaeus, *A Description of the East India Coast of Malabar and Coromandel*, vol. III, London, 1703, p. 573.

87. Mandelslo, in Adam Olearius, *The Voyages & travels of the ambassaddors sent by Frederick duke of Holstein to the great Duke of Muscovy, and the King of Persia. Began in the year MDCXXXIII and finish'd in MDCXXXIX . . .* , trans. John Davies, London, 1662, p. 87.

88. J.-B. Tavernier, *Travels in India*, ed. V. Ball and W. Crooke, New Delhi, 1977, 2 vols, II, p. 281, a number which is confirmed by Niccolao Manucci, *Storia do Mogor*, trans. W. Irvine, London, 1905-7, 4 vols, II, p. 45.

89. Sanjay Subrahmanyam, "Persians, Pilgrims and Portuguese: the Travails of Masulipatnam Shipping in the Western Indian Ocean, 1590-1665," *Modern Asian Studies*, XXII, 3, 1988, pp. 505, 509.

90. Saris in Purchas, *Purchas, His Pilgrimes*, III, 396; also see Middleton in *ibid.*, pp. 190-3; Sadashiv Gorakshkar, "An Illustrated *Anis al-Haj* in the Prince of Wales Museum, Bombay," in Robert Skelton, et al, eds, *Facets of Indian Art*, London, V and A Museum, 1986, p. 161.

91. C.R. Naik, "Abdu-r-Rahim, Khan-i-Khanan," MA thesis, University of Bombay, n.d., p. 203.

92. Jean Mocquet, *Voyages en Afrique, Asie, Indes Orientales et Occidentales*, Rouen, 1630, pp. 280-1.

93. Thomas Best, *The Voyage of Thomas Best to the East Indies, 1612-14*, ed. William Foster, London, Hakluyt, 1934, p. 234.

94. Qazvini, pp. 1-2, 64, 65, 70.

95. Ashin Das Gupta, "A Note on the Shipowning Merchants of Surat, c. 1700,'" in Denys Lombard and Jean Aubin, eds, *Marchands et hommes d'affairs asiatiques dans l'Océan Indien et la Mer de Chine 13ᵉ 20ᵉ siècles*, Paris, 1988, p. 112. I think I am right in saying that these 155 are all crew, for elsewhere in this article Das Gupta does specify passengers as distinct from crew [p. 113].

## Chapter 3  (Pages 59-78)

1. Kenneth Cragg, *The House of Islam*, Belmont, Cal., 1969, p. 69.

2. K.N. Chaudhuri, *Asia before Europe: Economy and Civilisation of the Indian Ocean from the Rise of Islam to 1750*, Cambridge, 1990, p. 353.

3. *The Independent* [London], quoted in the *Sydney Morning Herald*, June 20, 1991.

4. Clifford R. Geertz, *Islam Observed, Religious Development in Morocco and Indonesia*, Chicago, 1968, p. 67.

5. Pierre Belon, (Belon du Mans), *Les observations de plusieurs singularitez et choses mémorables trouvées en Grèce, Asie, Judée, Egypte, Arabie et autres pays estranges,* Paris, 1554, p. 189.

6. Geffrey Ducket in Richard Hakluyt, *The Principal Navigations, Voyages, Traffiques and Discoveries of the English Nation*, Glasgow, 1903-5, 12 vols., III, p. 162.

7. J.F. Richards, ed., *Precious Metals in the Late Medieval and Early Modern Worlds*, Durham, N.C., 1983, p. 202.

8. Henry Bigot, "Les strophes du pèlerin de Puey Monçon (Voyage à la Mecque à la fin du XVIe siècle) avec préface, traduction et commentaire," *Revue Tunisienne*, 1916, p. 106 for an example, from about 1600, of the impact of Mecca on a pilgrim.
9. R.M. Eaton, *Sufis of Bijapur, 1300-1700*, Princeton, 1978, p. 127.
10. Ibid., p. 127.
11. Alexander Hamilton, *A New Account of the East Indies*, ed. W. Foster, London, 1930, 2 vols, p. 18.
12. *Documentação para a história das Missões do padroado Português do Oriente: India*, ed. António da Silva Rego, Lisbon, 1947-58, 12 vols., VII, p. 78.
13. *Ibid.*, V, pp. 192-3.
14. Fernão Mendes Pinto, *The Travels of Mendes Pinto*, ed. and trans. Rebecca D. Catz, Chicago, 1989, pp. 30, 53, 455. See also Naimur Rahman Farooqi, *Mughal-Ottoman Relations* (A Study of Political and Diplomatic Relations between Mughal India and the Ottoman Empire, 1556-1748), Delhi, 1989, pp. 157-8.
15. Silva Rego, ed., *Documentação*, XII, 782, also in *Documenta Indica*, ed. J. Wicki et al, Rome, 1948-, 16 vols to date, to 1594, XII, pp. 679-80. Note that a Venetian was worth 320 reis, so the amount involved was Rs. 63,000.
16. Annemarie Schimmel, *Islam in the Indian Subcontinent*, Leiden, 1980, p. 164.
17. C. Snouck Hurgronje, *Mekka in the Latter Part of the Nineteenth Century*, Leiden, 1931, p. 244.
18. Fernão Mendes Pinto, *Travels*, p. 9.
19. *The Voyage of François Pyrard of Laval to the East Indies, the Maldives, the Moluccas and Brazil*, trans and ed. Albert Gray, London, Hakluyt, 1887-90, 2 vols, I, pp. 110, 165.
20. Jerónimo Lobo, *The Itinerary of Jerónimo Lobo*, trans. Donald M. Lockhart, London, Hakluyt, 1984, pp. 286-7.
21. William Foster, ed., *Letters Received by the East India Company from its Servants in the East*, London, 1896-1902, 6 vols., I, p. 215.
22. William Foster, ed., *The English Factories in India, 1618-1669*, Oxford, 1906-27, 13 vols., 1622-23, p. 273 f.n.; 1634-36, pp. xv, xxv; 1637-41, p. 99.
23. Hurgronje, pp. 243, 258, 256-86, and generally also pp. 153-212

for late nineteenth-century students in Mecca.

24. Muhammad ibn Ahmad ibn Jubair, *The Travels of Ibn Jubayr (1183-1185 AC),* trans. R.J.C. Broadhurst, London, 1952, pp. 119, 127.

25. Hurgronje, p. 222.

26. See two versions of his career by Johns: A.H. Johns, "Friends in Grace: Ibrahim al-Kurani and 'Abd al-Rauf al-Singkeli," in S. Udin, ed., *Spectrum: Essays Presented to Sutan Takdir Alisjahbana on his Seventieth Birthday,* Jakarta, 1978, pp. 471-2, and A.H. Johns, *The Gift Addressed to the Spirit of the Prophet,* Canberra, 1964, pp. 8-11.

27. John Voll, "Muhammad Hayya al-Sindi and Muhammad ibn 'Abd al-Wahhab: an analysis of an intellectual group in eighteenth century Madina," *Bulletin of the School of Oriental and African Studies,* XXXVIII, 1975, pp. 32-9.

28. Suraiya Faroqhi, *Herrscher über Mekka: Die Geschichte der Pilgerfahrt,* Munich, 1990, p. 176 notes a quarter in Mecca populated by poor Indian pilgrims.

29. S.A.A. Rizvi, *A History of Sufism in India,* New Delhi, 1978-83, 2 vols., II, pp. 146-7, 294, 167, and *passim* for many other examples.

30. *Ibid.,* I, p. 190.

31. Schimmel, pp. 94-5.

32. al-Badaoni, *Muntakhabu-t-tawarikh,* trans. G. Ranking et al., Patna, 1973, 3 vols., III, p. 127; I.H. Qureshi, *Ulema in Politics,* Karachi, 1972, p. 52.

33. S.C. Misra, *Muslim Communities in Gujarat,* London, 1964, p. 24.

34. Eaton, pp. 112-8.

35. S.A.I. Tirmizi, *Some Aspects of Medieval Gujarat,* Delhi, 1968, p. 112.

36. Rizvi, II, p. 320-3.

37. Nawwab Samsam-ud-daula Shah Nawaz Khan, *The Maathir-ul-Umara,* trans. H. Beveridge, ed. Baini Prashad, Patna, 1979, 2 vols., I, p. 74.

38. Khafi Khan, *Khafi Khan's History of Alamgir,* trans. S. Moinul Haq, Karachi, 1975, pp. 549-50.

39. Badaoni, III, pp. 19-20.

40. Niccolao Manucci, *Storia do Mogor,* trans. W. Irvine, London,

1905-7, 4 vols., IV, 118.

41. Farooqi, *Mughal-Ottoman Relations*, pp. 19, 118-9.

42. For a fuller study of this in Southeast Asia see my "Conversions in Southeast Asia: Evidence from the Portuguese Records," *Portuguese Studies*, VI, 1990, pp. 53-70. Political relations between the Portuguese and Muslim authorities will be discussed in the next chapter.

43. Silva Rego, ed., *Documentação*, VIII, pp. 192-3; also printed in *Documenta Indica*, IV, p. 777.

44. *Ibid.,* VIII, p. 195, and in *ibid.*, IV, pp. 779-80.

45. *Ibid.*, VIII, p. 235, and in *ibid.*, IV, pp. 831-2.

46. Diogo do Couto, *Da Asia*, Lisbon, 1778-88, IV, pp. vi, 9.

47. Gaspar Correa, *Lendas da India*, Coímbra, 1921-31, Lisbon, 1969, 4 vols, II, p. 348.

48. *Documenta Indica*, IV, p. 492.

49. Silva Rego, ed., *Documentação*, XII, p. 462.

50. Correa, I, 75-6; for conversion in East Africa, see João dos Santos, *Ethiopia Oriental*, Lisbon, 1891, 2 vols., book V, cap. 1, and *Documenta Indica*, IV, p. 591, for an interesting account of circumcism.

51. Zain-ud-din, *Tohfut-ul-Mujahideen*, trans. M.J. Rowlandson, London, 1833, pp. 48-50.

52. Silva Rego, *Documentação*, VII, pp. 74-5; VIII, p. 84.

53. *Ibid.*, VIII, p. 80.

54. *Ibid.*, X, p. 296.

# Chapter 4 (Pages 79-104)

1. F.E. Peters, *Jerusalem and Mecca: The Typology of the Holy city in the Near East* , New York, 1986, p. 46. For a detailed and discursive account of the rulers of Mecca, see Gerald de Gaury, *Rulers of Mecca*, London, 1951.

2. Diogo do Couto, *O Soldado Prático*, 3rd ed., Lisbon, 1980, p. 152.

3. João de Barros, *Da Asia,* Lisbon, 1778-88, I, vi, p. 3.

4. Fernão Lopes de Castanheda, *História do descobrimento e conquista da India pelos Portugueses*, 3rd. ed., Coímbra, 1924-33, 9 vols., III, p. cix.

5. Geneviève Bouchon, "Le premier voyage do Lopo Soares en Inde

(1504-1505)," *Mare Luso-Indicum*, III, 1976, p. 80 and f.n. 129.

6.  Barros, I, viii, 1. For copious detail on Portuguese-Muslim rela-
    tions around 1517 see Jean-Louis Bacqué-Grammont and Anne
    Kroell, *Mamlouks, Ottomans et Portugais en Mer Rouge:
    L'Affaire de Djedda en 1517*, Cairo, 1988. Other older general
    accounts still of use include M. Longworth Dames, "The
    Portuguese and the Turks in the Indian Ocean in the sixteenth
    century," *Journal of the Royal Asiatic Society*, 1921, pp. 1-28,
    and two articles by E. Denison Ross: "The Portuguese in India
    and Arabia between 1507 and 1517," *Journal of the Royal
    Asiatic Society*, 1921, pp. 545-62; "The Portuguese in India and
    Arabia, 1517-38," *Journal of the Royal Asiatic Society*, 1922,
    pp. 1-18.

7.  M.A. Muid Khan, "Indo-Portuguese Struggle for Maritime
    Supremacy (As gleaned from an Unpublished Arabic *Urjuza:
    Fathul Mubiyn*)," in P.M. Joshi and M.A. Nayeem, eds., *Studies
    in the Foreign Relations of India (From Earliest Times to 1947)
    Prof. H.K. Sherwani Felicitation Volume*, Hyderabad, 1975, pp.
    172, 176 [stanzas 90 and 278].

8.  Malik Ayaz, however, did not give up easily. In 1518 he was still
    so concerned with the Portuguese threat to the *hajj* that he
    wrote to the Ottoman sultan stressing the need for a joint offen-
    sive against them from Gujarat and the Ottomans. Naimur
    Rahman Farooqi, *Mughal-Ottoman Relations* (A Study of
    Political and Diplomatic Relations between Mughal India and
    the Ottoman Empire, 1556-1748), Delhi, 1989, pp. 12-13.

9.  Barros, II, pp. ii, 6.

10. See Farooqi, *Mughal-Ottoman Relations*, chapter 4, "The
    Problem of the Hajj Traffic: Mughal Response and Ottoman
    Reaction," pp. 144-72, for a discussion of Ottoman and Mughal
    relations with the Portuguese. While this chapter does well in
    its use of Ottoman records, it greatly exaggerates the actual
    impact of the Portuguese, and also, ironically, suffers from its
    failure to use Portuguese records.

11. Gaury, p. 124. For more detail on events consequent on the
    Ottoman conquest of Egypt, see Jean-Louis Bacqué-Grammont
    and Anne Kroell, *Mamlouks, Ottomans et Portugais en Mer
    Rouge*, pp. 17-18, and 74, f.n. 25. There is some variation in the
    details here. For example, Barakat's dates are given as 1497-

1525. This book is a detailed account of an attack on Jiddah, a farcical failure, by the Portuguese governor Lopo Soares, in April 1517, thus coinciding with the Ottoman conquest of the overlords of the Hijaz, the Mamluks.

12. Suraiya Faroqhi, *Herrscher über Mekka: Die Geschichte der Pilgerfahrt*, Munich, 1990, passim.

13. Carsten Niebuhr, *Travels through Arabia and other Countries in the East*, trans. Robert Heron, 2 vols, Edinburgh, 1792, II, p. 27. For an excellent modern discussion of Ottoman concern with the *hajj* in the eighteenth century, see Karl K. Barbir, *Ottoman Rule in Damascus, 1708-1758*, Princeton, 1980, pp. 108-77; for their comparable concern for the Cairo caravan see Stanford J. Shaw, *The Financial and Administrative Organization and Development of Ottoman Egypt, 1517-1798*, Princeton, 1962, pp. 239-71; and for excellent general accounts see Peters, *Jerusalem and Mecca,* pp. 199-206, and de Gaury, *Rulers of Mecca*, pp. 129-32.

14. Shaw, pp. 261-8.

15. Salih Ozbaran, "A Turkish Report on the Red Sea and the Portuguese in the Indian Ocean (1525)," *Arabian Studies*, IV, 1978, pp. 81-88, and for a fuller version see Michel Lesure, "Un document Ottoman de 1525 sur l'Inde portugaise et les pays de la Mer Rouge," *Mare Luso-Indicum*, III, 1976, pp. 137-60. See also Andrew C. Hess, "Piri Reis and the Ottoman Response to the Voyages of Discovery," *Terrae Incognitae*, VI, 1974, p. 22.

16. Diogo do Couto, *Da Asia*, Lisbon, 1778-88, V, pp. ii, 9.

17. Couto, V, ii, p. 7. For a sketchy account of relations between Gujarat and Turkey up to the 1550s, see Ghulam Muhammad Nizamuddin Maghrebi, "The Ottoman-Gujrat Relations (1517-1556)," in P.M. Joshi and M.A. Nayeem, eds., *Studies in the Foreign Relations of India (From Earliest Times to 1947) Prof. H.K. Sherwani Felicitation Volume*, Hyderabad, 1975, pp. 184-93. For the lead-up to the 1538 expedition, from the Ottoman side, see Salih Ozbaran, "The Ottomans in confrontation with the Portuguese in the Red Sea after the conquest of Egypt in 1517," *Studies on Turkish-Arab Relations*, Annual, 1986, Istanbul, 1986, pp. 207-14. He stresses the economic angle, seeing the Ottoman annoyance as mostly to do with the way the Portuguese had blocked trade to the Red Sea.

18. Fernão Mendes Pinto, *The Travels of Mendes Pinto*, ed. and trans. Rebecca D. Catz, Chicago, 1989, p. 37.
19. Muhammad Yakub Mughul, "The Expedition of Suleyman Pasha Al-Khadim to India (1538)," *Journal of the Regional Cultural Institute*, Tehran, II, 1969, p. 147.
20. Haji Khalifeh, *The History of the Maritime Wars of the Turks*, trans. James Mitchell, London, 1831, p. 66. He had only 40 days to wait until the beginning of Dhu al-Hijja.
21. Archivo Nacional da Torre do Tombo, Lisbon, "Corpo Chronologico," 3-14-44 [hereafter ANTTCC]. See also Hess, "Piri Reis," pp. 27-9. For an informed discussion of the rival merits of Turkish galleys as opposed to Iberian warships, see John Francis Guilmartin, *Gunpowder and Galleys: Changing Technology and Mediterranean Warfare at Sea in the Sixteenth Century*, Cambridge, 1974, especially pp. 7-15; 257-9.
22. al-Badaoni, *Muntakhabu-t-tawarikh,* trans. G. Ranking et al., Patna, 1973, 3 vols, I, pp. 480-1.
23. Farooqi, *Mughal-Ottoman Relations,* pp. 157-8.
24. Guilmartin, pp. 20, 259.
25. See Elaine Sanceau, "Uma Narrativa da Expedição Portuguesa de 1541 ao Mar Roxo," *Studia*, IX, 1962, pp. 199-234 [letter of D. Manuel de Lima to King, Goa, 18 Nov 1541]; the quotation is from pp. 225-6. According to Hess, in this same year the Portuguese proposed a truce to the Ottomans, which offer was rejected: Hess, "Piri Reis," p. 28.
26. Salih Ozbaran, "The Ottoman Turks and the Portuguese in the Persian Gulf, 1534-1581," *Journal of Asian History*, VI, 1, 1972, pp. 72, 73. See also on this matter the following very detailed study: Luís de Albuquerque, *Alguns Aspectos de Ameaça Turca sobre a India por meados do século XVI*, Coimbra, 1977 [sep from *Biblos*, LIII, 1977].
27. *Ibid., passim*; for detail on these incidents in the Portuguese records see Couto, VI, pp. ix, 3, 4, 14, 15 for 1550 events; VI, pp. x, 1-5, 10, 13 for the ill-fated "Pirbec," that is Piri Reis; VI, pp. x, 20 for another Ottoman attack in 1553; more skirmishes in the 1550s in VII, pp. i, 5; VII, pp. vii, 7-11, and for the 1580s X, pp. i, 11-13; X, pp. ii, 11-14. See also Hess, "Piri Reis," pp. 29-30.
28. Thus Ozbaran's generally excellent account in this article uses

only the shorter, published, version of Couto's *Decada* VIII, cap. 5, while Hess's account in "Piri Reis," p. 35 is based largely on Ozbaran.

29. M. Augusta Lima Cruz, "The 8th Decada of Diogo do Couto's Asia,", International Seminar on Indo-Portuguese History III, Goa, 1983, typescript, pp. 6-7, and see also Lima Cruz, "Década 8 da Asia de Diogo do Couto—informação sobre uma versão inédita," *Arquipelago*, Ponta Delgada, 1984, pp. 159-60 and Lima Cruz, "Para uma edição crítica da Década VIII de Diogo do Couto," *Arquivos do Centro Cultural Português*, Paris, 1982, pp. 93-114.

30. Ozbaran, "Ottoman Turks and the Portuguese," pp. 82-4.

31. Quoted in Farooqi, *Mughal-Ottoman Relations,* p. 144.

32. Farooqi, pp. 156-7.

33. See Hess, "Piri Reis," p. 35.

34. *Documentos remettidos da India, ou Livros das Monções*, ed. R.A. de Bulhão Pato, Lisbon, 1880-1935, 5 vols, I, p. 29, king to viceroy, March 6, 1605.

35. Riazul Islam, ed., *A Calendar of Documents on Indo-Persian Relations (1500-1750)*, Tehran and Karachi, 1979-82, 2 vols., II, p. 238; Riazul Islam, *Indo-Persian Relations. A Study of the Political and Diplomatic Relations between the Mughul Empire and Iran*, Teheran, 1970, p. 50.

36. Sidi Ali Reis, *The Travels and Adventures of the Turkish Admiral Sidi Ali Reis in India, Afghanistan, Central Asia and Persia during the years 1553-1556*, trans. A. Vambéry, London, 1899, pp. 86, 91, 97-9.

37. Muhammad Mujeeb, *The Indian Muslims*, London, 1967, p. 240 and f.n.; Islam, *Documents*, II, p. 238.

38. Norman Daniel, *Islam and the West the making of an image*, Edinburgh, 1960, and also of course more generally see Edward Said, *Orientalism*, London, 1978.

39. Castanheda, III, cxxiv.

40. Muid Khan, op. cit., pp. 171, 178, stanzas 54-59, 325-6, 330-41.

41. *Documenta Indica*, ed. J. Wicki et al, Rome, 1948- , 16 vols to date, to 1594, XV, p. 163.

42. *Bullarium Patronatus Portugalliae Regum in Ecclesiis Africae, Asiae atque Oceaniae*, ed. Vicecomite de Paiva Manso, I, Appendix, Concilia Provincialia Ecclesiae Goanensis, Lisbon,

1872, p. 13.

43. *Ibid.*, p. 14.

44. *Bullarium*, p. 66.

45. See *Documenta Indica*, XV, pp. 710, 741-2 for two slightly conflicting accounts of this matter, and vol. XVI *passim*.

46. See *Archivo Português Oriental*, ed. J.H. da Cunha Rivara, Nova Goa, 1857-77, 6 vols, III, p. 585.

47. Castanheda, II, lvii. "hu moçafo, qhe era hu liuro do alcorão do Mafamede, qhe foy aualiado e dozentos pardões." For "moçafo" see S.R. Dalgado, *Glossário Luso-Asiatico*, Coímbra, 1919-21, 2 vols, s.v.

48. *Ibid.*, III, lxxv.

49. Gaspar Correa, *Lendas de India*, Coimbra, 1921-31, Lisbon, 1969, 4 vols, III, pp. 476-9; Castanheda, VIII, caps. l, lxvii.

50. Castanheda, III, cxxxvi.

51. *Documenta Indica*, IV, p. 492. These figures seem to be quite fabulous, and designed merely for effect; nevertheless, the general point holds good.

52. Farooqi in *Mughal-Ottoman Relations* fails to discriminate in this way.

53. *Annaes Maritimos e Coloniaes*, Lisbon, 1840-46, 6 vols., V, p. 216.

54. Marechal Gomes da Costa, *Descobrimentos e Conquistas*, Lisbon, 1927-30, 3 vols., II, p. 110.

55. Castanheda, II, p. xvii.

56. Castanheda, II, p. xxxix.

57. *As Gavetas da Torre do Tombo*, Lisbon, 1960-75, 12 vols., IV, p. 82, 387-8; Barros, III, p. ix, 7.

58. ANTTCC, 1-33-3.

59. Castanheda, VII, p. xc.

60. See Hess, "Piri Reis," pp. 27-9.

61. For example, Barros, IV, pp. ii, 10; Castanheda, VIII, pp. xliii; Couto, V, pp. ii, 7.

62. British Library, Additional MSS 28433, ff. 174-5v; see also the treaty of 1535 with Bahadur in Couto, IV, pp. ix, 8.

63. See the case in 1538 in Couto, V, pp. ii, 8.

64. *Studia*, no. 10, p. 184.

65. ANTTCC, 1-62-154.

66. Correa, IV, p. 237.

67. ANTTCC, 1-81-93.
68. *Documenta Indica*, III, pp. 651, 712; IV, p. 427; V, pp. 263, 754.
69. Couto, *Soldado Pratico*, p. 83.
70. Jean Mocquet, *Voyages en Afrique, Asie, Indes Orientales et Occidentales*, Rouen, 1630, pp. 280-1.
71. D. João de Castro, *Cartas*, ed. Elaine Sanceau, Lisbon, 1954, pp. 227-30, 251, 257.
72. ANTTCC, 1-94-94.
73. Sanjay Subrahmanyam, "Persians, Pilgrims and Portuguese: the Travails of Masulipatnam Shipping in the Western Indian Ocean, 1590-1665," *Modern Asian Studies*, XXII, 3, 1988, pp. 503-30.
74. Vitorino Magalhães Godinho, *Les finances de l'état portugais des Indes Orientales, 1517-1635*, Paris, 1982, pp. 80, 146.
75. Bulhão Pato, ed., II, p. 290.
76. K.S. Mathew, "Indian Merchants and the Portuguese Trade on the Malabar Coast during the sixteenth century," Teotonio de Souza, ed., *Indo-Portuguese History: Old Issues, New Questions*, New Delhi, 1985, pp. 5-6, 10.
77. Archivo Nacional da Torre do Tombo, Lisbon, "Colecção da São Lourenço," III, ff. 160, 180.
78. Mathew, *op. cit.*; see also Silva Rego, ed., *Documentação*, X, p. 157.
79. Fernão Guerreiro, *Relação Annual das coisas que fizeram os Padres da Companhia de Jesus nas suas Missões*, ed. Artur Viegas, Coìmbra, 1930-31, Lisbon, 1942, 3 vols., II, p. 390; Couto, X, p. vii, 7; XII, pp. i, 7; XII, pp. iii, 10; Cunha Rivara, III, pp. 682-3.
80. Bulhão Pato, ed., I, p. 36.
81. Archivum Romanum S.I., Rome, Provincia Goana et Malabarica, Cartas etc., vol. XV, f. 18.
82. Couto, IX, cap. p. 13.
83. See *ibid.*; Arquivo Historico Ultramarino, India, caixa 3, no. 4; Guerreiro, II, pp. 389-90; *Documentos remettidos da India, ou Livros das Monções*, ed. R.A. de Bulhão Pato, Lisbon, 1880-1935, 5 vols., III, pp. 162-3.
84. Abul Fazl, *Akbar Nama*, trans. H. Beveridge, Delhi, 1972-3, 3 vols., III, pp. 409-10, 757-8.

## Chapter 5  (Pages 105-122)

1. al-Badaoni, *Muntakhabu-t-tawarikh*, trans. G. Ranking et al., Patna, 1973, 3 vols., I, p. 51.
2. Babur, *Babur Nama*, trans. A. Beveridge, New Delhi, 1970, pp. 228 and f.n.; 522-3.
3. S.A.I. Tirmizi, *Some Aspects of Medieval Gujarat*, Delhi, 1968, p. 11; *A Comprehensive History of India*, vol. V, The Delhi Sultanat, Delhi, 1970, pp. 887-8.
4. Jadunath Sarkar, *History of Aurangzeb*, Calcutta, 1973-4, 5 vols., V, p. 363.
5. Sikandar, *The Mirat-i-Sikandari,* Persian text ed. S.C. Misra, Baroda, 1961, p. 219.
6. Fazlullah Lutfullah Faridi, trans., *Mirati Sikandari.* Dharampur, n.d., p. 126.
7. Tirmizi, p. 11.
8. J.F. Richards, ed., *Precious Metals in the Late Medieval and Early Modern Worlds*, Durham, N.C., 1983, p. 202.
9. W.H. Moreland, ed., *Relations of Golconda in the Early Seventeenth Century*, London, Hakluyt, 1931, p. 37.
10. Abul Fazl, *Akbar Nama*, trans. H. Beveridge, Delhi, 1972-3, 3 vols., III, pp. 275-7. See also Naimur Rahman Farooqi, *Mughal-Ottoman Relations* (A Study of Political and Diplomatic Relations between Mughal India and the Ottoman Empire, 1556-1748), Delhi, 1989, pp. 19, 113-6.
11. Khwajah Nizamuddin Ahmad, *The Tabaqat-i-Akbari*, trans. B. De., Calcutta, 1911-40, 3 vols., II, pp. 472-3.
12. Farooqi, *Mughal-Ottoman Relations,* p. 115.
13. al-Badaoni, *Muntakhabu-t-tawarikh*, II, pp. 216-7.
14. Gulbadan Begam, *The History of Humayun,* trans. A. Beveridge, Delhi, 1972, pp. 69-75.
15. Riazul Islam, ed., *A Calendar of Documents on Indo-Persian Relations (1500-1750)*, Tehran and Karachi, 1979-82, 2 vols., II, pp. 155-6.
16. Niccolao Manucci, *Storia do Mogor*, trans. W. Irvine, London, 1905-7, 4 vols, II, p. 300. Suraiya Faroqhi, *Herrscher über Mekka: Die Geschichte der Pilgerfahrt*, Munich, 1990, pp. 205-6, notes a ship owned by the Queen Mother of Bijapur, possibly the same one, carrying 1500 pilgrim passengers.

17. William Foster, ed., *The English Factories in India, 1618-1669*, Oxford, 1906-27, 13 vols., 1661-4, p. 88 f.n.; R.B. Serjeant, *The Portuguese off the South Arabian Coast*, Oxford, 1963, pp. 120-1.

18. Historical Archives of Goa, "Livro da Fazenda," X, f. 131.

19. J.-B. Tavernier, *Travels in India*, ed. V. Ball and W. Crooke, New Delhi, 1977, 2 vols., I, p. 148. He visited Ispahan several times, but 1664-5 seems to be the most likely time for him to have seen her.

20. *Akbar-Nama*, II, pp. 534-5 and f.n.

21. *Ibid.*, III, p. 9.

22. Badaoni, II, pp. 275, 283.

23. *Comprehensive History,* p. 979.

24. Bamber Gascoigne, *The Great Moghuls*, London, 1971, pp. 64-5; Gulbadan, pp. 41, 49.

25. I.A. Khan, *The Political Biography of a Mughal Noble*, New Delhi, 1973, p. 65, f.n.

26. S.A.A. Rizvi, *A History of Sufism in India*, New Delhi, 1978-83, 2 vols., II, p. 321, and see pp. 266, 338-9, 372 for other examples.

27. S.A.A. Rizvi, *Muslim Revivalist Movements in Northern India in the Sixteenth and Seventeenth Centuries*, Agra, 1965, p. 394.

28. I.A. Khan, *Political Biography*, pp. 70-1.

29. Khafi Khan, *Khafi Khan's History of Alamgir*, trans. S. Moinul Haq, Karachi, 1975, p. 393.

30. Ishwardas Nagar, *Futuhat-i-Alamgiri*, trans. and ed. Tasneem Ahmad, Delhi, 1978, pp. 94, 116.

31. Nawwab Samsam-ud-daula Shah Nawaz Khan, *The Maathir-ul-Umara*, trans. H. Beveridge, ed. Baini Prashad, Patna, 1979, 2 vols., II, pp. 891-3.

32. Jahangir, *The Tuzuk-i Jahangiri*, trans. A. Rogers, ed. H. Beveridge, New Delhi, 1968, 2 vols., II, p. 213.

33. *Ibid*, II, p. 217.

34. William Foster, ed., *The English Factories*, 1622-23, p. 273 f.n.; 1634-36, pp. xv, xxv, 99.

35. *Maathir-ul-Umara*, II, pp. 662-3.

36. *Cambridge History of India*, vol. IV, The Mughul Period, Delhi, 1963, pp. 331, 341; Hajji ad-dabir, *An Arabic History of Gujarat*,

trans. M.F. Lokhandwalla, Baroda, 1970-74, 2 vols., Introduction, p. xix.

37. R.C. Majumdar, ed., *History and Culture of the Indian People; the Mughul Empire*, Bombay, 1974, p. 142.

38. Manucci, I, pp. 370, 374.

39. *Maathir-ul-Umara*, II, pp. 58-9.

40. Gerald de Gaury, *Rulers of Mecca*, London, 1951, p. 107.

41. *Ain*, I, pp. 467, 284; *Akbar Nama*, III, pp. 271-2. I am at a loss to explain this and other examples of the distribution of *khilats*, for normally these signified by their reception an acknowledgement of vassaldom or clientage vis à vis the bestower. For general Mughal relations with the Sharifs see Farooqi, *Mughal-Ottoman Relations*, pp. 107-43.

42. Abul Fazl, *Ain-i Akbari*, trans. H. Blochmann et al., New Delhi, 1977-78, 3 vols., I, p. 345.

43. Badaoni, II, p. 412; S.A.A. Rizvi, *Religious and Intellectual History of the Muslims in Akbar's Reign*, New Delhi, 1975, p. 199.

44. Farooqi, *Mughal-Ottoman Relations*, p. 144.

45. Ibid., pp. 153-4.

46. Ibid., pp. 161-2.

47. Sarkar, *Aurangzeb*, III, p. 67; Manucci, II, p. 3; according to Saqi Must'ad Khan, *Maasir-i-Alamgiri*, trans. J.N. Sarkar, Calcutta, 1947, p. 17, the articles of 1659 were worth Rs.6,30,000. See Farooqi, *Mughal-Ottoman Relations*, pp. 57-69 for Aurangzeb's diplomatic relations with the Ottomans and other powers.

48. *Cambridge History of India*, IV, p. 229.

49. Yet we may note that in 1662 the Shah of Persia sent presents worth only Rs.4,22,000 and Aurangzeb replied to this major ruler with only Rs.5,35,000; see *Maasir*, pp. 17, 22.

50. *Cambridge History of India*, IV, p. 229.

51. Manucci, II, pp. 114-5 and f.n.; *Maasir*, p. 32.

52. François Bernier, *Travels in the Mogul Empire*, ed. A. Constable and V.A. Smith, London, 1914, pp. 133-4. The echoes of the Chinese tribute system are obvious!

53. *Maasir,* pp. 48, 67, 87, 166.

54. *Cambridge History of India*, IV, p. 229; Sarkar, *History of*

*Aurangzeb*, III, pp. 67-8.

55. B. Schrieke, *Indonesian Sociological Studies*, The Hague, 1955-57, 2 vols, II, pp. 249-50.
56. Willem Floor, "A Report of the Trade of Jedda in the 1730s," *Moyen Orient & Océan Indien*, V, 1988, p. 162.
57. Manucci, I, p. 116.
58. Badaoni, I, pp. 480-1.
59. Sikandar, *Mirat*, Persian text, p. 219.
60. Sanjay Subrahmanyam, "Persians, Pilgrims and Portuguese: the Travails of Masulipatnam Shipping in the Western Indian Ocean, 1590-1665," *Modern Asian Studies*, XXII, 3, 1988, pp. 505-6.
61. Ibid., p. 505.
62. *Akbar Nama*, III, pp. 275-7, 409-10, 757-8.
63. *Arabic History*, introduction, p. xvii.
64. B.G. Gokhale, *Surat in the Seventeenth Century*, London, 1979, p. 68.
65. Ashin Das Gupta, *Indian Merchants and the Decline of Surat, c.1700-1750*, Wiesbaden, 1979, pp. 28, 128.
66. Aziz Ahmad, *Studies in Islamic Culture in the Indian Environment*, Oxford, 1964, pp. 26, 29-30.
67. *Tabaqat*, II, pp. 472-3.
68. Badaoni, II, p. 217.
69. *Ibid*, II, p. 246.
70. *Akbar Nama*, III, 306; *Maathir-ul-Umara*, I, p. 143.
71. Badaoni, II, pp. 275, 293.
72. C.R. Naik, "Abdu-r-Rahim, Khan-i-Khanan," MA thesis, University of Bombay, n.d., p. 203; Saris in Samuel Purchas, *Purchas, His Pilgrimes*, Glasgow, Hakluyt, 1905-7, 20 vols, III, 396; also see Middleton in *ibid.*, pp. 190-3; Sadashiv Gorakshkar, "An Illustrated *Anis al-Haj* in the Prince of Wales Museum, Bombay," in Robert Skelton, et al, eds, *Facets of Indian Art*, London, V and A Museum, 1986, p. 161. Gorakshkar also claims [ibid., p. 159] that Akbar provided a fleet of 100 ships, called *Jahaz-i ilahi*, for pilgrims, but I can find no evidence for this, which would have been truly massive patronage.
73. S.R. Sharma, *The Religious Policies of the Mughal Emperors*,

3rd. ed., New York, 1972, p. 106.

74. Manucci, II, p. 45.

75. J.-B. Tavernier, *Travels in India*, II, p. 281.

76. Ashin Das Gupta, "Gujarati Merchants and the Red Sea Trade, 1700-1725," in B.B. Kling and M.N. Pearson, eds., *The Age of Partnership.*, Honolulu, 1979, pp. 125-6.

77. John Fryer, *A New Account of East India and Persia*, London, Hakluyt, 1909-15, 3 vols., I, p. 267.

78. Sadashiv Gorakshkar, "Anis al-Haj," in Karl Khandalavala, ed., *An Age of Splendour: Islamic Art in India*, Bombay, 1983, p. 132.

# Chapter 6 (Pages 123-138)

1. Vitorino Magalhães Godinho, *Os descobrimentos e a economia mundial*, 2nd. ed., Lisbon, 1981-83, 4 vols., II, p. 223.

2. Mohammed Marmaduke Pickthall, trans., *The Meaning of the Glorious Koran*, New York, n.d., LXII, pp. 9-11, my emphasis.

3. *The Encyclopedia of Religion*, ed. Mircea Eliade, vol. XI, New York, 1987, s.v. "pilgrimage," pp. 327-54. The quotation from Richard Martin is on p. 340.

4. Clifford R. Geertz, *Islam Observed, Religious Development in Morocco and Indonesia*, Chicago, 1968, p. 68.

5. Pickthall, *Glorious Koran*, XXX, p. 46; XVII, p. 66; XLV, p. 12.

6. R.B. Serjeant, *The Portuguese off the South Arabian Coast*, Oxford, 1963, p. 5.

7. S.D. Goitein, *Studies in Islamic History and Institutions*, Leiden, 1966, p. 8; cf. S.D. Goitein, *A Mediterranean Society*, Berkeley, 1967-78, 3 vols., I, p. 55.

8. Goitein, *Studies,* pp. 123-4.

9. Karl K. Barbir, *Ottoman Rule in Damascus, 1708-1758*, Princeton, 1980, pp. 163-6.

10. Tenreiro in António Baião, ed., *Itinerarios da India a Portugal por terra*, Coimbra, 1923, pp. 83-4.

11. F.E. Peters, *Jerusalem and Mecca: The Typology of the Holy city in the Near East* (New York University Studies in Near Eastern Civilization, Number XI), New York, 1986, p. 48; H.A.R. Gibb and Harold Bowen, *Islamic Society and the West*, vol. I, 2 parts,

Oxford, 1950-7, I, p. 302.

12. William Foster, ed., *The Red Sea and Adjacent Countries at the Close of the Seventeenth Century*, London, Hakluyt, 1949, p. 158; Ludovico di Varthema, *The Itinerary of Ludovico di Varthema of Bologna from 1502-1508*, ed. Sir Richard Carnac Temple, London, 1928, p. 12.

13. Francis Gladwin, trans, *The Memoirs of Khojeh Abdulkurreem* (of Kashmir), Calcutta, 1788, pp. 135-6.

14. Henry Rooke, *Travels to the Coast of Arabia Felix and from thence by the Red-Sea and Egypt to Europe*, London, 1783, p. 38.

15. Henry Bigot, "Les strophes du pèlerin de Puey Monçon (Voyage à la Mecque à la fin du XVIe siècle) avec préface, traduction et commentaire," *Revue Tunisienne*, 1916, pp. 98-9.

16. Anon., "A Description of the yeerely voyage or pilgrimage of the Mahumitans, Turkes and Moores unto Mecca in Arabia," in Richard Hakluyt, *The Principal Navigations,* Glasgow, 1903-5, 12 vols, V, p. 340.

17. Varthema, *Itinerary*, p. 19.

18. Julien Claude Galland, *Recueil des rites et cérémonies du pèlerinage de la Mecque; auquel on a joint divers écrits relatifs à la religion, aux sciences & aux moeurs des Turcs*, Amsterdam, 1754, p. 11, f.n.

19. Muhammad ibn Ahmad ibn Jubair, *The Travels of Ibn Jubayr (1183-1185 AC),* trans. R.J.C. Broadhurst, London, 1952, pp. 55-6, 57-8, 59, 72-3, etc.

20. João de Barros, *Da Asia,* Lisbon, 1778-88, I, pp. viii, 1.

21. Dutch letter of February 20, 1649, quoted in Philip Baldaeus, *A True and Exact Description of the Most Celebrated East-Indian Coasts of Malabar and Coromandel as also of the Isle of Ceylon . . .* , in Churchill, *A Collection of Voyages and Travels*, 3rd ed., vol. III, London, 1745, p. 516.

22. Carsten Niebuhr, *Travels through Arabia and other Countries in the East*, trans. Robert Heron, 2 vols, Edinburgh, 1792, II, p. 37.

23. Comte de Modave, *Voyage en Inde du Comte de Modave, 1773-1776*, ed. Jean Deloche, Paris, 1971, p. 350.

24. Abdullah Ankawi, "The Pilgrimage to Mecca in Mamluk Times," *Arabian Studies,* I, 1974, p. 150.

25. Anon., in Hakluyt, V, pp. 340, 342, 346, my emphasis.
26. John Fullerton, "Commonplace Book," MS, English, c. 1727 [Bell Library, University of Minnesota, 1727 f Fu] Includes Memorandum of 1727, and Daily Journal, Jiddah, Tuesday July 23, 1728, of EIC people there. This quotation is from "Miscellaneous Transactions and Memoranda: of Judda, 1727."
27. Foster, ed., *Red Sea*, p. 158.
28. William Foster, ed., *The English Factories in India, 1618-1669*, Oxford, 1906-27, 13 vols., 1637-41, p. 277.
29. Eyles Irwin, *A Series of Adventures in the Course of a Voyage up the Red Sea . . . in the Year MDCCLXXVII*, London, 1780, pp. 58-9.
30. Gibb and Bowen, I, pp. 301-2.
31. Serjeant, p. 115.
32. *English Factories*, 1637-41, p. 303.
33. Sanjay Subrahmanyam, "Persians, Pilgrims and Portuguese: the Travails of Masulipatnam Shipping in the Western Indian Ocean, 1590-1665," *Modern Asian Studies*, XXII, 3, 1988, p. 509.
34. J.F. Richards, ed., *Precious Metals in the Late Medieval and Early Modern Worlds*, Durham, N.C., 1983, p. 202; W.H. Moreland, *India at the Death of Akbar: An Economic Study*, Delhi, 1974, p. 205.
35. Niebuhr, I, p. 237.
36. William Foster, ed., *Early Travels in India*, Delhi, 1968, p. 301.
37. John Ovington, *A Voyage to Surat in the Year 1689*, ed. H.G. Rawlinson, London, 1929, p. 275.
38. Ibn Jubayr, p. 31.
39. Ibn Battuta, *The Travels of Ibn Battuta,* trans. H.A.R. Gibb, Cambridge, Hakluyt, 1958-71, 3 vols., vol. I *passim*.
40. Ibn Jubayr, pp. 191-3.
41. Foster, ed., *Red Sea*, pp. 3, 5, 19, 44.
42. Ankawi, "The Pilgrimage to Mecca," pp. 146-8.
43. Mulla Safi-ud din Qazwini, "Anis-ul hujjaj, " trans. A. Jan Qaisar and Z. Islam, 71 pp. typescript, pp. 10-11, 11-15.
44. Niels Steensgaard, *The Asian Trade Revolution of the Seventeenth Century*, Chicago, 1974, generally for overland trade.

45. G. Levi Della Vida, "A Portuguese Pilgrim to Mecca in the Sixteenth Century," *Muslim World*, XXXII, 1942, pp. 288-9.
46. John Henry Grose, *A Voyage to the East Indies . . . to which is added A Journey from Aleppo to Busserah, over the Desert, by Mr. Charmichael* [lst French ed, 1758, lst English ed 1766, 2nd Eng ed 1772, which adds Charmichael] 2nd ed., 2 vols, London, 1772. This description is by Charmichael, which appears in vol. I, Appendix, pp. 1-53. The quotation is on p. 4.
47. *Documentação Ultramarina Portuguesa*, Lisbon, 1960-67, 5 vols, I, p. 7.
48. *As Gavetas da Torre do Tombo*, Lisbon, 1960-75, 12 vols., IV, p. 97.
49. A. Botelho da Costa Veiga, *Relação das plantas e descrições de todas as fortalezas, cidades e povoações que os Portugueses tem no Estado da India Oriental*, Lisbon, 1936, p. 16.
50. Poncet in Foster, ed., *The Red Sea*, p. 157.
51. Samuel Purchas, *Purchas, His Pilgrimes*, Glasgow, Hakluyt, 1905-7, 20 vols, III, pp. 152-5.
52. Modave, p. 342; this French traveler had a pronounced liking for the multiplication table.

## Chapter 7 (Pages 139-166)

1. Ashin Das Gupta, "Gujarati Merchants and the Red Sea Trade, 1700-1725," in B.B. Kling and M.N. Pearson, eds., *The Age of Partnership*, Honolulu, 1979, p. 124 and f.n. 24.
2. *Ibid.*, pp. 123, 136, and cf. 137.
3. *Ibid.*, pp. 135-6.
4. Ashin Das Gupta, "Indian Merchants and the Trade in the Indian Ocean," *Cambridge Economic History of India*, vol. I, Cambridge, 1982, p. 430.
5. *Ibid.*, p. 426.
6. *Ibid.*, p. 424.
7. Ashin Das Gupta, *Indian Merchants and the Decline of Surat, c.1700-1750*, Wiesbaden, 1979, pp. 68-9.
8. Ashin Das Gupta, "Introduction II: The Story," in Ashin Das Gupta and M.N. Pearson, eds., *India and the Indian Ocean, 1500-1800*, Calcutta, 1987, pp. 25, 27.

9. It was disturbing to read in Professor Wink's recent book on Islam that the *hajj* "usually coincided with the south-west monsoon". André Wink, *Al-Hind: The Making of the Indo-Islamic World Vol. I, Early Medieval India and the Expansion of Islam, 7th-11th Centuries* (Leiden, 1990), p. 33.

10. *The Voyage of François Pyrard of Laval to the East Indies, the Maldives, the Moluccas and Brazil*, trans. and ed. Albert Gray, London, Hakluyt, 1887-90, 2 vols, I, p. 134.

11. Julien Claude Galland, *Recueil des rites et cérémonies du pèlerinage de la Mecque; auquel on a joint divers écrits relatifs à la religion, aux sciences & aux moeurs des Turcs*, Amsterdam, 1754, p. 25, f.n.

12. William Foster, ed., *The Red Sea and Adjacent Countries at the Close of the Seventeenth Century*, London, Hakluyt, 1949, p. 107.

13. Elaine Sanceau, "Uma Narrativa da Expedição Portuguesa de 1541 ao Mar Roxo," *Studia*, IX, 1962, pp. 199-234 [letter of D. Manuel de Lima to King, Goa, 18 Nov 1541]. The account is from pp. 226-7.

14. Colonel James Capper, *Observations on the Passage to India through Egypt and across the Great Desert . . .* , 2nd ed., London, 1784, p. vi.

15. Henry Rooke, *Travels to the Coast of Arabia Felix and from thence by the Red-Sea and Egypt to Europe*, London, 1783, p. 63.

16. M. Lesourd, "Notes sur les Nawakid, Navigateurs de la Mer Rouge," *Bulletin de l'Institut Français d'Afrique Noire*, Série B, Dakar, vol. XX, 1960, pp. 346-355, especially pp. 349-50.

17. G. Bouchon, "Un microcosme: Calicut au 16e siècle," in Denys Lombard and Jean Aubin, eds, *Marchands et hommes d'affairs asiatiques dans l'Océan Indien et la Mer de Chine 13e-20e siècles*, Paris, 1988, p. 53.

18. Fernão Lopes de Castanheda, *História do descobrimento e conquista da India pelos Portugueses*, 3rd. ed., Coímbra, 1924-33, 9 vols, VIII, p. xiii.

19. William Foster, ed., *Early Travels in India*, Delhi, 1968, pp. 301-2.

20. Mandelslo in Adam Olearius, *The Voyages & travels of the ambassaddors sent by Frederick duke of Holstein to the great*

*Duke of Muscovy, and the King of Persia. Began in the year MDCXXXIII and finish'd in MDCXXXIX* . . . , trans. John Davies, London, 1662, p. 87. For an exact plagiarism of this account, admittedly in a compilation, see John Ogilby, *Asia, the first part, Being an accurate description of Persia, and the several provinces thereof. The vast empire of the Great Mogol, and other parts of India* . . . , [collected and translated from most authentic authors], London, 1673, p. 223.

21. Philip Baldaeus, *A True and Exact Description of the Most Celebrated East-Indian Coasts of Malabar and Coromandel as also of the Isle of Ceylon* . . . , in Churchill, *A Collection of Voyages and Travels*, 3rd ed., vol. III, London, 1745, pp. 510-793. This account is from p. 520.

22. John Ovington, *A Voyage to Surat in the Year 1689*, ed. H.G. Rawlinson, London, 1929, p. 261.

23. C.F. Beckingham, *Between Islam and Christendom. Travellers, Facts and Legends in the Middle Ages and the Renaissance*, London, 1983, "Dutch Travellers," pp. 79-81.

24. Mulla Safi-ud din Qazwini, "Anis-ul hujjaj, "trans. A. Jan Qaisar and Z. Islam, 71 pp. typescript, [Qazvini], pp. 55-6.

25. Pedro Barreto de Rezende, "Descripçoens das cidades e fortalezas da India Oriental," 2 vols, Biblioteca da Academia das Sciencias, Lisbon, Mss. Azuis, pp. 267-8, I, ff. 60-60v; 67.

26. W.H. Moreland, ed., *Relations of Golconda in the Early Seventeenth Century*, London, Hakluyt, 1931, pp. 37, 61.

27. G.R. Tibbetts, *Arab Navigation in the Indian Ocean before the Coming of the Portuguese,* London, 1971, p. 231, and cf. p. 375 for a gloss by Tibbetts on the dictatorship of the monsoons.

28. Willem Floor, "A Report of the Trade of Jedda in the 1730s," *Moyen Orient & Océan Indien*, V, 1988, p. 173. We should stress that this is an example of trade destined for Mecca, not Jiddah.

29. Floor's account mentions "pedlars and retailers" in Jiddah who dealt with European merchants. These are of course not agents, and in any case his account is not based on first hand experience, and at times is internally contradictory: cf. p. 165.

30. Pyrard, I, p. 143.

31. Xavier de Planhol, *The World of Islam*, Ithaca, 1959, p. 72.

32. John Fullerton, "Commonplace Book," MS, English, c. 1727

[Bell Library, University of Minnesota, 1727 f Fu] Includes Memorandum of 1727, and Daily Journal, Jiddah, Tuesday July 23, 1728, of EIC people there. This account is from the Daily Journal, dated 23 July, 1728.

33. Ashin Das Gupta, "Introduction II: The Story," in Das Gupta and Pearson, eds., *India and the Indian Ocean*, p. 34; Das Gupta, *Indian Merchants and the Decline of Surat*, p. 70.

34. Gaspar Correa, *Lendas de India*, Coímbra, 1921-31, Lisbon, 1969, 4 vols., IV, p. 237.

35. Henry Rooke, *Travels to the Coast of Arabia Felix*, pp. 51-5.

36. Abu Zaid Hasan ibn Yazid, *Ancient Accounts of India and China by Two Mohammedan Travellers who went to those Parts in the 9th Century; translated from the Arabic by the late Learned Eusebius Renaudot*, London, 1733, p. 93.

37. G.R. Tibbetts, "Arab Navigation in the Red Sea," *Geographical Journal*, vol. 127, 1961, pp. 322-34. See Syed Sulaiman Nadvi, *The Arab Navigation*, trans from Urdu by Syed Sabahuddin Abdur Rahman, Lahore, 1966 for an old but useful account of Arab navigation, and for other accounts of the hazards of Red Sea navigation see Albert Kammerer, *La Mer Rouge, l'Abyssinie et l'Arabie depuis l'Antiquité. Essai d'historique* (Mémoires de la Société royale de Géographie d'Egypte, tomes XV-XVI), 2 vols in 5 parts, Cairo, 1929-35, I, pp. 67-8; and John Ovington, *A Voyage to Surat*, p. 275.

38. Rooke, pp. 61-74.

39. William Foster, ed., *The Red Sea*, pp. 64-70.

40. Eyles Irwin, *A Series of Adventures in the Course of a Voyage up the Red Sea . . . in the Year MDCCLXXVII*, London, 1780, pp. 69-117.

41. Tomé Pires, *The Suma Oriental of Tomé Pires*, ed. A. Cortesão, London, Hakluyt, 1944, 2 vols., I, p. 9.

42. F.C. Lane, *Venice and History*, Baltimore, 1966, pp. 70-2.

43. Muhammad ibn Ahmad ibn Jubair, *The Travels of Ibn Jubayr (1183-1185 AC)*, trans. R.J.C. Broadhurst, London, 1952, pp. 61, 63.

44. João de Barros, *Da Asia*, Lisbon, 1778-88, II, vii, p. 8; Castanheda, III, ciii; Affonso de Albuquerque, *Cartas*, Lisbon, 1884-1935, 7 vols., I, p. 236.

45. Robert Coverte, *A True and Almost Incredible report of an Englishman, that (being cast away in the good Ship called the Assention in Cambaya the farthest part of the East Indies) Travelled by Land through many unknowne Kingdomes and great Cities* . . . , London, 1612, p. 20. This rare account, little known to historians, was published in a modern, but very limited, edition by Penrose: Boise Penrose, ed., *The Travels of Captain Robert Coverte*, Philadelphia, 1931. [Privately printed, 150 copies only]
46. Coverte, pp. 22, 39.
47. Samuel Purchas, *Purchas, His Pilgrimes*, Glasgow, Hakluyt, 1905-7, 20 vols., III, pp. 152-5.
48. Jerónimo Lobo, *The Itinerary of Jerónimo Lobo*, trans. Donald M. Lockhart, London, Hakluyt, 1984, p. 88, a report dating from 1625, supports this claim.
49. C.F. Beckingham, *Between Islam and Christendom. Travellers, Facts and Legends in the Middle Ages and the Renaissance*, London, 1983, "Dutch travellers," pp. 71-2, 79-81, also see *Recueil des voyages qui ont servi à l'établissement et aux progrez de la Compagnie des Indes Orientales formée dans les Provinces-Unies des Pais-Bas,* Rouen, 1725, VII, p. 462. It will be remembered that this great ship from Suez appears to have been atypical in that, unlike ships from the Arabian Sea, it was the only large ship which navigated the whole length of the Red Sea.
50. William Foster, ed., *The English Factories in India, 1618-1669,* Oxford, 1906-27, 13 vols., 1624-9, pp. 349-50; see also Historical Archives of Goa, "Ordens Regias," I, f. 191 for Mocha's trade in 1638.
51. William Foster, ed., *Early Travels in India*, pp. 301-2.
52. *Recueil des voyages*, VII, pp. 564-5.
53. See Ovington, in Foster, ed., *The Red Sea*, p. 173, for an account from the 1690s; and for his full description of Mocha (which he never visited) see Ovington, *Voyage*, pp. 268-72.
54. Baldaeus, in Churchill, *A Collection of Voyages*, III, p. 523.
55. Jean de la Roque, *Voyage de l'Arabie Heureuse par l'Océan Oriental, & le Détroit de la Mer Rouge. Fait par les Français pour la première fois, dans les années 1708, 1709 & 1710* . . .

Paris, 1716, p. 98.

56. ibn Jubair, *Travels*, p. 69.

57. G.W.F. Stripling, *The Ottoman Turks and the Arabs 1511-1574*, Illinois, 1942, p. 22. For the difficulties of the Portuguese governor Lopo Soares off Jiddah in April 1517, see Jean-Louis Bacqué-Grammont and Anne Kroell, *Mamlouks, Ottomans et Portugais en Mer Rouge: L'Affaire de Djedda en 1517*, Cairo, 1988, p. 40.

58. F.E. Peters, *Jerusalem and Mecca: The Typology of the Holy city in the Near East* (New York University Studies in Near Eastern Civilization, Number XI), New York, 1986, pp. 70-1. It will be remembered from the previous chapter that the merchants on an Aleppo-Basra caravan consisted of some 40 Christians and Jews, and about 20 Turks.

59. Ibid., pp. 227-9.

60. See G. Rex Smith and Ahmad 'Umar al-Zayla'i, trans and ed., *Bride of the Red Sea: A 10th / 16th century Account of Jeddah*, Durham, 1984, for a long and pious account of Jiddah and its association with Mecca, its walls, mosques, etc.

61. Barros, II, p. viii, 1; III, p. i, 3.

62. Barros, II, pp. vii, 8.

63. Barros, I, pp. viii, 1.

64. Affonso de Albuquerque, *Commentaries of the great Afonso Albuquerque,* London, Hakluyt, 1875-84, 4 vols, III, pp. 33-4.

65. Castanheda, II, p. lxxv.

66. Castanheda, II, p. xxxix.

67. Correa, I, p. 787.

68. Archivo Nacional da Torre do Tombo, Lisbon, "Colecção de São Lourenço," III, f. p. 160.

69. Correa, II, p. 494; Castanheda, IV, xii. For copious detail on this expedition see the exhaustive account of Jean-Louis Bacqué-Grammont and Anne Kroell, *Mamlouks, Ottomans et Portugais en Mer Rouge,* op. cit.

70. ANTT, "Corpo Chronologico," 1-62-154 (ANTTCC).

71. Anon., "A Description of the yeerely voyage or pilgrimage of the Mahumitans, Turkes and Moores unto Mecca in Arabia," in Richard Hakluyt, *The Principal Navigations,* Glasgow, 1903-5, 12 vols, V, pp. 340-65; for Jiddah see p. 360.

72. Saris in S. Purchas, III, 396; also see Middleton in *ibid.*, pp. 190-3. For a detailed description of these Indian Ocean ships see Correa, I, 122-4, an account which needs extended analysis by a Portuguese-reading scholar conversant with ship construction and design. For another detailed account of the rigging of a ship, in this case a Red Sea one, see Rooke, p. 65.

73. Lobo, pp. 89-90.

74. Suraiya Faroqhi, *Herrscher über Mekka: Die Geschichte der Pilgerfahrt*, Munich, 1990, pp. 201-3; however she is incorrect when she writes [p. 204] that the owners of these Indian ships were mostly Indian rulers.

75. Qazvini, pp. 1-2, 64, 65.

76. Dr. John Fryer, *A New Account of East India and Persia*, London, Hakluyt, 1909-15, 3 vols., I, p. 282.

77. Foster, *The Red Sea*, pp. 63-4. The confused switch from saying the voyage back was by sea, and then by land, is unfortunately rather typical of the quality of the sources we must rely on!

78. Alexander Hamilton, *A New Account of the East Indies*, ed. W. Foster, London, 1930, 2 vols, p. 30. Hamilton was a ship captain, and lived in Asia from 1688 to 1723. The French alternative is from La Roque, pp. 126-7.

79. Ovington, p. 274.

80. Carsten Niebuhr, *Travels through Arabia and other Countries in the East*, trans. Robert Heron, 2 vols, Edinburgh, 1792, I, pp. 235-6.

81. Comte de Modave, *Voyage en Inde du Comte de Modave, 1773-1776*, ed. Jean Deloche, Paris, 1971, pp. 340-1, 342, 348-9, 350.

82. Rooke, pp. 56, 65, 66, 71; Capper, p. vi.

83. Ali Bey, *Travels of Ali Bey in Morocco, Tripoli, Cyprus, Egypt, Arabia, Syria and Turkey, 1803-1807*, London, 1816, 2 vols., II, p. 43, my italics.

84. Quoted in William R. Roff, "Sanitation and Security: The Imperial Powers and the Nineteenth Century Hajj," *Arabian Studies*, VI, 1982, p. 145.

85. "Descrição das terras da India Oriental, e dos seus usos, costumes, ritos e leis," in Biblioteca Nacional, Lisbon, Mss. 9163, f. 37; Marechal Gomes da Costa, *Descobrimentos e Conquistas*, Lisbon, 1927-30, 3 vols., III, p. 75.

86. ANTTCC, 1-106-50.
87. ANTTCC, 1-107-9.
88. Letter to king in Madrid, 28 June 1627, a survey of Portuguese possessions in India, Biblioteca da Ajuda, Lisbon, 51-VII-30, f. 118v. This valuable account goes from f. 116 to f. 127.
89. Sikandar, *The Mirat-i-Sikandari,* ed. S.C. Misra, Baroda, 1961; Trans. E.C. Bayly, *History of Gujarat,* Delhi, 1970; and trans by Fazlullah Lutfullah Faridi as *Mirati Sikandari,* Dharampur, n.d; Persian text, pp. 436-7.
90. Barros, I, p. vi, 3; Correa, I, pp. 346-7.
91. *Alguns Documentos do Archivo Nacional da Torre do Tombo,* Lisbon, 1892, pp. 181-2.
92. Correa, II, p. 565. I use the original monetary units from the sources in this discussion. As a rough guide to equivalents, in terms of the contemporary Portuguese money of account of the time, *reis,* one Mughal rupee was worth 200 *reis,* one xerafim or one silver pardão 300, one gold pardão 360, one cruzado 400 *reis.* An English shilling (1/-) was very roughly equal to 100 *reis.* See for this C.R. Boxer, *The Great Ship from Amacon,* Lisbon, 1959, pp. 335-42; Niels Steensgaard, *The Asian Trade Revolution of the Seventeenth Century,* Chicago, 1974, pp. 415-22; K.S. Mathew, *Portuguese Trade with India in the Sixteenth Century,* Delhi, 1983, pp. 236-42.
93. *Documentação Ultramarina Portuguesa,* Lisbon, 1960-67, 5 vols., I, p. 473 (DUP).
94. Diogo do Couto, *Da Asia,* Lisbon, 1778-88, IV, pp. i, 7; IV, pp. iv, 9.
95. Correa, III, p. 419.
96. Couto, VII, pp. iii, 3.
97. DUP, I, p. 415.
98. Castanheda, VIII, cap. 1, lxvii for this incident.
99. ANTTCC, 1-100-28.
100. Couto, VII, pp. x, 3.
101. Letter to king in Madrid, 28 June 1627, Biblioteca da Ajuda, Lisbon, 51-VII-30, f. 118v. See f.n. 91.
102. Couto, IX, cap. 13.
103. Philip Baldaeus, *A Description of the East India Coast of Malabar and Coromandel,* vol. III, London, 1703, p. 573.

104. *Assentos do Conselho do Estado*, ed. P.S.S. Pissurlencar, Bastorá, 1953-57, 5 vols, and supplementary series, 1 vol. in 2 parts, Panaji, 1972, I, p. 291.

105. Fryer, III, p. 163.

106. *India in the 17th Century (Social, Economic and Political): Memoirs of François Martin (1670-1694)*, trans Lotika Varadarajan, vol. II, part 1, New Delhi, 1984, p. 966.

107. Khafi Khan, *Khafi Khan's History of Alamgir*, trans. S. Moinul Haq, Karachi, 1975, pp. 419-20; further data on Gujarat's trade with the Red Sea in M.N. Pearson, *Merchants and Rulers in Gujarat*, Berkeley and New Delhi, 1976, pp. 23, 100-101, and in Ashin Das Gupta, "Gujarati Merchants and the Red Sea Trade," op cit.

# Chapter 8  (Pages 167-186)

1. Russel King, "The Pilgrimage to Mecca: Some Geographical and Historical Aspects," *Erdkunde*, 26, 1972, p. 63, and for a revisionist view which downplays Mecca's economic importance at the time of the Prophet, see Patricia Crone, *Meccan Trade and the Rise of Islam*, Princeton, 1986.

2. Ali Bey, *Travels of Ali Bey in Morocco, Tripoli, Cyprus, Egypt, Arabia, Syria and Turkey, 1803-1807*, London, 1816, 2 vols, II, p. 101.

3. Ludovico di Varthema, *The Itinerary of Ludovico di Varthema of Bologna from 1502-1508*, ed. Sir Richard Carnac Temple, London, 1928, p. 19.

4. *Ibid.*, pp. 17, 19.

5. Bernard Lewis, ed., *Islam: From the Prophet Muhammad to the Capture of Constantinople*, New York, 1974, 2 vols., II, p. 32. For one contrary opinion, a very atypical one, see Anon., "A Description of the yeerely voyage or pilgrimage of the Mahumitans, Turkes and Moores unto Mecca in Arabia," in Richard Hakluyt, *The Principal Navigations*, Glasgow, 1903-5, 12 vols, V, p. 352, where it is claimed that there were gardens and orchards on the plains between the mountains and the town.

6. Suraiya Faroqhi, *Herrscher über Mekka: Die Geschichte der*

*Pilgerfahrt*, Munich, 1990, pp. 129-30.

7. Affonso de Albuquerque, *Cartas,* Lisbon, 1884-1935, 7 vols, I, p. 223.

8. John Ovington, *A Voyage to Surat in the Year 1689*, ed. H.G. Rawlinson, London, 1929, p. 274.

9. Carsten Niebuhr, *Travels through Arabia and other Countries in the East*, trans. Robert Heron, 2 vols, Edinburgh, 1792, II, p. 27.

10. Muhammad ibn Ahamd Ibn Jubair, *The Travels of Ibn Jubayr (1183-1185 AC),* trans. R.J.C. Broadhurst, London, 1952, pp. 48, 52, 116-21.

11. Ali Bey, II, p. 102.

12. King, p. 62; Robert Lacey, *The Kingdom*, London, 1981, p. 88.

13. F.E. Peters, *Jerusalem and Mecca: The Typology of the Holy city in the Near East* (New York University Studies in Near Eastern Civilization, Number XI), New York, 1986, p. 231.

14. C. Snouck Hurgronje, *Mekka in the Latter Part of the Nine-teenth Century*, Leiden, 1931, pp. 10, 23-4.

15. Richard Burton, *Personal Narrative of a Pilgrimage to al-Madinah and Meccah*, London, 1898, 2 vols., II, p. 235.

16. *The Independent* [London], quoted in the *Sydney Morning Herald*, June 20, 1991.

17. Ibn Jubayr, pp. 127, 131-2, 135-6, 165, 168.

18. Jean Aubin, "Un nouveau classique, l'Anonyme du British Museum," in *Mare Luso-Indicum*, III, 1976, p.185, and cf. J.F. Richards, ed., *Precious Metals in the Late Medieval and Early Modern Worlds*, Durham, N.C., 1983, pp. 202-3. For Ottoman patronage see Faroqhi, pp. 105-24.

19. Fernão Mendes Pinto, *The Travels of Mendes Pinto*, ed. and trans. Rebecca D. Catz, Chicago, 1989, pp. 10-11.

20. Ibid., pp. 30, 53, 455.

21. Eyles Irwin, *A Series of Adventures in the Course of a Voyage up the Red Sea . . . in the Year MDCCLXXVII*, London, 1780, p. 58.

22. João de Barros, *Da Asia,* Lisbon, 1778-88, II, pp. ii, 6.

23. William Foster, ed., *The Red Sea and Adjacent Countries at the Close of the Seventeenth Century*, London, Hakluyt, 1949, pp. 3-4.

24. Ibn Jubayr, pp. 116-7.

25. Varthema, p. 19.

26. Hakluyt, *The Principal Navigations,* Duckett's account in III, 161; see also G.W.F. Stripling, *The Ottoman Turks and the Arabs 1511-1574,* Illinois, 1942, pp. 21-22 and K.N. Chaudhuri, *Trade and Civilization in the Indian Ocean. An Economic History from the Rise of Islam to 1750,* Cambridge, 1985, p. 46.

27. Mulla Safi-ud din Qazwini, "Anis-ul hujjaj," trans. A. Jan Qaisar and Z. Islam, 71 pp. typescript, [Qazvini], p. 53.

28. F. Eugene Roger, *La Terre Saincte ou Description topographique très particulière des saincts lieux & de la terre de promission* . . . , Paris, 1646, pp. 234-5.

29. Faroqhi, pp. 216-9.

30. Qazvini, pp. 36, 49.

31. Ibn Battuta, *The Travels of Ibn Battuta,* trans. H.A.R. Gibb, Cambridge, Hakluyt, 1958-71, 3 vols., I, p. 206.

32. *Encyclopedia of Islam*, Leiden, 1960, 2nd. ed., s.v. hadjdj.

33. Anon., in Hakluyt, *The Principal Navigations,* V, p. 358.

34. Pitts in Foster, ed., *The Red Sea,* p. 38.

35. Niebuhr, II, pp. 35-6.

36. Burton, II, p. 225 and *passim*; for other accounts of mercantile activity in the nineteenth century, a time when we have argued the whole character of the *hajj* and Mecca had changed, see inter al Hurgronje, pp. 3-4, 220, and C.M. Doughty, *Travels in Arabia Deserta*, London, 1926, 1 vol ed., I, pp. 60, 71, 206, which seems to point to a trade in provisions and souvenirs only.

37. *The Independent* [London], quoted in the *Sydney Morning Herald*, June 20, 1991.

38. Ibn Jubayr, p. 188.

39. Qazvini, pp. 50, 53, 54.

40. Jafar Sharif, *Islam in India, or the Qanun-i-Islam*, ed. G.A. Herklots and William Crooke, London, 1975, p. 121.

41. Pitts in Foster, ed., *The Red Sea,* p. 25.

42. Jean Aubin, "Marchands de Mer Rouge et du Golfe Persique au tournant des 15$^e$-16$^e$ siècles," in Denys Lombard and Jean Aubin, eds, *Marchands et hommes d'affairs asiatiques dans l'Océan Indien et la Mer de Chine 13$^e$-20$^e$ siècles*, Paris, 1988, p. 87.

43. Peters, pp. 37, 66-67, 227, 229-32.

44. Peters, p. 163.
45. Pitts in Foster, ed., *The Red Sea*, p. 30.
46. Niebuhr, II, pp. 33-4.
47. Adam Olearius, *The Voyages & travels of the ambassaddors sent by Frederick duke of Holstein to the great Duke of Muscovy, and the King of Persia. Began in the year MDCXXXIII and finish'd in MDCXXXIX . . .* , trans. John Davies, London, 1662, p. 232.
48. Quoted in G.E. von Grunebaum, *Muhammadan Festivals*, London, 1976, pp. 37-8.
49. Anon., in Hakluyt, V, p. 342.
50. *Ibid.*, p. 351.
51. Qazvini, p. 34.
52. Pitts in Foster, ed., *The Red Sea.*, p. 31.
53. Qazvini, pp. 30, 33.
54. Peters, p. 231.
55. Pitts in Foster, ed., *The Red Sea.*, pp. 33-4.
56. Daniel in *ibid.*, p. 79.
57. Pitts in *ibid.*, pp. 38-9.
58. Comte de Modave, *Voyage en Inde du Comte de Modave, 1773-1776*, ed. Jean Deloche, Paris, 1971, p. 342.
59. Ali Bey, II, pp. 59, 60, 81.

## Chapter 9  (Pages 187-198)

1. For some of the general issues raised here, see also my short article "Pilgrims, Travellers, Tourists: the Meanings of Journeys," *Australian Cultural History*, no. 10, 1991, pp. 125-34.
2. Irawati Karve, "On the Road: A Maharashtrian Pilgrimage," *Journal of Asian Studies*, XXII, 1, 1962, pp. 13-29.
3. Surinder Mohan Bhardwaj, *Hindu Places of Pilgrimage in India (A Study in Cultural Geography)*, Berkeley, 1973. Among other studies of Hindu pilgrimage are E. Alan Morinis, ed., *Pilgrimage in the Hindu Tradition: A Case Study of West Bengal*, Oxford, 1984; Diana L. Eck, *Banaras: City of Light*, New York, 1982; Burton Stein, ed., *South Indian Temples: An Analytical Reconstruction*, New Delhi, 1978, especially Stein's Introduction; Nancy Gardner Cassels, *Religion and Pilgrim Tax*

*under the Company Raj*, New Delhi, 1988; David Sopher, "Pilgrim Circulation in Gujarat," *Geographical Review*, vol. LVIII, 1968, pp. 392-425 and R. L. Singh, and Rana P.B. Singh, eds., *Trends in the Geography of Pilgrimages: Homage to David E. Sopher*, Varanasi, 1987. Also on Hindu pilgrimage see Makhan Jha, ed., *Dimensions of Pilgrimage: An Anthropological Appraisal (Based on the Transactions of a World Symposium on Pilgrimage)*, New Delhi, 1986 (13 of the 15 chapters are about Hindu pilgrimage), and Ann Grodzins Gold, *Fruitful Journeys: The Ways of Rajasthani Pilgrims*, Berkeley, 1989.

4. Jonathon Sumption, *Pilgrimage: An Image of Mediæval Religion*, London, 1975.

5. Fernand Braudel, *The Mediterranean and the Mediterranean World in the Age of Philip II*, London, 1972, 2 vols, pp. 264, 615.

6. Sidney Heath, *Pilgrim Life in the Middle Ages*, London, 1971 [reprint of 1911 edition].

7. Alan Kendall, *Medieval Pilgrims*, London, 1970; Horton and Marie-Helene Davies, *Holy Days and Holidays: The Medieval Pilgrimage to Compostela*, Bucknell, 1982.

8. Donald R. Howard, *Writers and Pilgrims: Medieval Pilgrimage Narratives and their Posterity*, Berkeley, 1980.

9. F.E. Peters, *Jerusalem and Mecca: The Typology of the Holy city in the Near East*, New York, 1986.

10. *The Encyclopedia of Religion*, ed. Mircea Eliade, New York, 1987, 16 vols., XI, p. 328. For Victor Turner's views see "The Centre out there: Pilgrim's Goal," *History of Religions*, XII, 3, 1973, pp. 191-230, also published as "Pilgrimages as Social Processes," in Victor Turner, *Dramas, Fields and Metaphors: Symbolic Action in Human Society*, Ithaca, 1974, pp. 166-230, and also Victor and Edith Turner, *Image and Pilgrimage in Christian Culture*, New York, 1978.

11. V. Turner, *Dramas, Fields and Metaphors*, p. 293-8, and "Center out there," *passim*.

12. Turner, "Center out there," p. 221.

13. *The Encyclopedia of Religion*, XI, pp. 328-30.

14. Peter Brown, *The Cult of the Saints*, Chicago, 1981, p. 42.

15. Quoted *ibid.*, p. 147, f.n. 103.

16. *Ibid.*, p. 90.
17. Xavier de Planhol, *The World of Islam*, Ithaca, 1959, p. 74.
18. Brown, *Cult of the Saints*, p. 87 et seq.
19. Quoted in Peters, p. 226.
20. Braudel, *Mediterranean*, pp. 264, 615.
21. S.D. Goitein, *A Mediterranean Society*, Berkeley, 1967-78, 3 vols., I, p. 55.
22. *Encyclopedia of Religion*, XI, s.v. "pilgrimage," pp. 335, 346.
23. Turner, "Center out there," p. 192.
24. See Abdul Kadir Haji Din, "Economic implications of Moslem Pilgrimage from Malaysia," *Contemporary South East Asia*, IV, 1, June, 1982, pp. 58-75; Valene L. Smith, ed., "Pilgrimage and Tourism: the Quest in Guest," *Annals of Tourism Research*, Special Number, XIX, 1, 1992. See also Nelson H.H. Graburn, "Tourism: The Sacred Journey," in V. Smith, ed., *Hosts and Guests: The Anthropology of Tourism*, Philadelphia, 1977, pp. 17-31.
25. Turner, "The Centre out there," p. 196.
26. *Encyclopedia of Religion*, XI, s.v. "pilgrimage," p. 328.
27. Turner, "Center out there," p. 208.
28. Howard, *Writers and Pilgrims*, p. 14.
29. Benedict Anderson, *Imagined Communities: Reflections on the Origin and Spread of Nationalism*, London, 1983.
30. Turner, "Center out there," p. 219.
31. Anderson, pp. 55-6.

# Bibliography

NOTE: The more important of the sources listed here have been discussed in Chapter 1 of this book.

## PRIMARY SOURCES [INDIAN AND ISLAMIC]

Abul Fazl, *Ain-i Akbari*, trans. H. Blochmann et al., New Delhi, 1977-78, 3 vols.

Abul Fazl, *Akbar Nama*, trans. H. Beveridge, Delhi, 1972-3, 3 vols.

Al-Harawi, Abu al-Hasan Ali ibn Bakr, *Guide des Lieux de Pèlerinage*, trans. Janine Sourdel-Thomine, Damascus, 1957.

Ali Bey, *Travels of Ali Bey in Morocco, Tripoli, Cyprus, Egypt, Arabia, Syria and Turkey, 1803-1807*, London, 1816, 2 vols.

Babur, *Babur Nama*, trans. A. Beveridge, New Delhi, 1970.

al-Badaoni, *Muntakhabu-t-tawarikh*, trans. G. Ranking et al., Patna, 1973, 3 vols.

Bigot, Henry, "Les strophes du pèlerin de Puey Monçon (Voyage à la Mecque à la fin du XVIe siècle) avec préface, traduction et commentaire," *Revue Tunisienne*, 1916, pp. 87-124.

Bilimoria, J.H., *Ruka'at-i-Alamgiri, or Letters of Aurangzebe*, Delhi, 1972.

Donzel, E. van, *Foreign Relations of Ethiopia, 1642-1700. Documents Relating to the Journeys of Khodja Murad*, Leiden, 1979.

Gladwin, Francis, trans, *The Memoirs of Khojeh Abdulkurreem* (of Kashmir), Calcutta, 1788.

Gulbadan Begam, *The History of Humayun*, trans. A. Beveridge, Delhi, 1972.

Hajji ad-dabir, *An Arabic History of Gujarat*, trans. M.F. Lokhandwalla, Baroda, 1970-74, 2 vols.

Hasan ibn Yazid, Abu Zaid, *Ancient Accounts of India and China by Two Mohammedan Travellers who went to those Parts in the 9th*

*Century; translated from the Arabic by the late Learned Eusebius Renaudot*, London, 1733.

Ibn Battuta, *The Travels of Ibn Battuta,* trans. H.A.R. Gibb, Cambridge, Hakluyt, 1958-71, 3 vols.

Ibn Jubair, Muhammad ibn Ahmad, *The Travels of Ibn Jubayr (1183-1185 AC),* trans. R.J.C. Broadhurst, London, 1952.

Islam, Riazul, ed., *A Calendar of Documents on Indo-Persian Relations (1500-1750)*, Tehran and Karachi, 1979-82, 2 vols.

Jahangir, *The Tuzuk-i Jahangiri*, trans. A. Rogers, ed. H. Beveridge, Delhi, 1968, 2 vols in one.

Khafi Khan, *Khafi Khan's History of Alamgir*, trans. S. Moinul Haq, Karachi, 1975.

Khalifeh, Haji, *The History of the Maritime Wars of the Turks*, trans. James Mitchell, London, 1831.

Ma Huan, *The Overall Survey of the Ocean's Shores*, trans. J.V.G. Mills, Cambridge, Hakluyt, 1970.

al-Nahrawali, Muhammad ibn Ahmad, *Extrados da história da conquista do Yaman pelos Othmans. Contribuções para história do estabelecimento dos Portugueses na India*, trans. and ed. David Lopes, Lisbon, 1892.

Nagar, Ishwardas, *Futuhat-i-Alamgiri*, trans. and ed. Tasneem Ahmad, Delhi, 1978.

Nizamuddin Ahmad, Khwajah, *The Tabaqat-i-Akbari*, trans. B. De., Calcutta, 1911-40, 3 vols.

Norris, H.T., trans. and ed., *The Pilgrimage of Ahmad, Son of the Little Bird of Paradise. An Account of a 19th Century Pilgrimage from Mauritania to Mecca*, Warminster, 1977.

Pickthall, Mohammed Marmaduke, trans., *The Meaning of the Glorious Koran*, New York, n.d.

Qazwini, Mulla Safi-ud din, "Anis-ul hujjaj, " trans. A. Jan Qaisar and Z. Islam, 71 pp. typescript.

Reeland, Adrianus [1676-1718], *Four Treatises concerning the doctrine, discipline and worship of the Mahametans . . . III. A treatise of Babovius (sometime first interpreter to Mahomet IV) concerning the liturgy of the Turks, their pilgrimage to Mecca, . . .* , London, 1712.

Reis, Sidi Ali, *The Travels and Adventures of the Turkish Admiral Sidi Ali Reis in India, Afghanistan, Central Asia and Persia during the years 1553-1556*, trans. A. Vambéry, London, 1899.

Saqi Must'ad Khan, *Maasir-i-Alamgiri*, trans. Jadunath Sarkar, Calcutta, 1947.

Shah Nawaz Khan, Nawwab Samsam-ud-daula, *The Maathir-ul-Umara*, trans. H. Beveridge, ed. Baini Prashad, Patna, 1979, 2 vols.

Sharif, Jafar, *Islam in India, or the Qanun-i-Islam*, ed. G.A. Herklots and William Crooke, London, 1975.

Sikandar, *The Mirat-i-Sikandari,* ed. S.C. Misra, Baroda, 1961; trans. E.C. Bayly, *History of Gujarat*, Delhi, 1970; and trans by Fazlullah Lutfullah Faridi as *Mirati Sikandari*. Dharampur, n.d.

Smith, G. Rex, and Ahmad 'Umar al-Zayla'i, trans and ed., *Bride of the Red Sea: A 10th / 16th century Account of Jeddah*, Durham, 1984.

Zain-ud-din, *Tohfut-ul-Mujahideen*, trans. M.J. Rowlandson, London, 1833.

## PRIMARY SOURCES [EUROPEAN]

Albuquerque, Affonso de, *Cartas,* Lisbon, 1884-1935, 7 vols.

Albuquerque, Affonso de, *Commentaries of the great Afonso Albuquerque,* London, Hakluyt, 1875-84, 4 vols.

*Alguns Documentos do Archivo Nacional da Torre do Tombo*, Lisbon, 1892.

*Annaes Maritimos e Coloniaes*, Lisbon, 1840-46, 6 vols.

Anon, "A Description of the yeerely voyage or pilgrimage of the Mahumitans, Turkes and Moores unto Mecca in Arabia," in Richard Hakluyt, *The Principal Navigations,* Glasgow, 1903-5, 12 vols, V, 329-65.

*Archivo Português Oriental*, ed. J.H. da Cunha Rivara, Nova Goa, 1857-77, 6 vols.

Archivum Romanum S.I., Rome, Provincia Goana et Malabarica, Cartas etc., vols. 15, 16.

*Assentos do Conselho da Fazenda,* vol. I, part 1, 1613-1617, Panaji, 1979.

*Assentos do Conselho do Estado*, ed. P.S.S. Pissurlencar, Bastorá, 1953-57, 5 vols, and supplementary series, 1 vol. in 2 parts, Panaji, 1972.

Baião, António, ed., *Itinerarios da India a Portugal por terra*, Coimbra, 1923.

Baldaeus, Philip, *A Description of the East India Coast of Malabar and Coromandel*, vol. III, London, 1703.

Baldaeus, Philip, *A True and Exact Description of the Most Celebrated East-Indian Coasts of Malabar and Coromandel as also of the Isle of Ceylon* . . . , in Churchill, *A Collection of Voyages and Travels*, 3rd ed., vol. III, London, 1745, pp. 510-793.

Barbosa, Duarte, *Livro*, London, Hakluyt, 1918-21, 2 vols.

Barros, João de, *Da Asia*, Lisbon, 1778-88.

Belon, Pierre, (Belon du Mans), *Les observations de plusieurs singularitez et choses memorables trouvées en Grèce, Asie, Judée, Egypte, Arabie et autres pays estranges*, Paris, 1554.

Bernier, François, *Travels in the Mogul Empire*, ed. A. Constable and V.A. Smith, London, 1914.

Best, Thomas, *The Voyage of Thomas Best to the East Indies, 1612-14*, ed. William Foster, London, Hakluyt, 1934.

Bocarro, António, *Decada 13 da história da India*, Lisboa, 1876.

*Boletim da Filmateca Ultramarina Portuguesa*, nos. 1-41, 1954 - .

British Library, Additional Manuscripts, no. 28433.

Broecke, Pieter van dan, *Pieter van den Broecke in Azie*, ed. W. Ph. Coolhaas, The Hague, 1962-3, 2 vols.

*Bullarium Patronatus Portugalliae Regum in Ecclesiis Africae, Asiae atque Oceaniae*, ed. Vicecomite de Paiva Manso, I, Appendix, Concilia Provincialia Ecclesiae Goanensis, Lisbon, 1872.

Capper, James [Colonel] *Observations on the Passage to India through Egypt and across the Great Desert* . . . , 2nd ed., London, 1784.

Castanheda, Fernão Lopes de, *História do descobrimento e conquista da India pelos Portugueses*, 3rd. ed., Coímbra, 1924-33, 9 vols.

Castro, D. João de, *Cartas*, ed. Elaine Sanceau, Lisbon, 1954.

Castro, D. João de, *Roteiro da viagem que fizeram os Portuguezes ao Mar Roxo no anno de 1541*, Paris, 1833.

Castro, D. João, *Obras Completas*, ed. Armando Cortesão and Luis de Albuquerque, 3 vols, Coìmbra, 1968-76.

*Colecção de São Lourenço*, ed. Elaine Sanceau, Lisbon, 1973-75, 2 vols.

"Corpo Chronologico," Archivo Nacional da Torre do Tombo, Lisbon.

Correa, Gaspar, *Lendas de India*, Coímbra, 1921-31, Lisbon, 1969, 4 vols.

Correia-Afonso, John, trans and ed., *Intrepid Itinerant: Manuel Godinho and his Journey from India to Portugal in 1663*, Bombay, 1990.

Costa Lobo, A. de S.S., *Memórias de um soldado da India* (Francisco Rodrigues Silveira), Lisbon, 1877.

Costa Veiga, A. Botelho da, *Relação das plantas e descrições de todas as fortalezas, cidades, e povoações que os Portugueses tem no Estado da India Oriental*, Lisbon, 1936.

Couto, Diogo do, *Da Asia*, Lisbon, 1778-88.

Couto, Diogo do, *O Soldado Prático*, 3rd ed., Lisbon, 1980.

Couto, Diogo do, *Vida de D. Paulo de Lima Pereira*, Lisbon, 1903.

Coverte, Robert [Captain], *A True and Almost Incredible report of an Englishman, that (being cast away in the good Ship called the Assention in Cambaya the farthest part of the East Indies) Travelled by Land through many unknowne Kingdomes and great Cities . . .* , London, 1612.

*Documenta Indica*, ed. J. Wicki et al, Rome, 1948 - , 16 vols to date, to 1594.

*Documenta Malucensia*, ed. H. Jacobs, Rome, 1974-84, 3 vols.

*Documentação para a história das Missões do padroado Português do Oriente: India*, ed. António da Silva Rego, Lisbon, 1947-58, 12 vols.

*Documentação para a história das Missões do padroado Português do Oriente: Insulíndia*, ed. Artur Basílio de Sá, Lisbon, 1954-58, 5 vols.

*Documentação Ultramarina Portuguesa*, Lisbon, 1960-67, 5 vols.

*Documentos remettidos da India, ou Livros das Monções*, ed. R.A. de Bulhão Pato, Lisbon, 1880-1935, 5 vols.

du Jarric, P., *Akbar and the Jesuits*, ed. E.D. Ross and E. Power, trans. C.H. Payne, New Delhi, 1979.

*English Records on Shivaji (1659-1682)*, Poona, 1931.

Ficalho, Conde de, *Viagens de Pedro de Covilhan*, Lisbon, 1898.

Foster, William, ed., *Early Travels in India*, Delhi, 1968.

Foster, William, ed., *Letters Received by the East India Company from its Servants in the East*, London, 1896-1902, 6 vols.

Foster, William, ed., *The English Factories in India, 1618-1669*,

Oxford, 1906-27, 13 vols.

Foster, William, ed., *The Red Sea and Adjacent Countries at the Close of the Seventeenth Century as described by Joseph Pitts [c.1685], William Daniel [1700], and Charles Jacques Poncet [1698-1700]*, London, Hakluyt, 1949.

Fryer, Dr. John, *A New Account of East India and Persia*, London, Hakluyt, 1909-15, 3 vols.

Fullerton, John, "Commonplace Book," MS, English, c. 1727 [Bell Library, 1727 f Fu] Includes Memorandum of 1727, and Daily Journal, Jiddah, Tuesday July 23, 1728.

Galland, Julien Claude, *Recueil des rits et cérémonies du pèlerinage de la Mecque; auquel on a joint divers écrits relatifs à la religion, aux sciences & aux moeurs des Turcs*, Amsterdam, 1754.

*Gavetas da Torre do Tombo*, Lisbon, 1960-75, 12 vols.

Grose, John Henry, *A Voyage to the East Indies . . . to which is added A Journey from Aleppo to Busserah, over the Desert, by Mr. Charmichael* [1st French ed, 1758, 1st English ed 1766, 2nd Eng ed 1772, which adds Charmichael] 2nd ed., 2 vols, London, 1772. [Charmichael is in vol. I, Appendix, pp. 1-53.]

Guerreiro, Fernão, *Relação Annual das coisas que fizeram os Padres da Companhia de Jesus nas suas Missões*, ed. Artur Viegas, Coìmbra, 1930-31, Lisbon, 1942, 3 vols.

Hakluyt, Richard, *The Principal Navigations, Voyages, Traffiques and Discoveries of the English Nation*, Glasgow, 1903-5, 12 vols.

Hamilton, Alexander, *A New Account of the East Indies*, ed. W. Foster, London, 1930, 2 vols.

Harff, Arnold von, *The Pilgrimage of Arnold von Harff, Knight ... in the Years 1496-99*, ed. and trans. Malcolm Letts, London, Hakluyt, 1946.

Irwin, Eyles, *A Series of Adventures in the Course of a Voyage up the Red Sea . . . in the Year MDCCLXXVII*, London, 1780.

Jourdain, John, *The Journal of John Jourdain, 1608-17*, ed. William Foster, London, Hakluyt, 1935.

La Roque, Jean de [1661-1745], *Voyage de l'Arabie Heureuse par l'Océan Oriental, & le Détroit de la Mer Rouge. Fait par les Français pour la première fois, dans les années 1708, 1709 & 1710 . . .* Paris, 1716.

Linhares, Conde de, *Diário do 3rd Conde de Linhares, Vice-Rei da India*, Lisbon, 1937-43, 2 vols.

"Livro da Consulta," Historical Archives of Goa, no. 1043, 1618-21.
"Livro das Feitorias," Historical Archives of Goa, no. 2316, 1667-84.
*Livro do Pai dos Cristãos*, ed. José Wicki, Lisbon, 1969.
Lobo, Jerónimo, *The Itinerary of Jerónimo Lobo*, trans. Donald M. Lockhart, London, Hakluyt, 1984.
Lockyer, Charles, *An Account of the trade in India, containing the rules of good government in trade, price courants, and tables...* London, 1711.
Luillier-Lagaudiers, *Nouveau voyage aux grandes Indes, avec une introduction pour le commerce des Indes Orientales, et la description de plusieurs isles, villes, & rivières, l'histoire des plantes & des animaus qu'on y trouve; avec un traité des maladies particulières aux pays orientaux, et dans la Route, et de leurs remèdes* par Mr. D.L.F., Docteur en Medecine, qui a voyagé et sejourné dans les principales Villes des Indes Orientales, [pp. 199-236], Rotterdam, 1726.
Manucci, Niccolao, *Storia do Mogor*, trans. W. Irvine, London, 1905-7, 4 vols.
Mocquet, Jean, *Voyages en Afrique, Asie, Indes Orientales et Occidentales*, Rouen, 1630.
Modave, Comte de, *Voyage en Inde du Comte de Modave, 1773-1776*, ed. Jean Deloche, Paris, 1971.
Navarrete, Friar Domingo, *The Travels and Controversies of Friar Domingo Navarrete 1618-1686*, ed. J.S. Cummins, Cambridge, Hakluyt, 1962, 2 vols.
Niebuhr, Carsten, *Travels through Arabia and other Countries in the East*, trans. Robert Heron, 2 vols, Edinburgh, 1792.
Ogilby, John [1600-1676], *Asia, the first part, Being an accurate description of Persia, and the several provinces thereof. The vast empire of the Great Mogol, and other parts of India . . .* , [collected and translated from most authentic authors], London, 1673.
Olearius, Adam [d. 1671], *The Voyages & travels of the ambassaddors sent by Frederick duke of Holstein to the great Duke of Muscovy, and the King of Persia. Began in the year MDCXXXII and finish'd in MDCXXXIX . . .* , trans. John Davies, London, 1662.
Ovington, John, *A Voyage to Surat in the Year 1689*, ed. H.G. Rawlinson, London, 1929.

Penrose, Boies, ed., *The Travels of Captain Robert Coverte*, Philadelphia, 1931.

Pinto, Fernão Mendes, *The Travels of Mendes Pinto*, ed. and trans. Rebecca D. Catz, Chicago, 1989.

Pinto, Fernão Mendes, *The Voyages and Adventures of Ferdinand Mendez Pinto, the P:ortuguese*, ed. A. Vambéry, London, 1891.

Pires, Tomé, *The Suma Oriental of Tomé Pires*, ed. A. Cortesão, London, Hakluyt, 1944, 2 vols.

Purchas, Samuel, *Purchas, His Pilgrimes*, Glasgow, Hakluyt, 1905-7, 20 vols.

*Recueil des voyages qui ont servi a l'etablissement et aux progrez de la Compagnie des Indes Orientales formée dans les Provinces-Unies des Pais-Bas,* Rouen, 1725.

Ribeiro, Luciano, "Un Geografia Quinhentista," *Studia*, no. 7, 1961.

Roger, F. Eugene, *La Terre Saincte ou Description topographique très particulière des saincts lieux & de la terre de promission* . . . , Paris, 1646.

Rooke, Henry, *Travels to the Coast of Arabia Felix and from thence by the Red-Sea and Egypt to Europe*, London, 1783.

Sanceau, Elaine, "Uma Narrativa da Expedição Portuguesa de 1541 ao Mar Roxo," *Studia*, IX, 1962, pp. 199-234 [letter of D. Manuel de Lima to King, Goa, 18 Nov 1541].

Sanson, Nicolas [1600-1667], *L'Asie en plvsievrs cartes novvelles, et exactes; en divers traittes de geographie, et d'histoire* . . . Paris, 1652.

Santos, João dos, *Ethiopia Oriental*, Lisbon, 1891, 2 vols.

São Bernardino, Frei Gaspar de, *Itinerario da India por Terra ate este Reino de Portugal* . . . , Lisbon, 1611.

Sherley, Sir Athony, *Relation of Travels into Persia* [London, 1613], Amsterdam, 1974.

Tavernier, J.-B., *Travels in India*, ed. V. Ball and W. Crooke, New Delhi, 1977, 2 vols.

Varthema, Ludovico di, *The Itinerary of Ludovico di Varthema of Bologna from 1502-1508*, ed. Sir Richard Carnac Temple, London, 1928.

Wright, Thomas, ed., *Early Travels in Palestine, comprising the narratives of Arculf, Willibald, Bernard, Saewulf, Sigurd, Benjamin of Tudela, Sir John Mandeville, de la Brocquière, and Maundrell*, London, 1848.

# MODERN ACCOUNTS OF THE HAJJ

Ali, M.R., *My Umra* [1970], Dacca, n.d.

Amin, Mohamed, *Pilgrimage to Mecca,* London, 1978.

Ankawi, Abdullah, "The Pilgrimage to Mecca in Mamluk Times," *Arabian Studies,* I, 1974, pp. 146-70.

Badr-i Alam, Syed Muhammad, *How to Perform Hajj*, Lahore, 1971.

Begam, Sultan Jahan, nawab of Bhopal [1858-1930], *The Story of a Pilgrimage to Hijaz* [1903-4], Calcutta, 1909.

Birks, J.S., *Across the Savannas to Mecca: the overland pilgrimage route from West Africa,* London, 1978.

Birks, J.S., "Overland Pilgrimage from West Africa to Mecca: Anachronism or Fashion?" *Geography*, vol. LXII, 1977, pp. 215-7.

Birks, J.S., "The Meccan Pilgrimage by West African Pastoral Nomads," *Journal of Modern African Studies*, vol. XV, 1977, pp. 47-58.

Burkhardt, J.L., *Travels in Arabia*, London, 1829.

Burton, Richard, *Personal Narrative of a Pilgrimage to al-Madinah and Meccah*, London, 1898, 2 vols.

Din, Abdul Kadir Haji, "Economic implications of Moslem Pilgrimage from Malaysia," *Contemporary South East Asia*, IV, 1, June, 1982, pp. 58-75.

Doughty, C.M., *Travels in Arabia Deserta*, London, 1926, 1 vol ed.

Eickelman, Dale F., and James Piscatori, eds., *Muslim Travellers: Pilgrimage, Migration and the Religious Imagination*, London, 1990.

*Encyclopedia of Islam*, Leiden, 1st ed., 1934, s.v. 'umra; 2nd. ed., 1960, s.v. hadjdj.

Faroqhi, Suraiya, *Herrscher uber Mekka: Die Geschichte der Pilgerfahrt*, Munich, 1990.

Gaudefroy-Demombynes, Maurice, *Le pèlerinage à la Mekke: Etude d'histoire religieuse*, Paris, 1923.

Guellouz, Ezzedine, *Pilgrimage to Mecca*, London, 1980.

*Hajj Studies*, ed. Ziauddin Sardar and M.A. Zaki Badawi, 1978 - .

Hurgronje, C. Snouck, *Mekka in the Latter Part of the Nineteenth Century*, Leiden, 1931.

Husain, S.A., *A Guide to Hajj*, Lahore, 1972.

Jomier, Jacques, *Le Mahmal et la caravane Egyptienne des pèlerins de la Mecque (XIII-XX siècles)*, Cairo, 1953.

Jung, Nawab Sir Nizamat, "At the Haj," *Islamic Culture*, VII, 2, 1933, p. 195.

Jung, Nawab Sir Nizamat, "In the Kaaba," *Islamic Culture*, VII, 3, 1933, p. 379.

Jung, Nawab Sir Nizamat, "Round Mecca," *Islamic Culture*, VIII, 2, 1934, p. 178.

Kamal, Ahmad, *The Sacred Journey: being pilgrimage to Makkah*, New York, 1961.

Keane, T.F., *Six Months in Meccah*, London, 1881.

Khalifa, Saida Miller, *The Fifth Pillar: The Story of a Pilgrimage to Mecca and Medina*, Hicksville, N.Y., 1977.

Khan, Muhammad Zafrulla, *Pilgrimage to the House of Allah*, London, 1968.

King, Russel, "The Pilgrimage to Mecca: Some Geographical and Historical Aspects," *Erdkunde*, 26, 1972, pp. 61-73.

Levi Della Vida, G., "A Portuguese Pilgrim to Mecca in the Sixteenth Century," *Muslim World*, XXXII, 1942, pp. 283-97.

Long, David E., *The Hajj Today: A survey of the contemporary Makkah pilgrimage*, Albany, N.Y., 1979.

Majid, Haji Abdul, "A Malay's Pilgrimage to Mecca," *Journal of the Malayan Branch of the Royal Asiatic Society*, vol. IV, 1926, pp. 270-87.

Makky, G.A.W., *Mecca: the Pilgrimage City: A Study of Pilgrim Accommodation*, London, 1978.

Martin, Richard C., "Muslim pilgrimage," in *The Encyclopedia of Religion*, ed. Mircea Eliade, vol. XI, New York, 1987, pp. 338-46.

Matheson, Virginia, and A.C. Milner, *Perceptions of the Hajj. Five Malay Texts*, Singapore, 1984.

McDonnell, Mary Byrne, "Patterns of Muslim pilgrimage from Malaysia, 1885-1985," in Dale F. Eickelman and James Piscatori, eds., *Muslim Travellers: Pilgrimage, Migration and the Religious Imagination*, London, 1990, pp. 111-30.

McDonnell, Mary Byrne, "The Conduct of the Hajj from Malaysia and its Socio-Economic Impact on Malay Society: A Descriptive and Analytical Study, 1860-1981." Columbia University unpublished Ph.D. dissertation, 1986. [DAI XLVII, no. 7, Jan. 1987, p. 2701 A]

Metcalf, Barbara D., "The pilgrimage remembered: South Asian accounts of the *hajj*," in Dale F. Eickelman and James Piscatori, eds., *Muslim Travellers: Pilgrimage, Migration and the Religious Imagination*, London, 1990, pp. 85-107.

Meulen, D. van der, "The Mecca Pilgrimage and its importance to the Netherlands East Indies," *Muslim World*, XXXI, 1941, pp. 48-60.

Netton, Ian Richard, ed., *Golden Roads: Migration, Pilgrimage and Travel in Medieval and Modern Islam*, London, 1993.

Pakistan Central Haj Organization, *Haj Statistics, December 1974*, Islamabad, 1975.

Pickens, C.L., "The Mecca Pilgrimage," *Muslim World*, XXIV, 1934, pp. 229-35.

Rahim, J.A., *Report of the Special Hajj Inquiry*, [Indian Government report c. 1940].

*Report of the Haj Inquiry Committee*, Calcutta, 1930.

Roff, William R., "Pilgrimage and the History of Religions: Theoretical Approaches to the Hajj," in Richard C. Martin, ed., *Approaches to Islam in Religious Studies*, Tucson, 1985, pp. 78-86.

Roff, William R., "Sanitation and Security: The Imperial Powers and the Nineteenth Century Hajj," *Arabian Studies*, VI, 1982, pp. 143-60.

Roff, William R., "The Meccan Pilgrimage: Its Meaning for Southeast Asian Islam," in R. Israeli and A.H. Johns, eds., *Islam in Asia*, vol. II, Southeast and East Asia, Boulder, 1984, pp. 238-45.

Rowley, G., and S.A.S. El-Hamdan, "The Pilgrimage to Mecca: an exploratory and predictive model," *Environment and Planning A*, 1978, X, pp. 1053-71.

Rowley, Gwyn, and Soleiman A. El-Hamdan, "Once a Year in Mecca," *Geographical Magazine*, vol. 49, 1977, pp. 753-9.

Rutter, Eldon, *The Holy Cities of Arabia*, London, 1928, 2 vols.

Sardar, Ziauddin, "The Future of Hajj: Some Basic Considerations," *Islamic Culture,* vol. LVIII, no. 4, Oct. 1984, pp. 307-26.

Shair, I.M., and P.P. Karan, "Geography of the Islamic Pilgrimage," *GeoJournal*, III, 6, 1979, pp. 599-608.

Siraj ad-din, Abu Bakr, "Pilgrimage to Mecca," *Studies in Comparative Religion*, I, 1967, pp. 171-81.

Spiro, S. Bey, *The Moslem Pilgrimage*, Alexandria, 1932.

Stegar, Winifred, *Always Bells*, Sydney, 1969.

Tapper, Nancy, "*Ziyaret*: gender, movement, and exchange in a Turkish community," in Dale F. Eickelman and James Piscatori, eds., *Muslim Travellers: Pilgrimage, Migration and the Religious Imagination*, London, 1990, pp. 236-55.

Vredenbregt, Jacob, "The Haddj, some of its Features and Functions in Indonesia," *Bijdragen tot de Taal-Land-en Volkenkunde*, vol. 118, 1962, pp. 91-154.

Zafar, S.M., *Haj: A Journey in Obedience*, Lahore, 1978.

# OTHER PILGRIMAGE LITERATURE

Barber, Richard, *Pilgrimages*, Woodbridge, 1991.

Bhardwaj, Surinder Mohan, *Hindu Places of Pilgrimage in India (A Study in Cultural Geography,)*, Berkeley, 1973.

Bhardwaj, Surinder Mohan, "Non-Hajj Pilgrimage in Islam: a Neglected Dimension of Religious Circulation," typescript, 1989.

Cassels, Nancy Gardner, *Religion and Pilgrim Tax under the Company Raj*, New Delhi, 1988.

Davies, Horton, and Marie-Helene Davies, *Holy Days and Holidays: The Medieval Pilgrimage to Compostela*, Bucknell, 1982.

Eck, Diana L., *Banaras: City of Light*, New York, 1982.

El Moudden, Abderrahmane, "The ambivalence of *rihla*: community integration and self-definition in Moroccan travel accounts, 1300-1800," in Dale F. Eickelman and James Piscatori, eds., *Muslim Travellers: Pilgrimage, Migration and the Religious Imagination*, London, 1990, pp. 69-84.

*The Encyclopedia of Religion*, ed. Mircea Eliade, vol. XI, New York, 1987, s.v. "pilgrimage," pp. 327-54.

Foard, James, "The Boundaries of Compassion: Buddhism and National Tradition in Japanese Pilgrimage," *Journal of Asian Studies*, XLI, 1982, pp. 231-51.

Gold, Ann Grodzins, *Fruitful Journeys: The Ways of Rajasthani Pilgrims*, Berkeley, 1989.

Graburn, Nelson H.H., "Tourism: The Sacred Journey," in V. Smith, ed., *Hosts and Guests: The Anthropology of Tourism*, Philadelphia, 1977, pp. 17-31.

Heath, Sidney, *Pilgrim Life in the Middle Ages*, London, 1971 [reprint of 1911 edition].

Howard, Donald R., *Writers and Pilgrims: Medieval Pilgrimage Narratives and their Posterity*, Berkeley, 1980.

Jha, Makhan, ed., *Dimensions of Pilgrimage: An Anthropological Appraisal (Based on the Transactions of a World Symposium on Pilgrimage)*, New Delhi,1986.

Karve, Irawati, "On the Road: A Maharashtrian Pilgrimage," *Journal of Asian Studies*, XXII, 1, 1962, pp. 13-29.

Kendall, Alan, *Medieval Pilgrims*, London, 1970.

Morinis, E. Alan, ed., *Pilgrimage in the Hindu Tradition: A Case Study of West Bengal*, Oxford, 1984.

*Les Pèlerinages: Égypte Ancienne; Israel; Islam; Perse; Inde; Tibet; Indonésie; Madagascar; Chine; Japon* (Sources Orientales, III), Paris, 1960.

Shackle, C., "The Pilgrimage and the Extension of Sacred Geography in the Poetry of Khwaja Ghulam Farid," in Attar Singh, ed., *Socio-Cultural Impact of Islam on India*, Chandigarh, 1976.

Singh, R.L. and Rana P.B. Singh, eds., *Trends in the Geography of Pilgrimages: Homage to David E. Sopher*, Varanasi, 1987.

Smith, Valene L., ed., "Pilgrimage and Tourism: the Quest in Guest," *Annals of Tourism Research*, Special Number, XIX, 1, 1992.

Sopher, David, "Pilgrim Circulation in Gujarat," *Geographical Review*, vol. LVIII, 1968, pp. 392-425

Stein, Burton, ed., *South Indian Temples: An Analytical Reconstruction*, New Delhi, 1978.

Sumption, Jonathon, *Pilgrimage: An Image of Mediæval Religion*, London, 1975.

Toomey, Paul M., "Pilgrimage," in *The Encyclopedia of Asian History*, New York, 1988, 4 vols, III, 256-60.

Turner, Victor, "The Centre out there: Pilgrim's Goal," *History of Religions,* XII, 3, 1973, pp. 191-230 [also published as "Pilgrimages as Social Processes," in Victor Turner, *Dramas, Fields and Metaphors: Symbolic Action in Human Society*, Ithaca, 1974, pp. 166-230.

Turner, Victor, and Edith Turner, *Image and Pilgrimage in Christian Culture*, New York, 1978.

# GENERAL WORKS

Ahmad, Aziz, *Studies in Islamic Culture in the Indian Environment*, Oxford, 1964.

Albuquerque, Luís de, *Alguns Aspectos de Ameaça Turca sobre a Índia por meados do século XVI*, Coimbra, 1977 [sep from *Biblos*, LIII, 1977].

Al-Maamiry, Ahmed Hamoud, *Omani-Portuguese History*, New Delhi, 1982.

Anderson, Benedict, *Imagined Communities: Reflections on the Origin and Spread of Nationalism*, London, 1983.

Ashtor, Eliyah, *A Social and Economic History of the Near East in the Middle Ages,* London, 1976.

Aubin, Jean, "Un voyage de Goa à Ormuz en 1520," *Modern Asian Studies*, XXII, 3, 1988, pp. 417-32.

Bacqué-Grammont, Jean-Louis, and Anne Kroell, *Mamlouks, Ottomans et Portugais en Mer Rouge: L'Affaire de Djedda en 1517*, Cairo, 1988.

Barbir, Karl K., *Ottoman Rule in Damascus, 1708-1758*, Princeton, 1980.

Beckingham, C.F., *Between Islam and Christendom. Travellers, Facts and Legends in the Middle Ages and the Renaissance*, London, 1983.

Beckingham, C.F., "Some Early Travels in Arabia," *Journal of the Royal Asiatic Society*, 1949, pp. 155-76.

Beckingham, C.F., and R.B. Serjeant, "A Journey by Two Jesuits from Dhufar to San'a in 1590," *Geographical Journal,* 1950, CXV, pp. 194-207.

Benda, Harry J., *The Crescent and the Rising Sun: Indonesian Islam under the Japanese Occupation, 1942-5*, The Hague, 1958.

Berg, C.C., "The Islamization of Java," *Studia Islamica*, IV, 1955, pp. 111-42.

Bouchon, Geneviève, "Le premier voyage de Lopo Soares en Inde (1504-1505)," *Mare Luso-Indicum*, III, 1976, pp. 57-84.

Bouchon, Geneviève, *'Regent of the Sea.' Cannanore's Response to Portuguese Expansion, 1507-1528*, (French Studies in South Asian Culture and Society II), Delhi, 1988.

Brackenridge, Hugh, and Philip Freneau, *Father Bombo's Pilgrimage to Mecca, 1770*, ed. Michael D. Bell, Princeton, 1975.

Braudel, Fernand, *Civilization and Capitalism, 15th to 18th centuries*, London, 1981-84, 3 vols.

Braudel, Fernand, *The Mediterranean and the Mediterranean World in the Age of Philip II*, London, 1972, 2 vols.

Brown, Peter, *The Cult of the Saints*, Chicago, 1981.

*Cambridge History of India*, vol. IV, The Mughul Period, Delhi, 1963.

*Cambridge History of Iran*, vol. VI, The Timurid and Safavid Periods, ed. Peter Jackson and Laurence Lockhart, Cambridge, 1986.

Catão, Francisco Xavier Gomes, "Subsídios para a história de Chorão," *Studia*, 15, 1965, pp. 17-121; 17, 1966, pp. 117-250.

Chandra, Satish, ed., *The Indian Ocean: Explorations in History, Commerce and Politics*, New Delhi, 1987.

Chaudhuri, K.N., *Asia before Europe: Economy and Civilisation of the Indian Ocean from the Rise of Islam to 1750*, Cambridge,1990.

Chaudhuri, K.N., *Trade and Civilization in the Indian Ocean. An Economic History from the Rise of Islam to 1750*, Cambridge, 1985.

Chaudhuri, K.N., *The Trading World of Asia and the English East India Company, 1660-1760*, Cambridge, 1978.

*A Comprehensive History of India*, vol. V, The Delhi Sultanat, Delhi, 1970.

Costa, José Pereira da, *Socotorá e o domínio Portugues no oriente*, Coimbra, 1973.

Cragg, Kenneth, *The House of Islam*, Belmont, Cal., 1969.

Crone, Patricia, *Meccan Trade and the Rise of Islam*, Princeton, 1986.

Curtin, Philip, *Cross-Cultural Trade in World History*, Cambridge, 1984.

Dames, M. Longworth, "The Portuguese and the Turks in the Indian Ocean in the sixteenth century," *Journal of the Royal Asiatic Society*, 1921, pp. 1-28.

Daniel, Norman, *Islam and the West the making of an image*, Edinburgh, 1960.

Das Gupta, "Gujarati Merchants and the Red Sea Trade, 1700-1725," in Kling and Pearson, eds., *The Age of Partnership.*, pp. 123-58.

Das Gupta, Ashin, *Indian Merchants and the Decline of Surat, c.1700-1750*, Wiesbaden, 1979.

Das Gupta, Ashin, "Indian Merchants and the Trade in the Indian Ocean," *Cambridge Economic History of India*, vol. I, Cambridge, 1982, pp. 407-33.

Das Gupta, Ashin, "Indian Merchants and the Western Indian Ocean: The Early Seventeenth Century," *Modern Asian Studies*, XIX, 3, 1985, pp. 481-99.

Das Gupta, Ashin, "The Maritime Merchant and Indian History" *South Asia*, n.s. VII, 1, 1984, pp. 27-33.

Das Gupta, Ashin, "A Note on the Shipowning Merchants of Surat, c. 1700,'" in Denys Lombard and Jean Aubin, eds, *Marchands et hommes d'affairs asiatiques dans l'Océan Indien et la Mer de Chine 13ᵉ-20ᵉ siècles*, Paris, 1988, pp. 109-16.

Das Gupta, Ashin, and M.N. Pearson, eds., *India and the Indian Ocean, 1500-1800*, Calcutta, 1987.

De Gaury, Gerald, *Rulers of Mecca*, London, 1951.

Diffie, Bailey W. and George D. Winius, *Foundations of the Portuguese Empire, 1415-1580*, Minneapolis, 1977.

Drewes, G.W.J., "New Light on the Coming of Islam to Indonesia?" *Bijdragen Tot de Taal-, Land-, en Volkenkunde van Nederlandsch-Inde*, vol. 124, 1968, pp. 433-59.

D'Souza, B.G., *Goan Society in Transition*, Bombay, 1975.

Eaton, Richard M., "Approaches to the Study of Conversion to Islam in India," in Richard C. Martin, ed., *Approaches to Islam in Religious Studies*, Tucson, 1985, pp. 106-23.

Eaton, R.M., "Conversion to Christianity among the Nagas, 1876-1971," *Indian Economic and Social History Review*, XXI, no. 1, Jan-March 1984.

Eaton, R.M., *The Rise of Islam and the Bengal Frontier, 1204-1760*, Berkeley, 1993.

Eaton, R.M., *Sufis of Bijapur, 1300-1700*, Princeton, 1978.

Esposito, John L., ed., *Islam in Asia: Religion, Politics and Society*, New York, 1987.

Farooqi, Naim R., "Moguls, Ottomans, and Pilgrims: Protecting the Routes to Mecca in the Sixteenth and Seventeenth Century," *International History Review*, X, 2, May, 1988, pp. 198-220.

Farooqi, Naimur Rehman, *Mughal-Ottoman Relations (A Study of Political and Diplomatic Relations between Mughal India and*

262

*the Ottoman Empire, 1556-1748)*, Delhi, 1989.

Fok, K.C., "Early Ming Images of the Portuguese," in R. Ptak, ed., *Portuguese Asia*, pp. 143-55.

Gaborieau, Marc, ed., *Islam et société en asie du sud*, Paris, 1986.

Gellens, Sam I., "The search for knowledge in medieval Muslim societies: a comparative approach," in Dale F. Eickelman and James Piscatori, eds., *Muslim Travellers: Pilgrimage, Migration and the Religious Imagination*, London, 1990, pp. 50-65.

Gascoigne, Bamber, *The Great Moghuls*, London, 1971.

Geertz, Clifford R., *Islam Observed, Religious Development in Morocco and Indonesia*, Chicago, 1968.

Gibb, H.A.R., and Harold Bowen, *Islamic Society and the West*, vol. I, 2 parts, Oxford, 1950-7.

Godinho, Vitorino Magalhães, *Os descobrimentos e a economia mundial*, 2nd. ed., Lisbon, 1981-83, 4 vols.

Godinho, Vitorino Magalhães, *Les finances de l'état portugais des Indes Orientales, 1517-1635*, Paris, 1982.

Godinho, Vitorino Magalhães, *Mito e mercadoria, utopia e prática de navegar, séculos XIII-XVIII*, Lisbon, 1990.

Goitein, S.D., *A Mediterranean Society*, Berkeley, 1967-78, 3 vols.

Goitein, S..D., *Studies in Islamic History and Institutions*, Leiden, 1966.

Gokhale, B.G., *Surat in the Seventeenth Century*, London, 1979.

Gomes da Costa, Marechal, *Descobrimentos e Conquistas*, Lisbon, 1927-30, 3 vols.

Grunebaum, G.E. von, *Muhammadan Festivals*, London, 1976.

Guilmartin, John Francis, *Gunpowder and Galleys: Changing Technology and Mediterranean Warfare at Sea in the Sixteenth Century*, Cambridge, 1974.

Hall, K.R., "The Coming of Islam to the Archipelago: A Reassessment," in Karl L. Hutterer, ed., *Economic Change and Social Interaction in Southeast Asia*, Ann Arbor, 1977, pp. 213-31.

Hardy, Peter, *Historians of Medieval India*, London, 1966.

Hardy, P., "Modern European and Muslim Explanations of Conversions to Islam in South Asia: A Preliminary Survey of the Literature," in Nehemia Levtzion, ed., *Conversion to Islam*, New York, 1979, pp. 68-99.

Hardy, Peter, *The Muslims of British India*, Cambridge, 1972.

Hess, Andrew C., "Piri Reis and the Ottoman Response to the Voyages of Discovery," *Terrae Incognitae*, VI, 1974, pp. 19-37.

Hodgson, Marshall G.S., *The Venture of Islam*, Chicago, 1974, 3 vols.

Holden, David, and Richard Johns, *The House of Saud*, London, 1981.

Horton, Robin, "African Conversion," *Africa*, XLI, no. 2, April 1971, pp. 85-108.

Horton, Robin, "On the Rationality of Conversion," *Africa*, XLV, no. 3, 1975, pp. 219-35, no. 4, 1975, pp. 373-99.

Inalcik, Halil, *The Ottoman Empire: The Classical Age, 1300-1600*, London, 1973.

Islam, Riazul, *Indo-Persian Relations. A Study of the Political and Diplomatic Relations between the Mughul Empire and Iran*, Teheran, 1970.

*Islam in Asia*, vol. I, South Asia, ed. Yohanan Friedmann; vol. II, Southeast and East Asia, ed. Raphael Israeli and Anthony H. Johns, Boulder, 1984.

Johns, A.H., "Friends in Grace: Ibrahim al-Kurani and 'Abd al-Rauf al-Singkeli," in S. Udin, ed., *Spectrum: Essays Presented to Sutan Takdir Alisjahbana on his Seventieth Birthday*, Jakarta, 1978, pp. 469-85.

Johns, A.H., "From Coastal Settlement to Islamic School and City: Islamization in Sumatra, the Malay Peninsula and Java," *Hamdard Islamicus*, IV, 1981, pp. 3-28.

Johns, A.H., *The Gift Addressed to the Spirit of the Prophet*, Canberra, 1964.

Johns, A.H., "Sufism as a Category in Indonesian Literature and History," *Journal of Southeast Asian History*, II, 1961, pp. 10-23.

Jones, Russell, "Ten Conversion Myths from Indonesia," in Nehemia Levtzion, ed., *Conversion to Islam*, New York, 1979, pp. 129-58.

Kammerer, Albert, *La Mer Rouge, l'Abyssinie et l'Arabie aux XVIe et XVIIe siècles et La Cartographie des Portulans du Monde oriental* (Mémoires de la Société Royale de Géographie d'Égypte, tome XVII), 3 vols, Cairo, 1947-52. [First part: Abyssins et Portugais devant Islam; Second part: Les Jésuites Portugais et l'Ephémère triomphe du Catholicisme en Abyssinie (1603-32); Third part: La Cartographie du Monde Oriental, Mer Rouge,

Océan Indien et Extrême-Orient jusqu'au XVIIIe siècle. Cartographes Portugais et Français.]

Kammerer, Albert, *La Mer Rouge, l'Abyssinie et l'Arabie depuis l'Antiquité. Essai d'historique* (Mémoires de la Société royale de Géographie d'Egypte, tomes XV-XVI), 2 vols in 5 parts, Cairo, 1929-35. [Tome I, Les pays de la Mer Erythrée jusqu'à la fin du Moyen Age; Tome II, Les Guerres du poivre. Les Portugais dans l'océan indien et la Mer Rouge au XVIe siècle. Histoire de la cartographie Orientale.]

Kathirithamby-Wells, J., "The Islamic City: Melaka to Jogjakarta, c. 1500-1800," *Modern Asian Studies*, XX, 2, 1986, pp. 333-51.

Khan, I.A. *The Political Biography of a Mughal Noble*, New Delhi, 1973.

Khan, Dr. M.A. Muid, "Indo-Portuguese Struggle for Maritime Supremacy (As gleaned from an Unpublished Arabic *Urjuza: Fathul Mubiyn*)," in P.M. Joshi and M.A. Nayeem, eds., *Studies in the Foreign Relations of India (From Earliest Times to 1947) Prof. H.K. Sherwani Felicitation Volume*, Hyderabad, 1975, pp. 165-83.

Kissling, H.J., et al., *The Muslim World: A Historical Survey*, Part III, The Last Great Muslim Empires, Leiden, 1969.

Kling, Blair B., and M.N. Pearson, eds., *The Age of Partnership: Europeans in Asia before Dominion*, Honolulu, 1979.

Kumar, Ann L., "Islam, the Chinese, and Indonesian Historiography - A Review Article," *Journal of Asian Studies*, XLVI, 3, 1987, pp. 603-16.

Lacey, Robert, *The Kingdom*, London, 1981.

Lach, Donald F., *Asia in the Making of Europe,* vol. I, "The Century of Discovery," Chicago, 1965.

Launay, Robert, "Pedigrees and paradigms: scholarly credentials among the Dyula of the northern Ivory Coast," in Dale F. Eickelman and James Piscatori, eds., *Muslim Travellers: Pilgrimage, Migration and the Religious Imagination*, London, 1990, pp. 175-99.

Lombard, Denys and Jean Aubin, eds, *Marchands et hommes d'affairs asiatiques dans l'Océan Indien et la Mer de Chine 13ᵉ-20ᵉ siècles*, Paris, 1988.

Lane, F.C., *Venice and History*, Baltimore, 1966.

Lapidus, Ira M., *A History of Islamic Societies*, Cambridge, 1988.

Lapidus, Ira, ed., *Middle Eastern Cities,* Berkeley, 1969.

Lapidus, Ira, *Muslim Cities in the Later Middle Ages*, Cambridge, MA, 1967.

Lesourd, M., "Notes sur les Nawakid, Navigateurs de la Mer Rouge," *Bolletin de l'Institute Français d'Afrique Noire*, Série B, Dakar, vol. XX, 1960, pp. 346-355.

Lesure, Michel, "Un document Ottoman de 1525 sur l'Inde portugaise et les pays de la Mer Rouge," *Mare Luso-Indicum*, III, 1976, pp. 137-60.

Lewis, Bernard, ed., *Islam: From the Prophet Muhammad to the Capture of Constantinople*, New York, 1974, 2 vols.

Maghrebi, Ghulam Muhammad Nizamuddin, "The Ottoman-Gujrat Relations (1517-1556)," in P.M. Joshi and M.A. Nayeem, eds., *Studies in the Foreign Relations of India (From Earliest Times to 1947) Prof. H.K. Sherwani Felicitation Volume*, Hyderabad, 1975, pp. 184-93.

Majul, C.A., "Theories on the Introduction and Expansion of Islam in Malaysia," *Sulliman Journal*, XI, 1964, pp. 335-98.

Majumdar, R.C., *History and Culture of the Indian People; the Mughul Empire*, Bombay, 1974.

Martin, Richard D., *Islam and the History of Religions*, Berkeley, 1983.

Mathew, K.S., "Indian Merchants and the Portuguese Trade on the Malabar Coast during the sixteenth century," Teotonio de Souza, ed., *Indo-Portuguese History: Old Issues, New Questions*, New Delhi, 1985, pp. 1-12.

Mathew, K.S., *Portuguese and the Sultanate of Gujarat*, Delhi, 1986.

McPherson, Kenneth, *The Indian Ocean: A History of the People and the Sea*, Delhi, 1993

McPherson, Kenneth, "Maritime Passenger Traffic in the Indian Ocean Region before the Nineteenth Century," *The Great Circle*, X, 1, April 1988, pp. 49-61.

Misra, Rekha, *Women in Mughal India*, Delhi, 1967.

Misra, S.C., *Muslim Communities in Gujarat*, London, 1964.

Moreland, W.H., *India at the Death of Akbar: An Economic Study*, Delhi, 1974.

Moreland, W.H., ed., *Relations of Golconda in the Early Seventeenth Century*, London, Hakluyt, 1931.

Moreland, W.H., "The Ships of the Arabian Sea about A.D. 1500,"

*Journal of the Royal Asiatic Society*, 1939, pp. 63-74, 173-92.

Mortimer, Edward, *Faith and Power: the Politics of Islam*, New York, 1982.

*Mouvements de populations dans l'océan Indien*, Paris, 1979.

Mughul, Muhammad Yakub, "The Expedition of Suleyman Pasha Al-Khadim to India (1538)," *Journal of the Regional Cultural Institute*, Tehran, II, 1969, 146-51.

Mujeeb, Muhammad, *The Indian Muslims*, London, 1967.

Nadvi, Syed Sulaiman, *The Arab Navigation*, trans from Urdu by Syed Sabahuddin Abdur Rahman, Lahore, 1966.

Naik, C.R., "Abdu-r-Rahim, Khan-i-Khanan," MA thesis, University of Bombay, n.d.

Nizami, Khaliq Ahmad, *Some Aspects of Religion and Politics in India during the 13th Century*, Bombay, 1961.

Ozbaran, Salih, "The Ottoman Turks and the Portuguese in the Persian Gulf, 1534-1581," *Journal of Asian History*, VI, 1, 1972, pp. 45-87.

Ozbaran, Salih, "The Ottomans in confrontation with the Portuguese in the Red Sea after the conquest of Egypt in 1517," *Studies on Turkish-Arab Relations*, Annual, 1986, Istanbul, 1986, pp. 207-14.

Ozbaran, Salih, "A Turkish Report on the Red Sea and the Portuguese in the Indian Ocean (1525), *Arabian Studies*, IV, 1978, pp. 81-88.

Pearson, M.N., *Before Colonialism: Theories on Asian-European Relations 1500-1750*, Delhi, 1988.

Pearson, M.N., *Coastal Western India, Studies from the Portuguese Records*, New Delhi, 1981.

Pearson, M.N., "Conversions in Southeast Asia: Evidence from the Portuguese Records," *Portuguese Studies,* VI, 1990, pp. 53-70.

Pearson, M.N., *Merchants and Rulers in Gujarat: the Response to the Portuguese in the Sixteenth Century*, Berkeley and New Delhi, 1976.

Pearson, M.N., *The Portuguese in India*, Cambridge, 1987.

Peters, F.E., *Jerusalem and Mecca: The Typology of the Holy city in the Near East* (New York University Studies in Near Eastern Civilization, Number XI), New York, 1986.

Pissurlencar, P.S.S., *The Portuguese and the Marathas*, trans. P.R. Kakodkar, Bombay, 1975.

Planhol, Xavier de, *The World of Islam*, Ithaca, 1959.

Priolkar, A.K., *The Goa Inquisition*, Bombay, 1961.

Ptak, Roderich, ed., *Portuguese Asia: Aspects of History and Economic History (Sixteenth and Seventeenth Centuries)*, Stuttgart, 1987.

Qaisar, A. Jan,. "From Port to Port: Life on Indian Ships in the sixteenth and seventeenth centuries," in Ashin Das Gupta and M.N. Pearson, eds., *India and the Indian Ocean, 1500-1800*, Calcutta, 1987, pp. 331-49.

Qureshi, I.H., *Ulema in Politics*, Karachi, 1972.

Rao, R.P., *Portuguese Rule in Goa*, Bombay, 1963.

Raymond, André, *The Great Arab Cities in the 16th-18th Centuries: An Introduction*, New York, 1984.

Reid, Anthony, "The Islamization of Southeast Asia," in Muhammad Abu Bakar et al., eds., *Historia: Essays in Commemoration of the 25th Anniversary of the Department of History, University of Malaya*, Kuala Lumpur, 1984, pp. 13-33.

Reid, Anthony, "Sixteenth Century Turkish Influence in Western Indonesia," *Journal of Southeast Asian History*, X, 3, 1969, pp. 395-414.

Richards, D.S., ed., *Islam and the Trade of Asia*, Oxford, 1970.

Richards, J.F., ed., *Precious Metals in the Late Medieval and Early Modern Worlds*, Durham, N.C., 1983.

Richards, J.M., *Goa*, New Delhi, 1982.

Ricklefs, M.C., *A History of Modern Indonesia,* London, 1981.

Ricklefs, M.C., "Six Centuries of Islamization in Java," in Nehemia Levtzion, ed., *Conversion to Islam*, New York, 1979, pp. 100-28.

Rizvi, S.A.A., *A History of Sufism in India*, New Delhi, 1978-83, 2 vols.

Rizvi, S.A.A., *Muslim Revivalist Movements in Northern India in the Sixteenth and Seventeenth Centuries*, Agra, 1965.

Rizvi, S.A.A., *Religious and Intellectual History of the Muslims in Akbar's Reign*, New Delhi, 1975.

Rizvi, S.A.A., *Shah 'Abd al-'Aziz: Puritanism, Sectarianism, Polemics and Jihad*, Canberra, 1982.

Rizvi, S.A.A., *Shah Wali-Allah and his Times: a Study of Eighteenth-Century Islam,* Canberra, 1980.

Robinson, Francis, *Atlas of the Islamic World since 1500,* New York, 1982.

Roff, William R., ed., *Islam and the Political Economy of Meaning: Comparative Studies of Muslim Discourse*, Berkeley, 1987.

Roff, William R., "Islamic Institutions in Muslim Southeast Asia and cognate phenomena in the Indian sub-continent," in D. Rothermund, ed., *Islam in Southern Asia*, pp. 10-12.

Ross, E. Denison, "The Portuguese in India and Arabia between 1507 and 1517," *Journal of the Royal Asiatic Society*, 1921, pp. 545-62.

Ross, E. Denison, "The Portuguese in India and Arabia, 1517-38," *Journal of the Royal Asiatic Society*, 1922, pp. 1-18.

Rothermund, Dietmar, ed., *Islam in Southern Asia: a Survey of Current Research*, Wiesbaden, 1975.

Russell-Wood, A.J.R., "Men under Stress: the social environment of the Carreira da India, 1550-1750," *II Seminario Internacional de História Indo-Portuguesa*, Actas, Lisbon, 1985, pp. 19-35.

Russell-Wood, A.J.R., "Seamen Ashore and Afloat: the social environment of the Carreira da India, 1550-1750," *Mariners' Mirror*, LXIV, 1983, pp. 35-52.

Said, Edward, *Orientalism*, London, 1978.

Salibi, Kamal, *A History of Arabia*, Delmar, N.Y., 1980.

Sarkar, Jadunath, *History of Aurangzeb*, Calcutta, 1973-4, 5 vols.

Sarkar, Jadunath, *Studies in Aurangzib's Reign*, 3rd ed., London, 1989.

Sarkar, J.N., "Indian Merchants Ships and their Skippers in Red Sea Ports,, 1611," *Journal of Indian History*, XXVII, 1949, pp. 109-119.

Savory, Roger, *Iran under the Safavids*, Cambridge, 1980.

Schimmel, Annemarie, *Islam in the Indian Subcontinent*, Leiden, 1980.

Schrieke, B., *Indonesian Sociological Studies*, The Hague, 1955-57, 2 vols.

Schurhammer, Georg, *Francis Xavier: His Life, His Times*, vol. II, India, Rome, 1977.

Serjeant, R.B., *The Portuguese off the South Arabian Coast*, Oxford, 1963.

Serjeant, R.B., *Studies on Arabian History and Civilization*, London, 1982.

Sharma, S.R., *The Religious Policies of the Mughal Emperors*, 3rd.

ed., New York, 1972.

Shaw, Stanford J., *The Financial and Administrative Organization and Development of Ottoman Egypt, 1517-1798*, Princeton, 1962.

Shaw, Stanford, *History of the Ottoman Empire and Modern Turkey*, vol. I, "Empire of the Gazis: the rise and decline of the Ottoman Empire, 1280-1808," Cambridge, 1976.

Silva Rego, Antonio da, *História das missões do padroado portguês do Oriente*, Lisbon, 1949.

Steenbrink, K.A., "Indian Teachers and their Indonesian Pupils: On Intellectual Relations between India and Indonesia, 1600-1800," *Itinerario*, 1988/1, pp. 129-41.

Steensgaard, Niels, *The Asian Trade Revolution of the Seventeenth Century: The East India Companies and the Decline of the Caravan Trade*, Chicago, 1974.

Stripling, G.W.F., *The Ottoman Turks and the Arabs 1511-1574*, Illinois, 1942.

Subrahmanyam, Sanjay, "Persians, Pilgrims and Portuguese: the Travails of Masulipatnam Shipping in the Western Indian Ocean, 1590-1665," *Modern Asian Studies*, XXII, 3, 1988, pp. 503-30.

Sykes, Percy, *A History of Persia*, vol. II, 3rd ed., London, 1951.

Terpstra, H., *De Opkomst der Westerkwartieren van de Oost-Indische Compangie (Suratte, Arabie, Perzie), The Hague, 1918.*

Tibbetts, G.R., *Arab Navigation in the Indian Ocean before the Coming of the Portuguese*, London, 1971.

Tibbetts, G.R., "Arab Navigation in the Red Sea," *Geographical Journal*, vol. 127, 1961, pp. 322-34.

Tibbetts, G.R., "Early Muslim Traders in Southeast Asia," *Journal of the Malay Branch of the Royal Asiatic Society*, 30, 1, 1957.

Tirmizi, S.A.I., *Some Aspects of Medieval Gujarat*, Delhi, 1968.

Titus, Murray T., *Islam in India and Pakistan: A Religious History of Islam in India and Pakistan*, Calcutta, 1959.

Villiers, John, "Las Yslas de Esperar en Dios: The Jesuit Mission in Moro, 1546-1571," *Modern Asian Studies*, XXII, 3, 1988, pp. 593-606.

Voll, John, "Muhammad Hayya al-Sindi and Muhammad ibn 'Abd al-Wahhab: an analysis of an intellectual group in eighteenth century Madina," *Bulletin of the School of Oriental and African Studies*, XXXVIII, 1975, pp. 32-9.

Wallerstein, Immanuel, *The Modern World-System*, 3 vols, New York, 1974-89.

Whiteway, R.S., *The Rise of Portuguese Power in India*, London, 1899.

Winius, George D., *The Black Legend of Portuguese India*, New Delhi, 1985.

Wink, André, *Al-Hind: The Making of the Indo-Islamic World Vol. I, Early Medieval India and the Expansion of Islam, 7th-11th Centuries*, Leiden, 1990.

Wink, André, "'Al-Hind,' India and Indonesia in the Islamic World-Economy, c700-1800 A.D.," *Itinerario*, 1988/1, pp. 33-72.

Wolf, Eric R., *Europe and the People without History*, Berkeley, 1982.

Wolf, Eric R., "The Social Organization of Mecca and the Origin of Islam," *Southwestern Journal of Anthropology*, VII, 4, 1951, pp. 329-56.

# AIDS, GUIDES ETC

Arasaratnam, S., "Recent Trends in the Historiography of the Indian Ocean, 1500 to 1800," *Journal of World History*, I, 2, Fall 1990, pp. 225-48.

Aubin, Jean, "Un nouveau classique, l'Anonyme du British Museum," *Mare Luso-Indicum*, III, 1976, pp. 183-8.

Beckingham, C.F., "Hakluyt's Description of the Hajj," *Arabian Studies,* IV, 1978, pp. 75-80.

Dalgado, S.R., *Glossário Luso-Asiatico*, Coímbra, 1919-21, 2 vols.

De Silva, Daya, *The Portuguese in Asia: An annotated bibliography of studies on Portuguese colonial history in Asia, 1498-c.1800*, Zug, 1987.

*Encyclopedia of Asian History*, ed. Ainslie T. Embree, New York, 1988, 4 vols.

*Encyclopedia of Islam*, Leiden, 1960, 2nd. ed.

*Encyclopedia of Religion*, ed. Mircea Eliade, New York, 1987, 16 vols.

Freeman-Grenville, G.S.P., *The Muslim and Christian Calendars*, OUP, 1963.

Geddes, C.L., *An Analytical Guide to the Bibliographies on Islam,*

*Muhammad and the Qur'an*, Denver, 1973.

Gorakshkar, Sadashiv, "An Illustrated *Anis al-Haj* in the Prince of Wales Museum, Bombay," in Robert Skelton, et al, eds, *Facets of Indian Art*, London, 1986, pp. 158-67.

Gorakshkar, Sadashiv, "Anis al-Haj," in Karl Khandalavala, ed., *An Ag eof Splendour: Islamic Art in India*, Bombay, 1983, pp 132-5.

Lima Cruz, M. Augusta, "The 8th Decada of Diogo do Couto's Asia,", International Seminar on Indo-Portuguese History III, Goa, 1983, typescript.

Lima Cruz, M. Augusta, "Década 8 da Asia de Diogo do Couto — informação sobre uma versão inédita," *Arquipelago*, Ponta Delgada, 1984, pp. 159-60.

Lima Cruz, M. Augusta, "Para uma edição crítica da Década VIII de Diogo do Couto," *Arquivos do Centro Cultural Português*, Paris, 1982, pp. 93-114.

Marshall, D.N., *Mughals in India: A Bibliographical Survey*, London, 1967.

Pearson, J.D., *Index Islamicus*, London, 1958 - .

Polgar, Laszlo, *Bibliographie sur l'histoire de la Compagnie de Jésus 1901-1980*. II, Les Pays: Amérique Asie Afrique Océanie, Rome, 1986.

Richards, J.F., Review of *India and the Indian Ocean, 1500-1800*, and *The Indian Ocean* in *Journal of Asian Studies*, XLVIII, 3, Aug. 1989, 651-3.

Yule, Henry, and A.C. Burnell, ed William Crooke, *Hobson-Jobson: A Glossary* . . . , London, 1903, New Delhi, 1968.